RULES OF ESTRANGEMENT

RULES

of

ESTRANGEMENT

*Why Adult Children Cut Ties and
How to Heal the Conflict*

JOSHUA COLEMAN, PhD

HARMONY BOOKS

NEW YORK

To my father and mother, Steve and Corinne.

And to their parents: Robert and Edith,

Max and Lena.

And to all the parents and grandparents,

Children and grandchildren,

Who long to be in each other's lives

But haven't yet found a way.

Library of Congress Cataloging-in-Publication Data
Names: Coleman, Joshua, author.
Title: Rules of estrangement / Joshua Coleman, PhD.
Description: New York : Harmony Books, 2020. | Includes bibliographical references and index.
Identifiers: LCCN 2020010203 | ISBN 9780593136867 (hardback) |
ISBN 9780593136874 (ebook)
Subjects: LCSH: Alienation (Social psychology) | Parent and adult child. | Parents—
Psychology. | Adult children—Psychology. | Interpersonal conflict. | Conflict management.
Classification: LCC HM1131 .C65 2020 | DDC 306.874—dc23
LC record available at https://lccn.loc.gov/2020010203

ISBN 978-0-593-13686-7
Ebook ISBN 978-0-593-13687-4

Printed in Canada

Book design by Jennifer Daddio / Bookmark Design and Media Inc.
Jacket design by Pete Garceau

10 9 8 7 6 5 4 3 2 1

First Edition

CONTENTS

AUTHOR'S NOTE

For the sake of privacy and confidentiality, all of the case histories are composites of individuals and families, rather than the story of any one particular person or family. I have also changed the names of my own family members in the book to protect their privacy. Like any attempt to make sense of memories from the past, it is flawed and incomplete, but used with their permission.

INTRODUCTION

Sad, scared, and pissed off.

I assume you picked up this book because those words describe how you feel right now. *Sad* you haven't had any contact with your adult child or grandchild, *scared* you don't know if you'll ever see them again, and *pissed off* because you don't deserve to be treated this way by your own child, especially one to whom you've been so devoted.

Or maybe you picked up this book because you're reeling from the fact that your child wants nothing to do with you and you have no idea why.

Or maybe you know that you made some pretty big mistakes but assumed that the conflict was resolvable: "We'll get over it like we always do, no need to panic," to "What does he mean, he needs to take a break from our relationship?" to "Wait, how was I not invited to her wedding or the birth of my grandchild?!"

Every time I am interviewed in national media, I am besieged with referrals and emails from estranged parents who all say the same thing: "I thought I was the only one!" Parents don't talk about estrangement to their friends, coworkers, even their own family, because they fear judgment. They fear someone will say or think: "What did you do to your child? It must have been something terrible."

So let me start by saying: maybe you didn't do *anything* to cause it. While there are plenty of troubled parents in this world, many of those who contact me are some of the most dedicated, educated, and loving parents of any generation. They've read tons of parenting books; spent a record number of hours raising their children; provided their kids with a level of financial support far greater than that provided by their own parents; and tirelessly researched the causes of their children's anxiety, depression, learning disabilities, low self-esteem, ADD, and every other diagnosis known to have a URL. They have listened carefully to their children's dreams so that they could provision them with the safest, securest path to a happy and successful life. They have lived on a steady diet of worry, guilt, fear, sleep deprivation, and caffeine in order to become the absolute-best-parent-they-could-possibly-be—a goal that has been at the center of their consciousness since before their child was born.

Which doesn't mean that they were free from making mistakes. And to make matters worse, experts keep changing what's considered ideal parenting every three or four years, so it's hard to know which kind of mistake they might have made: small and predictable with little smiley faces around the edges? Medium and potentially forgivable with a "Keep Trying" sticker affixed to them? Or large and relationship-ending with a yellow and black hazmat warning?

Either way, dealing with an estrangement is no small task. Whatever the cause, rejection from the person whose opinion and love you care the most about—whom you love with a mightiness that only another estranged parent could understand—makes the certainties of life feel precarious and unraveled. Tender memories that seemed impervious to revision become infested with doubt and self-criticism. The times you know you were far from your best parenting self are thrust into a torturous spin cycle of *If only I hadn't said that, done that, wrote that.*

You might have thought: *This could never happen to me. I love my child too much. My child loves me too much. We can get through this, can't we? Look at the pictures of us together from before—we were so happy.*

You discover that nothing draws life more sharply into focus than the loss of a child's love and attention. Whether an estrangement is sudden or gradual, you'll find yourself flooded with images of rocking her in your arms while she was sleeping, swaddled in a blanket her grandmother gave her. You'll see her face on the day she was born, brought newly into the world. You'll remember crayoned Mother's Day/Father's Day cards (which you still have); you'll remember running behind her, holding the seat of her first bike as you let go and she sails down the street.

I understand because I've been there and those are my memories. And they came back to me when my daughter cut me off.

In her early twenties, my daughter Elena told me everything I knew and feared. She told me I had let her down. She told me I wasn't there for her. She told me I had a happy new family now, and that I never made her feel a part of it. She told me she was done with our relationship. It was the most painful experience I have ever had to go through or hope to go through again.

I was twenty-five when I met her mother, Rhonda, at City College of San Francisco. I transferred there after dropping out of the San Francisco Conservatory of Music, where I could no longer afford the tuition. In today's dollars, the amount was laughable—then again, so is everything in today's dollars. I sat next to her in a music theory class and exchanged goofy faces with her five-year-old son from a prior marriage. Within six months we were living together. The term *soulmate* finally meant something. I never had a girlfriend who was so hilarious and smart. Within less than a year she was pregnant and I was gearing up to be a dad.

We weren't married, weren't mature, weren't ready. We tied the knot anyway. We had a big party. We had a home birth. Despite the pain and gore suffered by the mother at the luxurious distance and repose of the father, I was witness to the first sight of my daughter's little head as she pushed through, her face red and squinting from the short, arduous journey into the world; her tiny pursed lips, her cerulean eyes opening with an expression that asked *Who the hell are you?* I felt the powerful compulsion of animals who nuzzle their just-born infants into contact guided by their scent, their innocence, their purity. Babies broadcast at an intoxicating frequency, a powerful proclamation of new life: Protect me.

Yet, despite the bond of parenthood, Rhonda and I separated within a year and a half. I moved out of our duplex in the outer Sunset District of San Francisco near Ocean Beach and into a walk-up Victorian with three other people in the inner Haight; mattress on the floor, portable crib in one hand, diaper bag in the other. Rita Rudner's observation that most single men live like bears with furniture was an apt description of my life at the time. We did shared custody, which meant that I saw Elena every other weekend and Wednesday nights. This was the preferred arrangement of family courts in the 1980s, a time before they received the memo that dads might have something to contribute to children's well-being.

But I adored my daughter. She was sunny, bold, not easily bossed around. She was opinionated about what she would or wouldn't wear. She threw her head back whenever she laughed. She was unafraid to race her Hot Wheels, then training wheels, then two-wheeler down the sidewalk; I had to race to keep up with her. She ate whatever I put in front of her, which was adaptive given my limited culinary skills. She goaded me to create scary bedtime stories with female protagonists who save the day.

When Elena was seven, I remarried. Her mother remarried, too.

The custody arrangement made it impossible to see her more than eight days a month. I missed her when she wasn't around and wanted our scarce amount of time together to be without tension. The stereotype "Disneyland dad" endures for a reason: If you only get to see your kid once in a while, who wants to clutter that up with limits or arguments? "Of *course* you can have another ice cream cone before dinner. They're delicious!" "Absolutely we can watch that scary R-rated movie. R means Really, Really Good!" "Yes, let's stay up way past your bedtime! I'll explain to your mom why you're always tired when I drop you off."

The last thing I wanted was conflict with my daughter. Conflict requires the luxury of time. Time to heal, to repair, to clarify. Monstrous things can fill the gaps between times that you see your child and times that you don't after divorce.

Because there's always the other home to contend with. Even if your ex was a decent person, they could still undermine your relationship with your child if they wanted to: ignore the happy reports of their days with you and attend more to their complaints. Upgrade their new spouse into the role of parent while downgrading you into someone more distant, avuncular, and irrelevant.

Studies show that divorce is sometimes less hard on children than their parents' remarriage. However, remarriages are also hard on exes—not because they're jealous, but because they have to contend with a person who takes on a role they assumed was uniquely and forever theirs. The first time my daughter referred to her stepfather as *her other daddy*, I almost smacked her across the face.

Instead, I said through clenched teeth, "Sweetheart, Rob is your stepfather, he's not your other dad. You only have one dad."

"I know," she said between bites of Raisin Bran. "You're Dad and he's Daddy," she continued, as if that explained everything.

"No," I persisted. Despite my years of therapy, I had no ability to calmly walk my way through this conversation. "I'm Dad *and* I'm Daddy. Like you're Elena and you're Leni. Daddy's just a different way to say Dad—like Leni's a different way to say Elena. Okay?"

She tilted her head at me with curiosity. At a precocious nine years, she was old enough to recognize that she had stumbled into a pit of vulnerability that she hadn't yet seen in me.

It didn't help that her mother had married a friend of mine who was decent and kind. If anyone was capable of replacing me as a father, he was. After he married my ex, we didn't stay close, because now he played for the other side. Rhonda and I weren't one of these "Oh, let's still be buddies and have Thanksgiving together" exes. We were more like this: "Hey, thanks for the regular updates on why breaking up was the best thing we ever did." We didn't try to be friends with each other's spouses. The teams had been formed and there was no mistaking for whom our new spouses were supposed to play. The problem was that our daughter had to play for both; however hard it was to be a divorced parent, it was even harder to be the kid who had to keep track of her parents' needs and moods.

Because we had scarce time together, I tried to make it count. Joint custody means spending a lot of time driving—picking up and dropping off, picking up and dropping off. Then again, driving had its benefits: It was private. It occurred without the distraction of others who could compete for attention.

Our relationship was in some ways made closer in the car, since we were both captive to whatever was in the cassette deck. And unlike the boozy, chummy Rat Pack music that adorned the stereos of my parents' generation, our generation's children actually liked our music. Listening to music with her, especially *loud* music, especially *loud, aggressive* music as she approached adolescence, allowed a lot to be said without having to say it. Soundgarden, Led Zeppelin, Public Enemy, Tupac, and Nine Inch Nails were the constants moving in and out of the console.

Then my twin sons were born, and at forty, I was more mature, more ready to parent. Being a full-time parent was healing. I could wake up to my sons every morning and put them to bed every night. But playing in the background was the contrast of what I wasn't giving to my daughter. Am I really a good father if I'm raising two of my kids and scarcely raising the other? And even though the arrangement was decided in court, I still felt guilt-ridden. I felt I had violated the agreement I made when I brought her into the world: that I would be with her at every moment and protect her. And now my kid was being raised by another man she called Daddy.

She was fourteen going on fifteen, and I had no idea what she was thinking or feeling. I could hear it in her voice when I called her at her mom's: bored, preoccupied, disconnected, irritated. Was she upset with me? Did her mom say something? Did something happen at school? Was it drugs? Was it a guy? I didn't know. I should have known what was going on with my own kid, but I didn't.

Hoping to get more time with her, I went back to court for a second time to get full-time custody. But I lost. The judge didn't see any reason to change what he thought was working. "What's working about it?" I asked. He said that since her mother and I weren't getting along, a change would make it even harder on Elena. I argued that the opposite was true: more time together would be better for everyone. He held firm and I went home.

Three more years passed and, at seventeen, Elena bucked the courts and moved in with my wife and me full-time. This was an answer to my prayers. Finally, I could be a real parent to her. I gave her the guitar that I'd played at my wedding with her mother; she learned one of the classical pieces I'd written for the Conservatory many years back. We made each other laugh, as we always had. We introduced each other to new bands. It seemed that we might have a new beginning—a new chance to heal.

But having her home didn't turn out exactly how I'd hoped. My wife, patient and good-natured in most ways, was unable to balance the cyclone of our twin boys and the needs of Elena. I didn't know how to reach my daughter when she seemed overwhelmed or depressed. And once again, she found herself on the short end of a parental stick.

I took her to college and was briefly buoyed: I felt like a real dad doing real things with his daughter. Yet a part of me knew that she wasn't really prepared for this next phase of life. She hadn't received the stable, consistent home that my twins had. She hadn't gotten to feel like the unambiguous priority.

And then, at twenty-two, she gave me the talk. The talk where she said she hadn't felt like a priority to me growing up; she didn't feel cherished or special or important. I don't remember her exact words—perhaps they're too excruciating to recall. What I do remember is her anger, her honesty. Her pain.

I defended myself; I explained, I rationalized, and I blamed others. None of this worked, of course—she withdrew even further.

And then, nothing. No contact. No returned calls. No visits. The car was now fully off the road, sailing over the cliff. It would take several years before we started to talk again.

My story may parallel yours. Or it may not. Maybe you never got divorced. Perhaps your relationship was great until your child got married. Or great until they had a kid. Or good enough until they got into therapy. Perhaps none of these applies. Regardless, the estrangement has made you feel lost and desperate for answers.

So you tried to get help with a variety of professionals. Maybe they were clueless, and their sensible-sounding advice only made things worse. Statements like "It's just a phase, give him time." "You need to remind her of everything that you've done for her and calling you up is the least she can do." "You should just show up there and demand that they see you!" So now you've dug yourself into a hole you have no idea how to dig your way out of.

I know how you feel because I got the same well-meaning, though ill-informed, advice. I don't fault any particular therapist or friend or family member for their bad counsel, because estrangement—unlike most of the terrible things that can happen to us—is still a largely closeted problem. Estrangement doesn't benefit from the surfeit of books, articles, and web pages that show up for more common problems like marriage, divorce, or depression.

So it was in some ways dumb luck that the consultant to my practice, wise and helpful with all of my difficult cases, turned out to be wise and helpful with the most difficult case of all: me and my heartbreaking estrangement. Over time, her recommendations helped me find a way back to my daughter. I wrote my last book, *When Parents Hurt*, to help other parents going through the hell of estrangement. My goal was to help them not make the same mistakes I did, and to find a way to heal the distance, as I was eventually able to do. As a result of the popularity of that book, I developed a large following of parents across the country and internationally, whom I've reached through weekly webinars on estrangement. Since I can't address all of the emails and questions that I receive on a daily basis, I started offering a free Monday Q&A for estranged parents, which is still ongoing. I also consult with parents in my office in Oakland, California, as well as parents and professionals in and outside of the United States.

I have learned an awful lot in the years since my last book was published and want you to benefit from the thousands of voices of parents who have informed my ideas about what works, what doesn't, and how to end the pain. These are voices that you will hear throughout these pages.

ISN'T IT THE PARENT'S FAULT?

When I'm consulted by a parent, I make no assumptions about their innocence or their guilt in regard to the claims of their adult child. Sometimes parents present themselves in a more idealized light than is obviously the case. Often, it's not until I read the correspondence with their adult child or talk to the child that I see how much the parent contributes to the child's need for distance. Sometimes it's clear that the parent is very reasonable and the adult child or their spouse is the more troubled part of the dynamic.

And to complicate matters further, sometimes the cause of the estrangement lies somewhere in that vast desert between—where the complexities of each person's personalities, histories, challenges, or genetics ping-pong back and forth off the other's, and conflict operates less as cause and effect and more like a feedback loop, endlessly amplifying the worst instincts of the parent, adult child, or anyone else who wants to step into the fray.

Part of what makes the discussion of estrangement challenging is the way that the tribal nature of our culture infects today's family relations. Spend a few minutes on the forums of either the estranged adult children or the estranged parents and you'll see a clannish approach as hostile as anything currently extant between the left and the right in our current political landscape.

Amid this new landscape, it is not your fault that you don't know how to navigate interactions with your adult children. But if you want a different relationship, it will require change on your part. Reconciling an estrangement requires an attitude unlike any you've ever experienced before. It's not easy, and frankly, my methods aren't for everyone. I've had parents fire me because they refused to reach out to the adult child in a way that I believe is critical for a potential reconciliation. I've also fired parents because they wanted to use the family therapy as a vehicle to blame their adult children rather than empathize or take responsibility.

My method requires a willingness and certain bravery on the part of the parent. You must strive to see yourself as your child sees you, and actively look for evidence that what they're saying may have a kernel of truth. And even when you think their ideas, perceptions, or accusations are bullshit or curated by their therapist, your ex, or their spouse, you must still start by saying: "Okay, let's look at this together." Not to prove them wrong, but to understand how they came to this point and why they have chosen not to be with you.

It is true that some parents have been destructive in how they raised their children—and that they continue to behave in ways that make it easy to see why distance is the best strategy for their now-grown son or daughter. But even here, hardly anyone talks about what to do for those parents who are trapped in the endlessly repeating cycles of despair, depression, and even violence that keep them on the fringes of support and understanding. It is these parents who are invariably the least equipped to navigate the high-wire communication techniques required of today's egalitarian parent–adult child relationships, where empathy, self-awareness, and self-reflection are key. The hurt, hapless, even destructive parent is also deserving of our help and understanding.

Is the best advice we can offer an adult child "Just walk away and protect yourself? Focus on your own needs—your spouse, friends, and children? Let the parent pay for the sins of their parenting?" Is a parent who didn't have the economic, social, or psychological supports to be a good parent really deserving of so little empathy, if not from their child, then from the rest of us?

I don't think so.

WHO IS THIS BOOK FOR?

This book is for anybody who is suffering from the loss of an adult child or a grandchild. While it's written for the parent and grandparent, adult children will also find a new perspective to consider—one that may foster empathy and understanding. Estrangement is painful and confusing. It's also complex: there are no one-size-fits-all solutions.

The first part of the book discusses the most common pathways to estrangement. These include abuse, divorce, mental illness, the contributions of today's psychotherapists to estrangement, and differences in values and personalities.

The second half includes familiar situations for estranged parents and grandparents. Grandparents who lose contact with grandchildren often come to me in despair, asking: "Will I ever see them again?" I look at how grandchildren are often a casualty of a parent–adult child estrangement and make recommendations for estranged grandparents. I also talk about siblings and how long-standing conflict can result in estrangement or ongoing conflict. Since estrangements often occur as a result of conflict between the parents and the spouse of the adult child, I have a chapter devoted to navigating that complex and often thorny relationship.

The final part of the book provides strategies and my own rules for parent–adult child relationships, drawn from my forty years of practice. I explain why failing to learn them puts you at risk for continued estrangement. I also address common questions crucial to your ongoing well-being and serenity: how to survive the holidays, how to make amends, how to handle disrespect and abuse, and how to heal from the pain, among others.

In my private practice, I've found that understanding the social causes of estrangement helps parents feel less alone, less guilty, and less ashamed. Throughout the book, I interweave the latest research on how families have changed and how those changes provide greater risk but also greater potential. But I also know that people want tools to help them heal their pain. So each chapter will provide all of the above: case studies, research to provide a framework for the observations, and some good old-fashioned advice.

In the past decade, my practice has become filled with estranged parents, leading me to wonder whether I'd uncovered a new trend. Was the rest of the country also experiencing an uptick in estrangement? In writing this book, I knew that I would need to dig deeper. I called colleagues around the country who worked with families and young adults—and discovered they were witnessing the same thing that I was. I began to read hundreds of studies in psychology, history, sociology, and economics and scores of books in those fields. I have also conducted my own research in affiliation with the University of Wisconsin at Madison.

My mission is to help you find a healthy way to reconcile. In general—and there are exceptions—I believe reconciliation is better than staying apart. Better for you and better for our society. And if a reconciliation isn't possible, I want to help you to have a happy, healthy life with or without your kid in it.

Chapter 1

CAN I SAVE THE RELATIONSHIP WITH MY ESTRANGED CHILD?

Sometimes parents do very little to cause an estrangement. And sometimes they do a lot . . .

Ralph wanted my help reconciling with his estranged son, but he didn't like my advice. He didn't believe that his son's view of him, however harsh, might have a little truth to it. In reality, I thought his son's assessment was more than a little true: Ralph was a gruff, self-centered Modesto developer who took his own opinions way too seriously. He expected a level of gratitude and deference from his son that was never going to happen. Ever. Especially challenging was Ralph's belief that the amount of financial help he'd provided his son afforded him the right to dictate the terms of the relationship.

Frank told me that he had grown up feeling controlled and dominated by his father. Among other things, Ralph was critical of Frank's desire to get an undergraduate degree in the humanities; he threatened to cut off his college funding if Frank didn't study something practical that could, as he put it, "actually support a family." Frank's temperament was more like his mother's—bookish, reclusive, drawn to the arts. While he ended up getting a BS in business, he went back to school for an MA in English lit shortly after. He had worked hard in his own therapy to stand up to his father's demands for time and availability. He'd also made it clear to his dad that there was no way he was going to give back an inch of that hard-won territory.

In my initial meeting with Frank he described feeling close to his mother but a constant disappointment to his father. It wasn't until he got into therapy that he began to connect his feelings of unworthiness to his relationship with his dad. "I just don't want to walk around feeling like that anymore. It sucks. I'm through with him treating me like that person. I feel a lot less stressed since I've cut off contact with him. I'm fine having a relationship with my mom, but she pretty much does whatever he says. You've met my father, so you probably get it."

I got it.

My work with estranged families typically takes place over two to five sessions. Most of the time parents contact me because they have no contact with their adult child and want strategies to pursue reconciliation. In our initial meeting, I ask about their own childhood history, so I can learn about experiences they may be repeating or that may continue to influence them. I also take a thorough developmental history of their adult child from the parent's perspective, which includes the child's academic performance, social life, drug and alcohol use or abuse, prior or current therapy, learning disabilities, temperament, and psychiatric issues. While I don't expect parents to be diagnosticians, I want to gain a sense of how they understand their child's strengths, vulnerabilities, temperament, level of insight, and self-reflection.

Of course the parent's view is sometimes colored by the limitations imposed by their own childhood history, their history of interactions with the child, and whatever other vulnerabilities or limitations they bring to the table. So a parent might wrongly assert that his or her adult child is overly sensitive or defensive because they can't see how much defensiveness they provoke.

In my initial meeting I suggested that Ralph consider making amends to his son. I stressed that Frank himself had indicated that the relationship wouldn't move forward unless his father could more deeply address his feelings about their relationship. It was clear that since childhood, Frank had felt controlled or criticized by his father.

"I have nothing to apologize for," Ralph said, annoyed. "He went to a good school and didn't have to pay a dime for it. I bought him and his wife a house; she won't even talk to me. I have money set aside so my grandchildren will have their college paid for. And now I'm not even allowed to see them. What exactly am I supposed to be sorry for again? I've got an idea: How about he apologizes to me for cussing me out the last time I was there?"

"Sounds like you did do a lot for him," I said. "I agree." And I did agree. But the exchange rate on parental investment has weakened over the past half century. Parents, for better or worse, can no longer demand contact as a return on time and money spent. Like many parents, Frank wasn't factoring that into his expectations.

Ralph's wife, Rachel, was small, quiet, and unbearably sad. I asked for her thoughts about the estrangement.

"Oh . . . ," she said slowly, as though gathering strength to respond, "I don't know. I just want this to end. My grandbabies, I don't know what they think, and you know, I just miss them so much. This isn't fair to them. He and his dad, they're probably more similar than different." Small smile. "Both a little too pigheaded for their own good."

I could see how some people would feel intimidated by Ralph. He was a big guy, used to getting his own way and to having people agree with him. His size, bluster, and arrogance would probably be daunting to a spouse, let alone a child. But I also recognized that he, like many estranged parents, was caught in a generational trap not of his own making.

"You know what?" he said when I asked him about his childhood. "Nobody gave me *anything* growing up. My old man used to beat my ass all the time. Is he calling me up and saying, 'Aww, son, I'm so sorry for beating your ass all the time. What was that like for you?' He's an ornery sonofabitch, but we still go see him and my mom 'cause that's what family does."

Rachel smiled at me apologetically.

"He also made me who I am today, so I kind of give the old man credit, as big of a dick as he was. When I'm in a meeting with a bunch of construction workers and I'm on the phone with some asshole who's holding up my building permits, even though I've already sent them everything for the tenth time, could they give a shit about what I'm feeling? So I just don't see how that's supposed to make things any better."

"I understand. I think a lot of the parents that I work with feel the same way," I said. "But it seems like the way you've been doing it isn't getting you what you want. Do I have that right?"

"Yep," he said begrudgingly.

"So I don't think there's a big chance of your seeing him or your grandchildren unless we can help you do it differently. Your son made that pretty clear to me in my individual session with him."

From my many years of experience, I can say that how a parent responds to this particular recommendation—that they try to empathize with the child's complaints or perceptions, however at odds these are with their own—is crucial: it often determines whether they ever see their children or grandchildren again.

"Well, I'm not apologizing to him. No way. For what?"

Rachel looked at him wearily. I could tell this was an old, tired interaction for her: she pleads with him to take a softer, less defensive approach and he aggressively shoots her down. In my experience with married couples, mothers are often willing to keep trying long after their husbands have stopped. I have worked with many desperately grieving mothers who said some version of this: "My life has no meaning without my children and grandchildren in it, so why go on living?" This reality causes them to keep trying sometimes well past the point of it being good for anyone. And sometimes they keep trying because they know that the child needs something different in order to reconcile.

A mother's desire to persevere may result from the fact that women are still held to a higher standard of responsibility for family relationships than are men. As a result, they have a much harder time letting themselves off the hook. Fathers are also deeply wounded by estrangements, but perhaps due to their roles being less socially prescribed, their identities may not suffer as intensely. And, unlike mothers, they may believe that giving up on reconciliation is an expression of pride or masculinity, rather than selfishness.

In Ralph's case, I also knew that his aggression and gruff bearing insulated him against his feelings of sadness and shame about his son's rejection.

"It's not exactly that you have to apologize," I tried again. "It's more like this: you're saying that you didn't know when you were raising him that you hurt him. And now you do. Now you wish you'd communicated differently. You don't have to say that you're a bad person or a bad father. Just that your behavior had an effect on him that wasn't your desire."

Rachel looked at her husband hopefully, waiting to see if this new approach was getting any purchase. "That seems like a good way to put it," she said.

But Ralph wasn't going to relent. Instead he seemed to grow hardened. "I *did* want him to be afraid of me: I wanted him to toughen up. He was such a whiny little mama's boy."

"He *wasn't* a mama's boy," Rachel said quietly, though with more resentment than I had heard from her up to that point. "He's not you. Not everyone goes charging through life like a bull, pushing aside everyone who gets in their way. He's just a gentler spirit. Why not try what Dr. Coleman's suggesting?"

I could feel Ralph getting more defensive. This was not the direction I wanted our session to go. Asking a parent to empathize with his son's complaint of mistreatment can be dicey territory if that parent was also abused in childhood, as Ralph apparently was. For some parents, feeling empathy for their child's allegations is a slippery slope, a route to experiencing long-warded-off feelings of hurt or fear from their own pasts. Their unconscious schema is that it is better to keep all of that neatly tucked away and sealed shut: *I raised him like my old man raised me and I turned out okay, so he should, too.*

I was also starting to feel discouraged. Most estranged parents will walk through fire to have a family session with their adult children. But Frank wasn't able to take even the most basic step. And I felt sad for Rachel. She didn't have the strength to tell her husband: *Nothing is more important to me than having my child and my grandchildren back in my life. If you don't try to change, I'll leave you. Or I'll make your life so miserable you'll give in and do as I ask you to do.* In marriage, people have to sometimes use their power to get what they need. And estrangements from adult children sometimes force a spouse to use that power.

"Like many couples," I said, trying to find a more direct alliance with Rachel, "it sounds like you two aren't in complete agreement about how to handle this. And it sounds like Frank's major complaints are with his father at this point, is that right?"

Rachel was quiet, letting Ralph take the lead.

"She can do whatever she wants," he said. "It's up to her. I'm not holding her back if she wants to go visit them. I've told her that."

"Well," Rachel said, repeating an obviously well-rehearsed line, "I think we probably have to stick together on this."

"You can," I offered. "But sometimes it makes sense for one parent to establish a separate peace with the child as a bridge toward a future relationship with the other. From my perspective, the fewer degrees of separation, the better."

Frank gave an "I don't give a damn" shrug to my suggestion, the disapproval of which was obvious to Rachel. "Mmm," she said, looking at him again. "I think we have to have a united front on this one." To her, defying a spouse was an unspeakable act of disloyalty.

"Okay," I said, "I understand what I'm asking you to do isn't easy. Having talked to your son, I do think I can help you. But the door is closing and some doors don't open up again. I wish I could offer you a different card to play, but this is all we've got. You're right that your parents didn't do that with you, Ralph, and you stayed in contact with them. And your grandparents probably didn't do it with your parents, and I'm guessing they stayed in contact with them as well?"

"Damn right," Ralph said.

"So I could see why you wouldn't want to do something that no one ever did for you—especially if you gave your son a better life than anyone ever gave you. It isn't necessarily fair, but family is very different today than it once was. In my experience, most parents who make these changes feel like it's worth it if it means getting their child and grandchildren back."

I had several more sessions with Ralph and Rachel. But I wasn't able to help them reconcile with Frank. It wasn't because their son was unwilling; rather, he was unwilling to do it on the terms set forth by his father.

FINDING RECONCILIATION

A very different outcome happened with another family with whom I worked. Karina was a twenty-six-year-old software developer in Oakland referred by her therapist for potential therapy with her mother. She had a warm, easy bearing that communicated comfort of being in close quarters with therapists. She sat down and apologized for her post-workout attire. Since running shoes, yoga pants, and a Gore-Tex hoodie are now standard couture in the Bay Area, I just smiled and said something about the importance of being properly warmed up if you're considering family therapy.

When I asked about her goals, she said that she wasn't sure that she even wanted to do family therapy with her mother. Moreover, she wondered if she *should.* "I get that my mother had a really hard childhood. I really do. Nobody should have to go through what she did. But it doesn't give her the right to demand I have a relationship with her if I don't want one. It also puts a lot of strain on my marriage because every time I talk to her or go see her, it takes me a week to start feeling normal again. Here, check out this email," she said, handing me her phone. "This is typical."

Dear Karina,

I am so sick and tired of you and your brother's self-centered bullshit. It's bad enough that you barely can condescend to return a phone call to me or invite me out to visit you and my grandchildren in the past three years, but now I get to hear about how hard your childhood was? You know what? Boo-hoo. Your childhood was a picnic compared to what I had growing up. You did not have a hard childhood. I went to every one of your soccer games, school plays and now I get to hear about how a relationship with me stresses you out and is bad for your marriage? Give me a break. I don't know what your therapist is saying but I doubt she's giving you very good advice if this is what she's telling you to do. Forget you.

Mom

"Pretty harsh," I said, handing back the phone.

"I just don't know what to do at this point. I haven't talked to her now for a year and I really don't want to talk to her. It makes me feel like a terrible person—but I'm just much happier without her in my life. Does that make me a bad person?"

I'm sometimes contacted by adult children who want to do due diligence and determine whether their position of estrangement is reasonable or severe. I don't think adult children are obligated to have a relationship with a parent, especially in those cases where there's a history of abuse. However, I *do* think that both parents and adult children should try for some period of time to empathize with the other's position in order to see if a more mutually satisfying relationship can be built. Parents should do this because the buck stops with them, and one never completely relinquishes the title of parent. Adult children should do it because working through childhood issues provides a better foundation for healthy relationships and the ability to parent. In addition, most parenting occurs in a fog where seemingly good decisions can later appear clueless, selfish, or damaging—and the parent deserves a chance to repair.

But directly confronting a hurtful parent takes courage. As I listened to Karina, it was clear that her mother was greatly downplaying, out of guilt or lack of awareness, how hurtful she had been in her parenting. Karina recounted many incidents of her mother's repeated use of shame and humiliation, especially during adolescence. This had left Karina feeling highly anxious and insecure in adulthood, a complex of emotions that were never too far from the surface of her daily life.

At the climax of Russell Banks's novel *Affliction*, the father rises up and assumes a terrifying height and power right before he dies in the fire intentionally set by the tormented protagonist son. In that moment, Banks illustrates the dominion some parents continue to have over the adult child's psychic life, often well into adulthood. In killing his father, he imagines an end to the internalized suffering experienced at his father's hand.

Estrangement is often a similar attempt to reduce the hold that the parent continues to have over the adult child. However painful the separation, many adult children report that ending the relationship with the parent was the only way they could find to take control over their own lives. To consider reconciling, an adult child needs to feel assured that they can return to the estrangement if they decide that reconciliation was a bad idea.

Estranged parents are often confused by my willingness to deeply empathize with the adult child's version of the parent. They worry that I am ceding to a view of them that is wrong, distorted, or unfairly curated by their spouse, therapist, or the parent's ex-spouse. But

I have good reason to empathize, one that ultimately helps estranged parents: the truth is that no adult child will step into a therapy office with a formerly estranged parent until they feel that their interests are protected, and that the person (me) leading them into potential battle will shield them from the ways that the parent could still be hurtful.

Many estranged adult children also worry their voices will be lost if they empathize with their parent. They worry they'll feel guilty once they fathom how much the estrangement hurt the parent—and, they fear the result of reconciling out of guilt instead of genuine desire. They worry that they're giving a pass on the parent's prior hurtful behavior by agreeing to be back in contact. They're concerned that the strength they need to counter the parent's authority will be overwhelmed by their feelings of responsibility for them.

I could tell that Karina possessed the capacity to forgive her mother, assuming that her mother was sincere about attempting to change. Karina felt sad for her mother, guilty about their estrangement, and aware of the emotional cost to both. Since Karina had contacted me in the spirit of due diligence, I suggested that a few sessions of family therapy might be worth pursuing. I stressed that she set the terms of a relationship with her mom, such as the length and frequency of visits. I told her it was reasonable to ask her mother to take responsibility for the hurt she had caused as a condition for reconciliation. I said that agreeing to family therapy didn't obligate her to reestablish contact with her mother beyond the meetings. In addition, I emphasized that if there were to be more contact post-therapy, we would set guidelines for going forward.

TEACHING PARENTS A NEW LANGUAGE

When I met Sinead, Karina's mother, she was slow to get up to greet me. It was as if she were still considering whether the appointment was a good idea. She stood up with effort, taking time to fold her newspaper and tuck it into her bag. She followed me into my office with her head down, as if she were heading into an execution. In my office, Sinead sat down on my couch. Facing me, she announced, "Well, I guess you got to hear all about what a terrible mother I was." Her tone was a mix of fear and contempt.

I smiled sympathetically. "I did hear some pretty big complaints."

"Oh, I bet you did. I've heard them all before, so I can only imagine what she said to you." She examined me to see when the inquisition would begin. If parents haven't read my work, they sometimes assume that I'll start lecturing them as soon as they sit down.

I kept it upbeat and affectionate, which is where I like to exist with families. Though I try to be lighthearted, my attitude is never dismissive—rarely, "Oh, that's not so bad," but rather: "Yep, life can be challenging, can't it?" My belief is that parents genuinely did the best they could, even if that best was very hurtful to their child. This disposition allows me to feel nurturing and caring for a parent, even when he or she is diminishing the consequences of their problematic behavior.

Sinead told me about growing up in Florida in a chaotic and violent household. Her father sometimes punched her in the stomach without warning and said, "That's to keep you from thinking whatever you were thinking." Diagnosed with paranoid schizophrenia, he was in and out of mental institutions before he finally took his own life at forty-two. Her mother cruelly compared Sinead's weight and appearance with that of her more attractive and socially aspiring older sisters. Not infrequently, her mother contemptuously referred to Sinead as "my little ugly duckling."

Sinead reported the difficulties of her past in a dismissive way, waving off my obviously concerned expressions. "Oh, gosh, that was so long ago," she said. "Does it really even matter? I haven't thought about that in years." I said that it matters because her childhood might make her daughter's complaints seem mystifying in comparison. I also observed that—having felt so rejected and unloved by her parents—the rejection of her daughter must feel much more unfair. She looked at me with an expression that conveyed skepticism about the utility of this line of inquiry.

I then told her about my own experience of being estranged from my daughter. That got her interest.

I don't typically talk about my own history or struggles with my clients, but I do with those whose adult children won't talk to them. My prior estrangement and reconciliation with my daughter positions me as a peer rather than another know-it-all parent or therapist.

Feeling understood rather than blamed allowed Sinead to consider the value in acknowledging her daughter's pain. More important, to accept the possibility that in so doing, she wasn't giving her daughter a platform for more reasons to hate her. To the contrary, it was the only path to credibility she possessed.

In Tara Westover's memoir, *Educated,* she describes the power of having her mother acknowledge the ways that she neglected her.

> I know only this: that when my mother told me she had not
> been the mother to me that she wished she'd been, she became
> that mother for the first time.

But that kind of frank acknowledgment is challenging for most parents to do. It's challenging to say, "Yes, I failed you, I hurt you, I let you down." It requires exposing your beating heart where your child could fatally wound you. At least it feels like that. I know it does.

These are hard sessions for both parents and adult children. Hard for the adult child to take the risk of baring their emotions to the very person who, they believe, caused their suffering. Hard for the parent to confront the possibility that he or she has deeply hurt, betrayed, or failed his or her own child. *Hard, hard, hard.* But: worth it if each can get to the other side.

Parents have to go first. They have to give their child the space and time to talk about why the estrangement was necessary. They have to sit there and tolerate the pain, sorrow, and guilt it evokes; they have to empathize, mirror, find the kernel if not the bushel of truth. My role is to steer them away from defending, explaining, rationalizing, blaming the child, blaming the ex, blaming whomever. Some parents need a whole lot of steering and I am not afraid to tell parents in a session: *If you keep communicating this way, you will convince your adult child that staying away was the right choice.*

But Sinead was courageous. She grasped how her fear and shame made it hard for her to acknowledge, in a straightforward way, the truth of her daughter's complaints about the ways that she shamed, neglected, and humiliated her. And she sobbed out her apologies in the session with Karina. Long, hard cries of regret and longing and sorrow. Of not being the mother she had always dreamed of being, given how much pain she had suffered as a child. Of causing her daughter to suffer despite wanting her to feel secure. Of failing to understand how much her own unresolved pain had infiltrated her own parenting. And her daughter tearfully, gratefully, thanked her. And asked her to be part of her life again.

The two cases I've described in this chapter mirror family dynamics that people commonly think of when they discuss estrangement: adult children with reasonable complaints who end contact because the relationship felt too hurtful and disruptive. And in both, the chance for a reconciliation hinged on the parent's capacity to dig deep, empathize, and make amends for the ways that their child had felt neglected, hurt, or abused.

However, there are other reasons why adult children cut off contact with parents and refuse to reconcile—reasons that have little to do with parental abuse or neglect. Regardless of the cause, a close parent–adult child relationship requires quite a bit more psychological health from both parent and child than it did in prior generations where there was less aspiration for a close lifelong friendship and where the rules of engagement weren't predicated on such a psychologically intensive framework. From this perspective, a close parent–adult child relationship often requires the following.

From the parent:
- An ability to respond to the adult child's negativity, complaints, criticisms, or rejections in a nonretaliatory way.
- An ability to disagree with the adult child's values without being rejecting.
- A willingness to see that the adult child has their own life separate from that of the parent. To that end, that the adult child is not obligated to spend more time than that wanted by the adult child.
- An ability in the parent to be sufficiently distant from their own childhood hurts or other life wounds and disappointments to recognize that:
  a) the adult child is not the same person as the one who shaped the parent's identity and
  b) the adult child is not obligated to make up for what the parent hasn't received in their lives.
- The ability to communicate their feelings in a noncritical, non-guilt-inducing, non-shaming way.
- The capacity for some measure of self-reflection.

From the adult child:
- The ability to be close to the parent without a fear of losing himself or herself in the relationship. This requires the capacity to be aware of the parent's thoughts, emotions, or needs without feeling unduly influenced to comply with the parent's wishes.

- The ability to state complaints or feedback to the parent without excessive fear of reprisal, even if the parent is prone to that.
- The ability to accept the parent's limitations as a parent and as a person.
- To recognize that the parent's inability to provide what he wanted or needed was more about the parent's deficits and less about the parent's inherent desire to have the child suffer.
- To see that the parent's inability to provide her what she needed was not a reflection of the child's inherent value or worth.
- The capacity for some measure of self-reflection.

In the upcoming chapters we'll answer the following questions: Does the term *parental abuse* sometimes mean one thing to today's adult children and something entirely different to parents? Can a divorce permanently cause rifts between parents and their children? While the parent's mental illness is an obvious contributor, in what ways might an adult child's mental illness or their spouse's also raise the probability? Do today's individual therapists increase the intensity and authority of the adult's complaints and raise the probability of estrangement? Are there such things as irreconcilable differences in values, personalities, or attitudes between parents and adult children? Can grandparents become estranged despite being good grandparents? Are there solutions to ongoing sibling estrangements? If reconciliation isn't possible, is it possible to have a meaningful life without your children or grandchildren? We have a lot to talk about.

Chapter 2

THE MANY PATHWAYS
TO ESTRANGEMENT

I'm often asked how successful I am in getting adult children to reconcile with their parents. The answer is that I'm consistently successful if both the parents and the adult child are willing and able to do the work. Parents typically have to take leadership because they are often more motivated for a reconciliation to occur. If reconciliation doesn't happen, sometimes it is because the parent is unwilling to engage in the kind of humility, self-reflection, and effort that are required—as was evident in Ralph's estrangement from his son.

But sometimes it won't go forward because no matter how expert and compassionate the parent, the adult child isn't able or willing to reconcile. Here are some common reasons:

A Parent's Divorce at Any Age

In a highly individualistic culture such as ours, divorce may cause the child to see the parents and others in a family less as members of a unit of which they're a part, and more as individuals with their own relative strengths or weaknesses. It can also increase the likelihood of an eventual estrangement in any of the following ways:

- It may cause the child to take sides against one parent over the other, whether the children are still minors or have reached adulthood.
- It may cause one parent to covertly or overtly alienate the child against the other parent.
- It may cause the child to worry more about the well-being of one parent over the other, which may cause them to shift toward or away from a parent depending on their gender, temperament, or other influences.
- Divorce brings new people into the family such as stepchildren, stepparents, girlfriends, or boyfriends who can create multiple family estrangements over the division of financial and emotional resources.

A Difficult Daughter-in-Law or Son-in-Law

I have worked with many families who had close, confiding relationships with their adult child but found their relationship completely upended by the child's new spouse. This was especially true if the new husband or wife was psychologically troubled. In those situations, the spouse feels threatened by the attachment of the adult child to his or her parents and eventually says, "Choose them or me, you can't have both."

Mental Illness or Addictions in the Child

If your child suffers from addiction or mental illness, they may experience contact with you as too challenging, confusing, or dysregulating. Their mental illness may cause them to misinterpret your intentions, the past, or your feelings about them. It may also cause them to interact with you in ways that make it difficult or impossible to respond in a consistently loving or affectionate way.

Their Therapist

It's not unusual for estrangements to begin as a result of the adult child entering psychotherapy. This can occur for several reasons: because the therapist makes faulty or exaggerated attributions of causality between your past behavior and your adult child's present state of mind; because your adult child wants to discuss their childhood and you don't or didn't have the skills to navigate that conversation; or because the therapist recommends estrangement as a worthwhile intervention to address your adult child's feelings about you.

Feeling Too Close to the Parent

Your child may have felt too dependent on you growing up and may know no other way to feel in charge of their own lives than to reject you. From this perspective, the parent is too important in the mind of the adult child; estrangement is an attempt to reduce that importance.

Disagreements About Choices, Values, and Lifestyles

Some estrangements occur because the parent and the adult child are too mismatched in values and political beliefs. This can occur if the parent doesn't approve of the child's gender or sexuality or when the child disapproves of the parent's. It can also occur as a result of differences in political orientations, choice of romantic partners, or more simply, a fundamental incompatibility of personalities.

A SOCIETAL SHIFT

In my clinical work over the past forty years with parents, adult children, and their extended families, I have found that estrangements reflect a broader cultural transformation. Emphasis on loyalty to the family unit has been replaced with the pursuit of individual fulfillment. Honor thy mother and thy father has been replaced by the idea that family is who you make it. Parents who were once advised to stay together for the sake of the children are now told: If you're not happy, then your kids won't be happy. The belief that one should respect his or her elders has been replaced with the truism that respect isn't given, it's earned. Values that once prioritized the family—these include obligation, responsibility, loyalty—have been radically reconfigured to emphasize the happiness and well-being of the individual.

Many of these shifts have been positive. There is now far more equality between the sexes, which has created the opportunity for more intimate, mutually respectful marriages and romantic relationships. There's more freedom to terminate relationships with hurtful siblings, parents, or grown children, which allows individual family members more insulation from psychologically destructive or overly meddlesome relatives. There's greater acceptance about the need to leave a meaningless or abusive marriage, which means that people are freer to form unions more in line with their own ideals or sexualities, and to protect their children from the costs of a destructive marriage. A majority of parents today are in far more contact with their adult children than were prior generations.

Yet when family members use this relatively newfound freedom, they can forever alter their lives and the lives of those around them. Estrangements can pit sibling against sibling in Shakespearean-worthy dramas over the spoils of kingdoms: fathers cast off their ungrateful and unsolicitous sons; grandchildren get used as ransom to compel better behavior from errant parents; a grown child's love is withheld as an object of torment more excruciating than anything used in the Inquisition; a daughter-in-law becomes obsessed with fantasies involving her mother-in-law, a locked garage door, and a car whose engine can't be shut off.

It's Because You Abused Me and Now I Need
to Focus On Myself

A common thread in the perspective of estranged children is allegations of harm committed by the parent. This is challenging terrain
for today's parents of adult children because much of what younger
generations consider hurtful or neglectful parental acts would barely
be on the radar for parents of almost any generation before. However,
it's important to understand that however loving, dedicated, or invested you were, your adult children have their own scale to weigh
your behavior as a parent, one calibrated in a way far different from
the one you brought into the nursery. Their measurements are based
on a much more curated concept of childhood, where identities and
emotions are more investigated, more complex, and more parsed.

For example, in a recent *New York Times* article, "Generation Z:
Who They Are in Their Own Words," a young woman remarked:
"We have the tools and language to understand identity in ways our
parents never really thought about." That's for sure. But why should
it matter? It matters because parents are more important than ever
in the narrative of how young adults understand themselves. The
language of psychotherapy permeates our culture through *Oprah,
Dr. Phil,* or thousands of self-help sites for every diagnosis known to
inhabit the *Diagnostic and Statistical Manual.* Even more strikingly,
in the past decade, younger generations are going to therapy more
frequently and with much less stigma than any generation before—
causing a writer in the *Wall Street Journal* to refer to millennials as
"the Therapy Generation."

Many parents are completely unprepared for the reflection of their
parenting seen through the eyes of their child's therapist. "I used
to think I had a pretty good childhood," one young adult told his
mother, "but since I've been in therapy I'm learning that it was really
all about you, not me." This disparity in perspectives may result from
changing definitions of what constitutes a good childhood, and by

extension, good parenting. According to psychologist Nick Haslam, definitions of abuse, trauma, and neglect have grown in the past three decades to incorporate more and more symptoms and to pathologize experiences that were once considered normal. "Phenomena that might previously have been understood as moral failings (e.g., substance abuse), bad habits (e.g., eating problems), personal weaknesses (e.g., sexual dysfunctions), medical problems (e.g., sleep disturbances), character foibles (e.g., shyness), or ordinary vicissitudes of childhood," writes Haslam, "now find shelter under the umbrella concept of mental disorder." The proliferation of mental disorders in successive editions of the DSM went from 47 conditions in 1952 to 300 in the DSM-IV, causing some to accuse the authors of the DSM and the field of psychiatry of disease mongering.

Unlike the definitions of trauma that existed three decades ago, the bar for qualifying as a trauma today is much lower. An event no longer has to involve serious threats to life or limb, nor does it need to exist outside of normal experience. It doesn't have to create marked distress in almost everyone, nor does it need to produce obvious distress in the traumatized person. In other words, if I say that you abused, neglected, bullied, or traumatized me, then you did. As Haslam writes, evaluations about whether emotional abuse, trauma, or neglect occurred are today based on the child's perception of that behavior, even if that behavior would look benign to an outside observer or exist independently of the parent's intentions or emotions. *It's what I feel that matters.*

Identities Around Suffering

Younger generations are also more likely to weave these hurtful childhood experiences into a narrative of their identities, which is also historically new. Stresses, struggles, and painful incidents once viewed as existential problems in families (and something better kept to oneself) are now seen, for better and worse, as life altering and transforming.

On the positive side, this orientation can create greater self-awareness and provide a language and road map to stronger relationships, not only with parents but with friends and romantic partners. On the other hand, it may increase the salience of emotions that are sometimes better left unspoken or tolerated.

Of course, many children *are* victimized by their parents through physical or sexual abuse, verbal abuse, and abject neglect and may carry lifelong scars as a result. In addition, the expansion over the past three decades in what's considered hurtful or traumatizing is useful in helping people put words to feelings that may not have before existed.

However, we have become so preoccupied with parents as the causal focus of life's outcomes—and what is diagnosable, pathological, and traumatizing now encompasses so much of what should be considered normal, expectable parenting—that adult children may feel that they have a much bigger complaint than is fair to the parent regardless of the seriousness of the parental behaviors.

This isn't good for anyone. Studies show that expanding the list of mental disorders to incorporate more and more experiences can create a feeling of decreased agency, increased pessimism about the potential for recovery, and decreased confidence in one's capacity to exert control over his or her challenges. This feeling of helplessness could make the bold move of estrangement look appealing as an act of empowerment. While there's nothing especially modern about family conflict or a desire to feel insulated from it, conceptualizing the estrangement of a relationship with a family member as an expression of personal growth and achievement is almost certainly new.

And herein lies the problem: the premises of many talk therapies and self-help books are still founded on ideas of child development that position the parent as the most important determinant of how children turn out. These suppositions are rooted in the outdated "blank slate" musings of Locke and Rousseau, Freud's now-discredited psychosexual stages and ideas about repression and memory, Maslow's theories of self-actualization, and John Watson's grandiose claims that behaviorism could create any kind of adult wanted by a parent.

Contemporary research challenges this received wisdom, yet families are being torn apart on the weight of its faulty propositions. As developmental psychologist Alison Gopnik wrote about parents in *The Gardener and the Carpenter: What the New Science of Child Development Tells Us About the Relationship Between Parents and Children:* "They're not architects. They're more like gardeners." Behavioral geneticist Robert Plomin goes further, arguing that parents are "not even gardeners if that implies nurturing and pruning plants to achieve a certain result."

The current model of how we become who we are puts adults on a path of self-discovery where the quest is to hunt down and eliminate—not only those traits that stand in the way of happiness, but the individuals they believe to have put those problems there in the first place. The family, more than any other institution, is the place Americans tend to go sniffing when they want to root out the inhibitions, anxieties, or propensities to failure that appear to block their path to growth and achievement. As cultural sociologist Eva Illouz writes, today our suffering is plotted backward: "What is a dysfunctional family? A family where one's needs are not met. And how does one know that one's needs were not met in childhood? Simply by looking at one's present situation." Or as Lillian Hellman wrote in *Pentimento,* "Some people supply too many past victories or pleasures with which to comfort themselves, and other people cling to pains, real and imagined, to excuse what they have become."

Especially powerful is the way that today's therapy, self-help, and even twelve-step groups have adopted the neoliberal logic of success achieved through overcoming inner obstacles. These concepts have become our way of making sense of life and our perceptions of causality, directing people to find and solve the dysfunction of their past to allow for future success. In so doing, they direct people away from other, more probable causes. As family historian Stephanie Coontz observes in *The Way We Never Were: American Families and the Nostalgia Trap*, blaming parents for how children turn out is especially unfair when applied to the poor and working classes, since research shows that the social dynamics of poverty and low status give them less influence over their children in relation to peer groups than parents in other classes.

LOSE YOUR PARENT, FIND YOURSELF

Culture powerfully influences our perceptions and the ways that we attribute causality, interpret the meaning of others' actions and intentions, and enact the aims of the self in relation to the rest of society.

A recent article in *HuffPost* illustrates our cultural preoccupation with narcissism in the form of the narcissistic parent: That is, the parent who is preoccupied with their own needs at the expense of the child's.

How to "Break Up" with a Narcissistic Parent

First, don't blame yourself for the state of the relationship.
Sometimes loving a narcissist means doing so at a safe
    distance—even if the narcissist in question is your parent.

The following items of advice were offered to the adult child:
1. Recognize that your health and well-being come first.
2. Learn to detach and create boundaries.
3. Try not to be confrontational, but do set clear boundaries.
4. Accept that your parent may make it extremely difficult to initiate a break.
5. Don't blame yourself for the state of the relationship.

The importance of boundaries, mentioned twice in the advice portion of the article, is a frequent topic that I hear from adult children (wanting more) and from their parents (wanting less). Maintaining one's boundaries is important if becoming an individual is a goal—and we Americans care very much about being individuals. According to the Hofstede cultural dimensions model, Americans rank higher on scores of individualism than any other culture, as measured by valuing independence, freedom from outside influences, self-expression, and self-realization.

But why is the desire for better boundaries such a common request from today's adult children of their parents? Why are so many young adults claiming they have narcissistic or borderline-personality-disordered parents?

In part, this stems from how families have become more enmeshed in recent decades: parents are more worried, more stressed out, and more educated about child-rearing; all too aware that their mistakes could interfere with their child's successful adulthood. Or so they believe. They're also spending a lot more time with their children. All of this may create a more intense family environment than prior generations where children were seen and not heard, the lines of authority were more spelled out, and parents were less concerned with what their children thought about the job they were doing as parents. In addition, many ways that technology allows families to stay in contact make for a family that is never more than a millisecond text away from one another.

As a result of all of these factors, many, if not most, children know quite a bit about the interior lives of their parents: their dreams, their frustrations, their failures, and their successes. All of the careful and mutual communication and disclosure that parents have been doing with children over the past few decades has created a lot of information about who we all are. Many parents and adult children feel closer because they know each other, arguably, more intimately than did any other generation of parents and adult children in the United States.

However, children have come to be the stand-in relationship that once was performed by community, religion, and friends. While prior generations of parents may have made the mistake of being insufficiently involved, at least as measured against current standards, today's parents are more likely to be *highly* involved with their children. This may be because today's parents are spending far less time with friends or anyone else outside of the family. Sociologist Paul Amato found that couples born in the 1940s had 51 percent more friends, were 39 percent more likely to share friends with their spouse, 168 percent more likely to have organizational memberships, and 133 percent more likely to share those with their spouse than those born in 1960. Sociologist Robert Putnam made a similar observation in his influential book *Bowling Alone.* I maintain that one of the reasons some adult children estrange themselves, or claim to have narcissistic parents, is that they experience their parents' demand for intimacy as more than they can fulfill, and in some cases, more than they should be asked to bear.

Children may also factor more centrally in a parent's system of meaning and pleasure, because they may be one of the few areas where today's climate of incivility is kept at bay: "Childhood has become the last bastion of kindness, the last place where we may find more love in the world than there appears to be," writes psychoanalyst Adam Phillips and historian Barbara Taylor, in *On Kindness.* "Indeed, the modern obsession with child-rearing may be no more and no less than an obsession about the possibility of kindness in a society that makes it harder and harder to believe in kindness."

Where the family and the identity of its members once existed in a rich ecosystem fed and nourished by a community of supports, American families have more and more begun to stand alone; as a result, the intimacy that is required from children is necessarily larger. This may confer benefits to their offspring during the child-rearing years and for those adult children who would like an ongoing relationship—but it may not work as well for those who, for a variety of reasons, don't want as much contact with the parent. While it may be the parent's desire to be besties for life, that doesn't mean that it's always that of the adult child. Nor does it mean that the adult child's smaller appetite for contact is indicative of a pathology.

Because today's parents have often invested more in their children, financially and emotionally, than previous generations, they may feel entitled to a kind of availability that is at odds with what their adult child can reasonably or sanely provide. This entitlement can make parents communicate in ways that work against them—and, in turn, cause the adult child to push back. A negative feedback loop sometimes ensues: the child moves further and further away to escape the feelings of guilt and responsibility for the parent. As they feel their child becoming more and more distant or angry, the parent pursues them even more aggressively. In research on marriage, this feedback loop is referred to as the "pursuer-distancer dynamic" and is associated with greatly increased risk of divorce.

THE CHANGING MEANING OF CONFLICT

The meaning of family turmoil has also changed. Engaging in conflict with family members stops being seen as purely stressful or painful, but rather an opportunity to express agency, display autonomy, and promote the drive for happiness. Staying in contact with family over the life course becomes based not on a presumed sense of obligation or duty, however problematic those may also be, but rather upon the way that the relationship makes the other *feel* about him or herself.

In contrast to prior generations, conflict is no longer seen as an unavoidable, and perhaps even necessary, component of family life, but rather a referendum on each person: *Does my parent limit my potential? My happiness? My distinctiveness? What does it say about me to stay in contact? To end contact? What kind of person does that make me?*

If today's role of parents in the United States is to raise individuals who are assertive and uncompromising in their pursuit of their happiness and individuality, then family conflict takes on a very different meaning than it might in other cultures.

For example, a large international study of nearly 2,700 parents over the age of sixty-five found that parents in the US have almost twice as much conflict with their adult children when compared with parents in Israel, Germany, the UK, and Spain. Merril Silverstein, a social gerontologist at the University of Southern California, summarized his findings by stating that in comparison with parent–adult child relationships in other countries, "American families can be characterized by greater strain."

The difference between American families and families of other industrialized nations may stem from a style of individualism that's unique to the United States. Sociologist Amy Schalet observed that American parenting practices are based on the idea that children learn to become adults by pushing hard against the parents' limits around authority, sex, and alcohol consumption. She terms this "adversarial individualism" and contrasts it with Dutch parenting practices where teens are brought into adulthood by permitting sleepovers in the parents' home with their boyfriends or girlfriends starting at around the age of sixteen, as well as drinking moderately with the family.

While American parents believe that rebellion against the parental order is a normal, even expectable, set of behaviors on the path to adulthood, Dutch parents believe that teens should be eased into the world of adulthood with the parents' knowledge and collaboration, a process she calls "interpersonal individualism." These differences, Schalet notes, stem from contrasting national values—freedom in the United States, and *gezelligheid* (cozy togetherness) in the Netherlands. Whereas children in the US struggle to escape the chains of parental constraint, Dutch children expect that they'll continue to rely on their parents even as they move into adulthood.

MERITOCRACY IN THE FAMILY

Parents are also vulnerable to a new kind of suffering where the meaning of an adult child's love and attention has become much more important to a parent's sense of self, identity, and security. In earlier generations, the job of a parent, however affectionate, was to launch the child into adulthood and send them on their way. Today, in a culture where the highest aspiration for both mothers and fathers is to be best friends with a child for life, a distant or estranged child marks the parent as a failure. Sociologist Carl Bowman notes that in 1985, when Robert Bellah wrote his influential book about the influence of American individualism on the family—*Habits of the Heart*—parents' biggest fear was that their children would never leave home. Now it's that they'll never return.

While some degree of loyalty and obligation to parents were *de jure* for prior generations, today's parents live in a familial meritocracy where they're required to be constantly attuned to the mood and needs of their adult children in order to earn a continued connection to them. This requires a level of psychological sophistication and communicative dexterity that would have been unheard of in any other generation of parents.

British sociologist Anthony Giddens observed that part of the strain of modernity results from our becoming "disembedded" from the traditional institutions of church, neighborhood, marriage, community, and gender. In its stead has been left an intensely personal, day-to-day, moment-to-moment appraisal of the self: its moods, desires, thoughts, and aspirations. This self-appraising project requires constant monitoring. How much or how little to engage with others—with friends, with romantic partners? Do they satisfy our ambition of self-actualization? "Personal growth," writes Giddens in *Modernity and Self-Identity: Self and Society in the Late Modern Age*, "depends on conquering emotional blocks and tensions that prevent us from understanding ourselves as we really are." Social psychologist Eli Finkel's observation of what is required for a successful marriage today also mirrors Giddens's observation: "Success typically requires not only compatibility but also deep insight into each other's core essence, the sort of insight that helps us know what type of support is most beneficial under which circumstances." I say, ditto parenting adult children.

SOULMATE PARENTING

Many, if not most, of today's parents have worked hard to create assertive, empowered people who are uncompromising in the pursuit of their dreams. In so doing, they've created an environment where they are expected to comport themselves much like a soulmate: sensitive but not intrusive, tolerant but not neglectful, supportive but not smothering, forgiving but not indulgent, current on child development though not a pedant, a good playmate but not trying to live their lives through the child, and a good mentor, without using the word *mentor*.

Many adult children are comfortable criticizing or rejecting their parents because they're doing exactly what their parents raised them to do. In her study comparing middle-class and working-class parents, sociologist Annette Lareau noted how common it was for middle-class children to make demands of their parents and insist that they prioritize the child's needs over theirs. Most young adults have been raised by parents who told them they can be anything that they want; their opinions matter, their dreams are vitally important, and their emotions are a source of interest and concern to Mom or Dad, as they will inevitably be to the world. A follow-up study of the same children ten years later found that young adult children of the middle class felt far less grateful to their parents than did the children of the working class. They also valued extended family less than did the working-class young adults.

However, recent research by sociologist Jennifer Silva finds that young adult children of the working class can also be very critical of their parents today as they struggle to find identity and meaning, now that established pathways to adulthood have become far less guaranteed. Silva was surprised to find how commonly working-class adults employed the language of psychotherapy and family dysfunction to explain their lack of success in finding decent paying jobs or intimate relationships. "Many draw unforgiving boundaries against their family members and friends who cannot transform their selves—overcome addictions, save money, heal troubled relationships—through sheer determination alone," writes Silva in her book *Coming Up Short: Working-Class Identity in an Age of Uncertainty*. "[A]t the center of the therapeutic coming of age narrative are not more traditional sources of identity such as work, religion, or gender, but instead the family—as the source of one's individuality, the source of the self, and the source of the neuroses from which one must liberate oneself."

Parenting doesn't occur in a void. It is constantly shaped and directed by economic, social, and cultural forces well outside of our awareness. The decision to estrange a parent or reconcile with a parent, to reach out to a child or let them go is similarly influenced in these ways. In the next few chapters we'll look at common causes of estrangement and the ways that these social forces create new possibilities but also new tensions in parent–adult child relationships.

Chapter 3

MARRIED, DIVORCED, ESTRANGED

Every divorce is a unique tragedy because every divorce brings
an end to a unique civilization—one built on thousands
of shared experiences, memories, hopes, and dreams.

E. Mavis Hetherington and John Kelly,
For Better or for Worse: Divorce Reconsidered

Mark's two grown daughters hated his new wife. She was everything that their mother wasn't: young, pretty, unblemished by years of child-rearing. They also hated her because they believed, wrongly, that their dad was sleeping with her before he divorced their mother. Since the divorce, neither of his daughters has answered his texts, emails, or calls. His younger daughter also cut him off from contact with his grandson, to whom he was very close.

"It's killing me that I'm not even invited to my older daughter's upcoming wedding," he told me in our first session. "I've been begging them to speak to me. Begging! I have lost all self-respect. I don't care. I saw on her Facebook page that she plans to have her uncle, my ex-wife's brother, walk her down the aisle. She doesn't even like him! I don't know if I can survive not going to her wedding. I've never been so sad about anything in my whole life."

Like most divorces, Mark's situation was complicated. Their mother, Martha, told her daughters they could have a relationship with their dad if they wanted, and that she supported it. Despite that, they knew that having a relationship with him was nothing short of a betrayal of her. This wasn't something they said or even thought about. It was just a fact. While both daughters used to say that Mark was a great father prior to the divorce, they were reconsidering their opinion of him based on things they'd learned from their mother since the divorce: the intimation of prior affairs; her depiction of him as being emotionally unavailable to her; his preoccupation with work at the expense of time with her, and—by implication—his daughters.

Their mother's complaints about Mark had been there on and off throughout their marriage but had been constrained by the gratitude she felt for the lifestyle he afforded the family. Since the divorce, her grievances colored the air of every conversation with her daughters, oxidizing into something much harsher now brought to the light of day. His daughters rallied around their mother, virtuous in their desire to protect her from the shame and insult of their father's rejection of her. So even though Martha said that she supported their having a relationship with their father, her constant complaints about him, as well as her portrayal of being victimized by him throughout the marriage, made being close to their dad an impossible task.

And Dad didn't make it any easier. By the time Mark made it to my practice, he had dug himself into a very big hole with his daughters— one that would be hard to dig his way out of. He'd told his kids that their mother was a liar; wrote to tell them how cruelly and selfishly they were behaving; reminded them of all of the privileges he'd provided them; and blamed their estrangement on their mother. Layer upon layer of soil he tossed onto his own grave.

I listened with empathy to this fairly typical scenario. After I took most of the hour to get a sense of his psychology and that of his ex and his two daughters, it was time to talk strategy.

"Okay, first thing is, no more blaming their mother for anything. Anything!"

"Why not? I'm just calling a spade a spade. I was a good father. I used to do everything for those girls," he said. "Coached their sports, helped them with their homework, traveled with them. What am I supposed to do, just go along with their mother that I was this self-centered, cheating asshole?"

"That is an awful position to be in. I get it. And she does sound motivated to bring you down in the eyes of your daughters, so you have every right to complain. Just not to them. At this point, your ex has all of the power and you have none. They won't talk to you, you're not invited to your daughter's wedding, and you can't get them to return a text."

"So what should I do?"

"I think you have to start by showing them you're willing to see this from their perspective—not yours."

As I do with all of the parents in my practice, I asked to see any emails or texts that he had. While the complaints of estranged adult children are sometimes surprisingly rigid and hurtful, often they are plaintive, even desperate, in their limits, requests for boundaries, even ultimatums. At least they can start that way. Over time, in response to the parent's defensiveness or hostility, they become more rigid and rejecting. Reading the string of texts from both daughters, I could tell that their communication had turned the corner to contempt and threat. We had very little time.

I told Mark that he needed to acknowledge their new harsher view of his prior parenting, even if he believed that this perspective was created or influenced by his ex: they now believed that he cared more about his work than his family when he was raising them, and that he had behaved selfishly during his marriage to their mother. He needed to address their new view of him, even if he believed it was incorrect.

I learned about addressing wrongful attributions of causality early in my career working on locked inpatient psychiatric wards; the first two years at Kettering Medical Center in Kettering, Ohio, and the remaining six years at California Pacific Medical Center in San Francisco. I worked with patients with varying degrees of paranoia and other severe disturbances and learned a lot about how to sit with those occupying a state of mind and existence radically different from my own.

One of the most important lessons I discovered was to take people where they were in the moment. If someone was a paranoid schizophrenic, I was never going to be able to reassure them that the CIA hadn't planted bugs in their garden or that aliens weren't sending them messages unless I first accepted those possibilities as both reasonable and plausible. I had to suspend my own disbelief and knowledge about the probabilities of certain outcomes. I had to first say without a shred of patronizing, "That sounds terrifying. Why are they pursuing you? How are they doing it? What do you think that they're trying to achieve?" And I had to occupy that space where such things could exist—to feel that in my mind and body—to let them know that I could enter their world before I earned any credibility that I could ever show them a way out of theirs. Instead of saying, "Well, that's certainly not true, let me show you how irrational you're being," I learned to say, "Wow, if that is happening of course you're scared. I'd be scared, too." And I would be if that was happening to me.

But once I could show them that I could feel what they were feeling, I was in a much better position to ask questions like "Are there other possible explanations? What are the chances that it's not that but something else?" In other words, I had to be able to live in their world, if even for the briefest moments, before I could invite them to take a step into mine. It didn't always work, of course. But those who were treated with empathy and seriousness—even in the florid throes of psychosis—would later seek out those of us who showed a concern and willingness to enter their world, even if they couldn't yet step into ours.

A comparable process is required of parents who feel wrongly or unjustifiably accused by their adult children. While most of the misperceptions faced by parents pale in comparison to those faced with schizophrenia or other serious psychiatric conditions, a similar mindset is required.

Mark, like many estranged parents, was worried about this recommendation.

"Won't that just strengthen her claim that I was this terrible father when I wasn't? I feel like I'm just playing into her hands so my ex can say, 'See, even he's admitting he was a shitty dad.'"

"No, it doesn't work that way. You strengthen your own authority by showing your willingness to see it from their perspective and finding a kernel of truth in it. And as tragic as it is, this is their current view of you, so telling them they're wrong won't get you anywhere; it will just make them more angry and shut down. Your willingness to show empathy and self-examination will help them feel like they can relax their guard a little and consider letting you in more."

"Okay, well, at this point I don't have anything to lose."

I also told Mark that he had to stop insisting that his daughters have a relationship with his new wife. He chose her—they didn't— and they shouldn't feel obligated to spend time with her, especially if they saw her as a homewrecker. He wasn't obligated to leave her, but he didn't need to insist that he and his wife were a package deal.

In my survey of more than 1,600 estranged parents, roughly 75 percent of them became estranged after their divorce from the other biological parent. My experience is that divorce can cause a radical realignment of long-held bonds of loyalty, gratitude, and obligation. It can cause children to reexamine their lives prior to divorce and shift their perspective so that they now support the other parent. It can swing the perception of the child away from viewing the family as a singular unit and instead to a loose affiliation of individuals with their own relative strengths and weaknesses.

Divorce can also alter the gravitational trajectories so that, over time, family members spin farther and farther out of each other's reach. While some parents do a good job of trying to prevent a child from being overly allied with them, children of all ages have their own needs, goals, and even agendas that can cause them, independently of a parent's preferences, to ally with one parent over the other. And even the most conscientious parent would be lying to himself if he couldn't admit to feeling some small tug of pleasure at hearing his child disparage the other parent, however loudly he might protest that child's depiction.

Few children miss either those small displays of happiness or the opportunity to integrate that data into their knowledge of their parent, how best to support them or to use that information to better their own position in the family. Tragically, cutting off contact with a parent is not infrequently part and parcel of this dynamic; a way to support one parent against the other, demonstrate their love or loyalty for the non-estranged parent, or ensure their place in a parent's life.

NEW WIVES/NEW LIVES

Like many remarried parents, Mark found himself hopelessly trapped between the powerful attachment to his new wife and his attachment to his daughters. Mark worried about his ability to convince his new spouse to stop insisting on being included in communications or potential family events. He was also concerned about how to best address her feelings about being portrayed by his ex-wife as the cause of his divorce.

"I don't blame her at all," I said. "She's in a terrible position. But the first priority is getting your kids back in your life. Maybe your daughters will one day be able to welcome her in, maybe not. Some kids forever hold the new partner in contempt, and sadly, not all family dynamics are fixable. Saying that you and your new wife are a package deal is a recipe for failure with your daughters. Once we see some progress with them, we can begin to think about ways to reintroduce your new wife into the family system, but not until then. It's simply too radioactive."

It's not uncommon for new wives to have strong opinions about how much emotional or financial support should be provided to the children from the husband's prior marriage. I've worked with plenty of families where the estrangement was either caused by this dynamic or persisted because of it. While the newer wife has her own understandable needs to be prioritized, valued, and cherished, those needs are sometimes on a collision course with the husband's desire to maintain a connection with his children, something that an alarmingly high number of men fail at. And sometimes when men fail, it's because they allow their new wives to have more authority or influence over their parenting decisions than is good for anybody.

Why do so many men defer? For most, their wives are their best friends, if not their only friend. This means that a withdrawal of her support might cost him more than it would if he had the same kind of extended social network that exists for most women. (This disparity in social networks may also explain why men have higher rates of illness and mortality postdivorce.)

In addition, many men come into marriage already compromised in their ability to label their emotions. Their greater awkwardness in talking about feelings may limit their ability to use them as a platform of advocacy and self-understanding. This inability to navigate their emotional worlds may exist because parents, even today, use less emotion language with boys than girls.

The fragile nature of male identity also means that most men are only one shameful comment away from feeling emasculated. Therefore, if a wife suggests that he's somehow failing her—with his lack of prioritization or attention—he'll feel more obligated to abide by her wishes rather than face the feelings of failing as a man—even if this sometimes means less time with his children.

Finally, many courts weaken the attachment between fathers and their children after a divorce by providing them with far less custody than is provided to mothers.

MOTHERS AND STEPMOTHERS, DAUGHTERS AND STEPDAUGHTERS

On the other hand, being a stepmother is no small task. Many stepmothers feel like they have to bear all of the costs of parenting—the responsibility for the children's well-being, the feelings that they should be doing it better, the blame of their spouses, the resentment of the stepchildren—without enjoying any of the benefits. Stepmothers not only have their own understandable concerns about money going out the door to the husband's ex or children, but they're in the frustrating role of having strong beliefs about what constitutes good parenting and not being able to voice those opinions. At least not without alienating their husband or stepchildren.

Stepchildren, in turn, may resist even the most affectionate entreaties from the stepmother. Grief, guilt, and feelings of loss linger from their parents' divorce or the death of a parent. They may be unable or unwilling to allow a positive relationship to occur out of fears of being disloyal.

In Mark's case, the fact that he had daughters rather than sons also increased his and his new wife's risk for conflict with them. Studies show that the mother-daughter dyad, however challenging, is potentially the most resilient. This matrilineal advantage, according to professor Karen Fingerman at the University of Texas at Austin, causes mothers and daughters to have more frequent phone contact and exchange more support and advice than fathers do with daughters or mothers with sons.

———

Mark made headway with his younger daughter with my strategy, but his older daughter was more reluctant. This seemed to result from the older daughter's stronger feelings of worry about the mother along with a temperamentally more volatile and unforgiving nature. While his younger daughter responded within a few months of Mark's new strategy, his older daughter kept him at arm's length for another three full years before she slowly began to open the door as a result of his changes: he continued to reach out to her on a monthly basis, restrained from criticizing or complaining about his ex, and actively sought to avoid making her feel guilty about her estrangement.

Estranged parents always want to know how long it will take before it ends. Sadly, we never know. Our children have their own timeline; parents sometimes have only so much power or ability to influence it. Your main task is to make it clear that you're available, you're willing to work on yourself and the relationship, and you're willing to respect your child's needs for a relationship that's more in line with their ideals.

GRAY DIVORCE

Sophie, a sixty-five-year-old mother, stayed with her husband for much longer than she wanted. "I knew before my kids were even teenagers that I wanted out of my marriage," she told me. "But I didn't want to put them through a divorce, so I figured I'd wait until they were in college and then I'd be done: time for the next chapter of my life. But then we lost our business and couldn't afford to get a divorce and also send our last child to the school she got into. We agreed that it wasn't fair to her to tell her we couldn't afford it since we were able to pay for the other two to go where they wanted, so we waited four more miserable years till she was out and then we told them.

"My older two kids took the announcement of the divorce pretty well, probably because they'd both been out of the house for a while and they're about as easygoing as kids can be. But my daughter, Lisa, who was always the most sensitive, had a much harder time of it. Which surprised me because, of the three kids, she was the one who used to tell my husband and me that we had a terrible marriage and should end it. Frankly, I thought she'd be relieved. At the very least I thought if she would turn against anyone it would be him, since I was much more involved as a parent than he was, and we were always really close."

Which was partly the problem: for some adult children, the parent's new status as a single person makes them feel guilty if they're less available than the parent wants. An adult child may be confused about how responsible she is for a parent's happiness and may limit or cut off contact as a way to feel independent.

This dynamic, where Lisa felt responsible for her mother's happiness, was created as a result of conflicts that existed long before in the marriage. It's not uncommon that—in unhappy marriages—children sense a parent's loneliness or lack of fulfillment and, accordingly, develop an orientation toward helping that parent feel more valued, loved, and fulfilled. This can allow a sensitive child to outcompete her siblings for a position of attention and attachment that might not otherwise exist. The closeness may also provide a needed source of meaning and identity for the child as he or she is growing up.

However, it may also outlive its utility and later burden the child, especially after a parent's divorce, when the feelings of responsibility feel magnified. In addition, what looked like and may have been a mutually beneficial relationship may later look to the child—rightly or wrongly—like something exploitative on the part of the parent.

While she was still married, Sophie's husband provided a kind of upper limit on her mother's needs—where Lisa could assure herself that it was her father's job to take care of her mother, not hers. Once the two divorced, no such understanding existed. Lisa's natural inclination toward caretaking her mother became much more onerous when the responsibility felt like it was hers and hers alone, especially with her older siblings out of the picture.

In this scenario, and in many like it, an adult child may need the clean lines of an estrangement to test out whether the parent (or she) can survive in this new system. This is why I often tell parents that protesting too loudly, acting wounded or outraged—as understandable as these reactions are—just signal that you're too needy to tolerate the new, more bounded rules of engagement. Put another way, sometimes families have to break up before they can get back together.

As part of my work, I sometimes offer to email the estranged son or daughter to see if they would be open to speaking with me. The letter I wrote to Lisa is a format that I typically use.

Subject: Sophie Garner

Dear Lisa,

    Please forgive my intruding into your privacy.

    I'm a psychologist and was contacted by your mother because of my expertise in parent–adult child conflict. I'm wondering if you'd consider touching base with me briefly about her?

    I know from my practice that adult children don't cut off contact with a parent unless they have very good reasons for doing so. To that end, I'm not writing to encourage you to reconcile, more to help me to help her better understand what happened. Would you consider talking to me on the phone for a bit about that?

                        All the best,

                        Josh

                        Joshua Coleman, PhD

Roughly 60 percent of the adult children I write to write me back: of those who do, roughly 20 percent say they're not interested in speaking to me, another 20 percent write a long, often angry explanation and then request that I never contact them again, and the remaining 60 percent agree to speak with me. Most adult children don't choose estrangement lightly and probably hold, someplace in their hearts and minds, a wish that it could be otherwise, even those who refuse to speak to me.

For those who do talk to me, the majority end up agreeing to doing a few sessions with me and the parent. Why would they be willing to do family therapy at that point if they weren't before? I believe that an adult child who's willing to get on the phone with their parent's therapist is already in a position that's less shut down than one who either wouldn't return the email or only writes an angry defense. However, it's also because I do what I tell parents to do: I listen, I empathize, and I assume that they have good reasons for their feelings. In addition, because most are understandably worried I'll take their parent's side, I make it clear that the goal of the therapy is to help their parent take responsibility and to better understand why the adult child needed to estrange themselves. I state that the other goal of the therapy is to make clear what the parent would need to do going forward if there's any chance of reconciliation.

I also coach the parent prior to the family therapy session that those are the goals of our work together, and if I hear them veering off these, then I'm going to steer them back, strongly if I have to. Most parents understand this instinctively (or out of desperation) but some are surprisingly unable to stop themselves from blaming, shaming, or guilt-tripping their adult child. Which just sets the starting clock of reconciliation back to zero. Or worse.

Fortunately, despite a four-year estrangement, Lisa agreed to do a few family sessions with her mother. In my initial solo session with Lisa, it became clear to me that the huge amount of anger and contempt she exhibited toward her mother was a defense against profound feelings of guilt and responsibility.

"Look, I get it. My mom and my dad should never have gotten

married. He's a nice man, but he's clueless. She's like this supersensitive needy person and he's this out-to-lunch scientist-type guy who wouldn't know an emotion if he was hit over the head with one. Which, probably, is why she was attracted to him."

Her observation struck me as reasonable. It's not uncommon that highly emotional and highly unemotional people are sometimes drawn to each other. Sometimes emotional people like the stability and low reactivity that an unemotional partner provides. And the less emotional partner likes the excitement of accessing the feelings of the more emotional one.

Lisa continued. "I'm not a psychologist, so who am I to psychoanalyze my own mother, but if you knew the kind of family that she grew up in, you can see why she'd want to find the most quiet, unemotional guy you could possibly get your hands on."

"Why, what was her family like?" She might not have been a therapist, but she was a good observer.

"Oh my God. I would've killed myself if they were my parents. Look up the definition of 'guilt-tripping Jewish parents' and you'll find a picture of my grandparents Max and Dell. There's only one audio volume at that house and it's loud. I'm surprised my mother isn't deaf from all the yelling. And that's when they were old. I can't imagine what they were like when she was growing up, when they had even more energy. Don't get me wrong. I adore them, they're amazing grandparents, but loud and guilt tripping played daily on the radio in that house."

I smiled at her affectionate and critical description.

"Sounds like you actually have a certain amount of empathy for your mother."

"I do. I have a lot of empathy for her. She's this brilliant, amazing, powerful woman, but when she gets around me she becomes this whiny little needy, pathetic person—especially since the divorce."

"Worse since the divorce or always that way?"

"Well, she's always been a serious martyr, like my grandparents.

She studied with the best. But since the divorce it's like she expects me to suddenly be there for her all of the time. I do actually have my own life."

"Well, that makes sense. You feel like you're supposed to fill in now for whatever role your father filled before?"

Quick nod. "Which is weird, because, like I said, they did not have a good marriage and I used to beg her to leave him because she was so obviously unhappy. But, yeah, at least he was a warm body to keep her company. Now she's just living alone in an apartment."

"You feel sorry for her?"

She paused for a long time before answering. People rarely know how powerful sorrow is as a motivator of avoidance.

"It's her life. I didn't tell her to marry my dad, have three kids, and then get a divorce."

"Right, but sounds like you feel more burdened by her since the divorce."

"Yes, definitely more burdened. I think I feel more *mad* at her than sorry for her. It's just not my job to make my mother happy."

"That's true. That is her job."

Lisa and Sophie were caught in a common spiral of mothers and daughters, especially exacerbated with a divorce. For the same reasons that the mother-daughter dyad can be the most close and resilient of any family relation, it can also be the most fraught. As journalist Ruth Whippman observed: "At both its best and its worst, the mother-daughter relationship can at times be as close as two humans can get to telepathy. With two people who are both heavily socialized to anticipate and meet everyone else's emotional needs, the dynamic can become a kind of high-alert empathy, each constantly attempting to decode what the other might be thinking, hypersensitive to any change in pitch or tone, like a pair of high-strung racehorses."

The more that Lisa asserted her right to be separate and independent of her mother, the more Sophie felt rejected and frightened. The more that Sophie telegraphed feeling rejected by her daughter, the more Lisa felt burdened. This sequence of emotions commonly goes like this:

1. Empathy: my mother is in pain.
2. Evaluation of that emotion:
   a. It feels burdensome to feel my mother's pain.
   b. I have no immunity to it. If she's in pain, I'm in pain.
3. Attempt to reduce the feelings of empathy by redirecting the arrow of accountability:
   a. This is her responsibility, not mine.
   b. It's selfish of her to make me feel her pain.
   c. She should be in therapy dealing with this, not burdening me with it.
   d. There must be something really wrong with her to make me feel like that. Maybe she's a narcissist.

From the mother's perspective the sequence might go as follows:

1. My daughter's complaints and her rejection make me feel hurt, humiliated, and scared.
2. Since I've been a dedicated parent, it would be good for me to tell her how her behavior makes me feel.
3. I should intensify my efforts to tell her how hurt I am. If she sees it more clearly, she'll be able to be nicer and more supportive than she has been.
4. The fact that I can't just tell her how I feel and have her react in a kind way proves that she doesn't really care about me.

It's easy to see how this feedback loop is a recipe for disaster; one is not calibrated to the other. Which is why I'm always glad to get an estranged parent and their adult child in the same room or conference call because it can allow a much more rapid revelation of these or other problematic feedback loops.

GETTING TO THE HEART OF THE ESTRANGEMENT

When I met with Lisa and Sophie, I asked about their goals for the session and for the relationship. Both Lisa (daughter) and Sophie (mother) stated similar goals: less conflict, better communication, and—as is almost always the request of the adult child—better boundaries. In my solo sessions with the parent or adult child, I ask them if there's anything that they don't want brought up in the family session when we're all together. That way I can cut to the chase if I feel like one or both are avoiding the thorny subjects.

> Lisa (started off the conversation): I just feel like my mother needs her own life.
>
> Sophie (annoyed): I have my own life, Lisa.
>
> Me: Maybe clarify what you mean by wishing your mom had a life.
>
> Lisa: Sorry.
>
> Me: No, I think you're trying to express something important about your feelings. [I wanted to make it clear that I wasn't scolding her—more encouraging her to try to express herself in a less provocative way.] I know in our individual session you said you feel more responsible for her happiness than you want to. Is that what you're referring to here?
>
> Lisa: Yes, I just feel like her whole world revolves around me and what I'm doing and I just don't need the responsibility. I have my own life.
>
> Me: So, if she did have her own life, what would that look like?

How would your relationship with her be different? She'd be happier? Call you less? Complain less?

Lisa: Yes, all of the above.

Sophie (annoyed): When do I ever complain about you? I never talk to you. I haven't talked to you in four years.

Lisa: Are you serious? Gee, I don't know. How about all of the time?? That's why I cut off contact with you. It was the only way to get any space from you, because you never listen.

Me [I chose to ignore the dig for the moment.]: Any specific examples come to mind?

Lisa: Well, before I cut off contact with you I asked you to not call me almost every single day, and you pretty much ignored that request.

Me: True, Sophie?

Sophie: Well, I'm her mother. It seems like if I want to call my daughter, I should be able to call her. She doesn't have to pick up the phone.

Me: But she's right that she asked you to not call her every day and you did anyway?

Sophie: Is that such a crime?

Me: I don't know if it's a crime. I'm just trying to make sense of what's happening in your relationship. Here it sounds like Lisa made a request, and you couldn't do it or wouldn't. I just want to understand what it felt like on your end. Was that because it made you anxious to not talk to her? Lonely? Scared?

Sophie: Well, I was definitely scared when she stopped returning any of my calls.

Lisa: Right, but that's the point, Mom. It didn't start out that way. It's like it always is. You don't listen until I'm screaming at you; then you just act all victimized, like I'm the cruelest daughter in the world.

Sophie: You said it; I didn't.

Me: Lisa's the cruelest daughter in the world? [I didn't want to avoid commenting on this but said it with a small smile to indicate that she was crossing a line.]

Lisa: Yes, I am. Definitely!

Sophie: No, I'm not saying that.

Lisa: You just did!

Me: Okay, let me give your mother the floor for a second. It sounds from Lisa's perspective like she started out with some pretty reasonable requests about how much contact there would be, and you weren't able to do that. I assume you have your reasons and I want to understand them. But from her perspective, you ignored those requests, which might feel like you're not open to her setting the terms of the relationship.

Sophie: What terms? I haven't talked to her in four years.

Me: But she's here now so I assume that's because she also wants a better relationship or to see if one can be made. I suspect that Lisa's account has some validity: that she starts out with a reasonable request and then, when you don't respond, she feels like you're not willing to hear what she wants.

Lisa: Exactly.

MOVING TOWARD INSIGHT

In order for a therapy to go forward, both have to accept some responsibility for the dynamic. The session continues:

Me: And I think, Lisa, that your worry about whether or not your mother has a life has to do with your feeling too responsible for her happiness. Maybe your anger is a kind of firewall against feeling responsible for her.

Lisa: That's possible. I have to think about it.

Me: So, for you, Sophie, when you can't or don't respect Lisa's requests, it makes her feel like you're way too needy and dependent on her for your happiness. I get that it doesn't feel that way to you, but that's how it feels to her.

Sophie: I don't think that's true. Is that true, Lisa?

Lisa: Yes! That's what I've been trying to tell you for the past three years. It's not like you're a bad mom. You were a great mom and there's a lot about you that I admire. I just feel like ever since you and Dad split up, that you expect me to fill that void and I have no desire to be that person.

The fact that Lisa can say Sophie was not only not a bad mom but a great mom allowed a very different conversation to occur. At stake wasn't a defense of her value as a mother, but rather how to agree to the terms for the relationship going forward. It also allowed a kind of breakthrough to occur in Sophie's ability to shift away from being defensive into being empathic.

Sophie: Really? I'm sorry, honey. You're not responsible for my happiness. You're just so mad all the time that I stopped knowing how to talk to you.

Me: Well, I think there's a feedback loop here. So Lisa may start out with a reasonable request for less contact; you feel hurt or rejected by that request, Sophie, so you complain about it or ignore it. This makes Lisa feel worried that you can't tolerate her independence of you. Which makes her feel guilty—and she responds to that with anger or criticism. And, Sophie, you feel rejected and then the ball keeps moving along. I think there would have to be an agreement that Sophie, going forward, you would be more responsive to Lisa's requests, and that you, Lisa, would work on putting those requests or limits in as mild and as nonrejecting of a tone and language as possible. It's a feedback loop because you're both contributing to it. The goal is to interrupt the loop: replace your reaction with something that's more in tune with the other's underlying emotions.

I knew that however understandable Lisa's gripes were about her mother, she wasn't really correct about her. Sophie did really miss her daughter, and I could see why: Lisa was funny, smart, and insightful. But Sophie was stronger than her daughter knew. She did have a life with good friends, two book clubs, and regular Italian classes at the local community college.

Why couldn't she get an equal vote in terms of how much contact there will be? A parent and an estranged adult child have very different goals. Put simply, most parents want to have as much contact as possible with their adult child. But that's not the goal of estranged adult children. Their goals tend to be the following: How can I feel like a happy, healthy person in the context of spending time with my parent(s)? From that perspective, adult children need to go slowly and be in charge of the terms; the psychological territory they're attempting to navigate is more complex.

Sophie was able to acknowledge quickly the way that her behavior contributed to her daughter's need for distance. This was also a strength. But she definitely could act victimized, and that needed to change. And Lisa needed to learn how to respond to her feelings of guilt and worry with more affectionate detachment, rather than with anger and criticism.

While Lisa was wrong in believing her mother wasn't a resilient person, this perception may be correct in other families. This in turn poses a larger problem in a reconciliation. As with marriage, a close and healthy relationship between parent and adult child does often require that both people are able to bring a certain amount of resiliency to the relationship. They have to be able to manage their moods and not rely on the other for more validation than the other can reasonably provide. While Sophie and Lisa were able to put their relationship back on track, some adult children (daughters of single mothers especially) feel so overwhelmed by their mother's unhappiness that they don't know any other way to focus on themselves other than to reject their mother.

When I've worked with parents who are burdened in this way, I counsel them to tell their child or children that they're getting help with their depression, anxiety, or other problems. I tell them that they must show their children they are creating a meaningful life for themselves. And I tell them that if they're not, then they should try to start. If the children have given any indication that they've felt too responsible for the parent's happiness, I encourage the parent to acknowledge their own contributions to that perception and to express a desire to have a relationship with the adult child where he or she doesn't feel so responsible.

DISCOVERING THE AFFAIR

Rick was thirteen when he saw the texts on his mother's phone. "Last night was so hot with you. I can't wait until tonight." Initially he thought it was a text to his dad and started to put it down with some feeling of TMI disgust. Then he realized that his mother hadn't been home the night before and said she would be going out *without* his dad for a work event that evening. With a feeling of curious dread, he scrolled through the string of explicit texts to someone who clearly wasn't his father—texts that became more graphic and detailed as he went through them. "I really need you inside me right *now!*" He felt punched to the floor. Rick imagined his father reading these texts from her to another man and felt protective. He was shocked, too, at his mother, since she always talked about the importance of honesty.

Rick walked numbly into the kitchen where she was eating breakfast, resolving not to say anything to anyone.

"Hi, honey," his mother said, looking up. "You okay? What's wrong?"

Rick wanted to lie. He wished he could rewind the clock to the time before he discovered the texts, when he naively believed that his parents loved each other and were who they showed themselves to be.

"Nothing. School."

Clara was used to the monosyllabic, emotionless tone of her teenage boy, so she looked back down at her breakfast.

Then it happened. He couldn't help exploding.

"What the hell is this?" He thrust her phone into her view. The color dropped from her face. She quickly tried to recover.

"What are you doing on my phone?"

"I was looking up something and I'd left mine in the other room. Who is Jim Osborne, who you're obviously fucking, so don't act all shocked."

"Rick, don't talk to me like that. And I'm not *fucking* anyone. He's a friend that I work with and I'd appreciate it if you'd stay off of my phone and out of my bedroom."

"Oh, so if it's all cool and he's just a friend from work, then I'm sure Dad won't mind if I just show him your phone when he gets home."

"Show it to him! He's met Jim before." Clara was a terrible liar.

"Seriously? I'm not a child." His voice fringed with tears. "Just admit you're having an affair and that you don't give a shit about anybody but yourself!"

"Rick, I understand you're mad, but this is not at all what you think. I'm your mother and you can't talk to me this way."

"You're *not* my mother!" Rick was sobbing now and running out of the room. Before he slammed his door shut, he yelled, "You're a whore, and I don't ever want you to talk to me again!"

Little did Clara realize how real the demand that she never talk to her son again would become. She *was* having an affair but hadn't planned on divorcing his dad. She had tried for years to have more intimacy in her marriage, to no avail. She loved her husband, even romantically. He was a decent person, and she was proud of the family they'd created together. But their sex life had dropped down to nothing, and after trying for several years to revive it, she gave up. She almost envied her middle-aged women friends who complained that their husbands still wanted to have sex and they just wanted to be left alone. That wasn't her. She had always considered herself a highly sexual person, but in the past her best lovers were often ill-equipped to be solid partners. She had married her husband in part because he was safe, secure, and available in ways that her previous boyfriends weren't.

And for most of her marriage, she felt like she'd made the right choice. Yes, Bob wasn't a very active lover when they actually did have sex, which was only a few times a year. But he more than made up for those deficits in his steadiness and commitment as a husband and father. Her own parents were divorced; she'd already decided she would never blow up a marriage with children just because her husband didn't like sex as much as she did. It was a compromise worth making: she'd achieved a degree of serenity over the years by circulating in her consciousness a *can't have everything with one person* mantra.

But when her coworker started flirting with her, she found herself preoccupied with fantasies about him. Seven months later they were still involved in an affair that was fun and passionate but which she knew would one day end. He was a great lover, but she had no illusions he'd be a great husband. She'd made it clear to him that she loved her husband and her family and that she'd never leave her husband for him. For her, the affair was a stopgap measure that allowed her to reclaim a part of herself that she valued, without breaking up her family.

She also knew that cheating on her husband was a risk. He was not one of those "We can get through anything" men: He would not let her beg her way back into his trust, nor would he examine how his lack of availability might have opened the door to another man's interest. He was good-hearted and generous to a fault if you were on his side—but completely done with you if you crossed him. She had witnessed this in his behavior with his brother.

Not that she had any need to blame him. She knew that her affair was very perilous to engage in, so she'd been scrupulous with her co-worker about concealing their identities and the content of their exchanges. She was furious at herself for not keeping her phone locked and for not erasing the most recent string of texts, as she always had before.

Despite a tumultuous and painful round of couples therapy, Clara's husband decided that he could never trust her again. He wanted out. One year later they were divorced and her son—true to his word—refused to visit or talk to her. Clara was heartbroken not only about the end of the marriage but about the devastating change in her relationship with her children.

While the custody arrangement gave her fifty-fifty legal and physical custody, the judge said her son could decide for himself, given his age of fourteen. Despite the fact that parenting orders generally apply until the age of eighteen, courts often defer to the desire of younger teens. Her daughter, now ten, was court-ordered to weekly visitation but had turned cold and distant. When she visited, she refused to talk to her mother beyond one- or two-word answers. She was also rebellious and oppositional around the simplest of requests.

COURTS, LAWYERS, AND JUDGES

While the revelation of a parent's affair is a lot for a child of any age to work through, it's especially difficult if the other parent uses the affair to punish their ex by poisoning the children's opinion of that parent. If anything can drive a parent to madness, it can be watching their own child slowly disappearing from their grasp and influence, replaced by a child who suddenly parrots the accusations and feelings of the other parent.

In psychology this dynamic is commonly referred to as *parental alienation*. Developmental psychologist Amy Baker notes seventeen primary parental alienation strategies that have been identified through research studies, which fall into five general categories: (1) poisonous messages to the child about the targeted parent in which he or she is portrayed as unloving, unsafe, and unavailable; (2) limiting contact and communication between the child and the targeted parent; (3) erasing and replacing the targeted parent in the heart and mind of the child; (4) encouraging the child to betray the targeted parent's trust; and (5) undermining the authority of the targeted parent. Taken together, these parental alienation strategies often foster conflict and psychological distance between the child and the targeted parent.

Treatment for parental alienation is often difficult to obtain because many judges lack sophistication as to how easily alienation can occur and how it can be perpetuated. In addition, once an alienation starts to occur, it can evoke behavior in parents that can cause them to look more troubled or dysfunctional. A judge or motivated lawyer could paint the targeted parent as less competent or deserving of a shared custody arrangement than the parent who is working behind the scenes against that parent.

When Clara consulted with me, her son was twenty-two and her daughter had just turned eighteen. She hadn't spoken directly to her son since the divorce, and her daughter also refused to see her after her thirteenth birthday. She reached out to me to get my advice about whether to attend the upcoming college graduation of her son and the high school graduation of her daughter. Both had told her she wasn't welcome at their graduations, but should she go anyhow? Meanwhile, her former husband had remarried within two years of their separation. He was distant and unwilling to facilitate any kind of rapprochement between her and the children. He also denied that he was in any way complicit with their rejection of her. Clara, fearing further alienation from her children, hadn't dated since the loss of her marriage.

Worsening the situation was the terrible legal and psychological advice she received. Her therapist at the time of her divorce told her to respect her children's request for distance. He interpreted their distance as a form of age-appropriate independence. Like many therapists, he wrongly assumed that the estrangement and her ex's weaponizing of the affair would all be resolved over time. "Don't worry. You were a good mom. They'll be back when they're older."

Yet time and distance are frequently enemies, not allies. They can allow a kind of ossification to occur. Parent and child become strangers to each other in the absence of shared life experiences. Parents who are actively being alienated by the other parent need to act quickly and decisively.

While parents of adult children rarely can use the courts to their advantage, parents of minors sometimes can. If Clara had reached out to me early in the estrangement, I would've told her to fire her lawyer, who knew nothing about parental alienation, and get one who did. I would have also encouraged her lawyer to ask the court for reunification therapy: structured, directive, or court-supervised to directly address the distance between the parent and the child. Reunification therapy is important after a divorce because it assumes that both parents and their children benefit when thoughts, feelings, and reactions can be discussed, worked on, and worked through. While it takes seriously the complaints and perceptions of the child, it doesn't idealize them or blindly accept the truth or reliability of those assertions above those of the parent. It acknowledges that some parents need more help learning how to create a better relationship with the child, and accepts the reality that children can be easily influenced by a motivated ex.

Typically, the court needs to also require that the alienating parent commit to the goals of the therapy, because the alienating parent sometimes has little motivation to move the children in the direction of the alienated parent. Judges and therapists often make the mistake of recommending individual therapy for children in these situations, because some children are clearly in distress after a divorce. However, individual child therapy without collaborative therapy with the parent's involvement does little to penetrate the powerful way that one parent can negatively influence a child against the other parent. Individual therapy can also work against the goals of the reunification therapy because of conflicting messaging.

In more extreme cases, a knowledgeable judge may recommend that a brainwashed child have *no* contact with the alienating parent for a sufficient period of time in order for the child to be freed to re-attach to the alienated parent. Of course, a judge wouldn't make this recommendation if the child has been abused and where being left alone with the parent is not in the child's best interest.

But even when a parent has committed some form of abuse or ne-glect, courts and professionals are far too quick to wash their hands of that parent rather than view her as someone equally in need of compassion, protection, and guidance. Further traumatizing an al-ready traumatized parent by isolating her from a child does little to repair their bond. It teaches the child that the parent is someone who not only can but *should* be discarded. This message may have special weight in the mind of both the rejected parent and child since it's done with the moral imprimatur of the legal and psychological institutions. These legal and psychological configurations may be es-pecially oppressive, since studies show that Native American and Af-rican American parents are far more at risk for having their children taken out of their homes and placed in foster care after any kind of allegation of harm, compared with white parents.

According to attorney Brian Ludmer, coauthor of *The High-Conflict Custody Battle*, "In intractable family situations, nothing is going to break through these dynamics except the power of the court. There has to be discipline in the process, which means that there need to be upcoming court dates that can be used to enforce good behavior on the part of the obstructionist parent." He observed that therapists often do more harm than good in the following ways:

1. They get co-opted by one of the parents or their attorney and filter everything that they hear through that narrative rather than assuming that both parents have legitimate perspectives.
2. They fail to identify the psychological or forensic signs of an intractable family such as refusing to transport the child to the other parent's house, showing up late for reconciliation therapy, or not attending.
3. They fail to require a mandate from the court that the goal is to heal the relationship between the parent and child.
4. They are unwilling to report to the court how one parent is blocking progress, such as refusing to take the child to reconciliation therapy or undermining the therapeutic process.
5. They view the estranged parent as beyond redemption, rather than as someone who needs help.
6. They do not understand that the process needs to be conducted with speed, urgency, and objective milestones of goals and progress.

What can parents do in those cases where the courts won't help or the parent can't afford the therapy? And what can be done when the children are grown and the courts are no longer relevant?

Here are some recommendations that are useful for both young and grown children:

1. Stay out of the mud. Just because your ex is saying terrible things about you doesn't mean that you have to respond.

Children of all ages need to have at least one sane person when they're going through the confusing firestorm of parental alienation. Trading insults through your children won't help them and will make you look unsafe.

2. Try to find a kernel of reality to the complaints that your children have about you, even if you know for a fact that your ex is behind them. The goal isn't to validate or invalidate their perceptions. Rather, it is to position yourself as someone who is willing and able to be self-reflective. Acknowledging the potential truth in a complaint is far more likely to cause children to relax their defenses than protests that they're wrong. In addition, your child isn't aware that their memories are false, coached, or curated. So getting into the truth or falsity of it is the wrong approach. You want to show your resilience, dedication, and capacity for affection.

3. The most powerful antidote to your ex's lies about you is not to be the person that she presents you as. Therefore, the more you can be loving, resilient, dedicated—and the more you can avoid doing to your children what your ex is doing—the better it is for your kids and the more you'll look like a person they can return to. Think of yourself as a kind of beacon of light shining far off in the distance. They may need to travel far before they can return to you, but your ability to adhere to these principles will show them the way back.

WHEN YOU SHOULD COUNTER LIES OR UNTRUTHS ABOUT YOU FROM THE OTHER PARENT

In general, tread cautiously. This may be one of the most common pitfalls in the case of a divorce at any age. Parents can sometimes, intentionally or otherwise, diminish the regard that the child has for the other parent in the following ways:

1. Reveal aspects of the other parent's behavior in the marriage that is generally unrelated to their role as a parent. For instance, when a parent tells the children of the other parent's affair when the child or children wouldn't have otherwise known. Another instance is when Mark's ex told the children that he was emotionally unavailable to her. In doing so, she's inviting them to feel sorry for her and to join her in her disdain of him. (There are plenty of people who are good spouses and difficult parents and plenty who are good parents and difficult spouses.)
2. Tell the children that the other parent engaged in shameful behavior unrelated to his or her parenting.
3. Lie about whether child support or alimony payments were made or received.

This isn't an exhaustive list, because there's no upper limit to the number of lies that can be told after a divorce. The point is less about what than how you respond. As with other responses, make your response about your children, not about you. For instance, resist the urge to say, "I can't believe that your mother told you I never paid her child support. I paid her thousands and thousands of dollars. What a liar!" Instead, say, "Hmm, I'm not sure why your mom is saying that. I do have the canceled checks if you'd like to see them, but right now I'm more concerned about how it felt to you to hear that. It must have been very upsetting to think that I wasn't making child support payments." Stay calm, count to ten.

On the other hand, some so-called memories should be directly countered, such as false allegations of sexual abuse. If your child is grown and you've been newly accused of abuse, respond quickly and unambiguously. Say: "I can tell you with one hundred percent clarity that that never happened. I'm not capable of molesting any child, especially my own." If your adult child is psychologically inclined, you could add, "I know that sometimes people remember events from the past in a certain way because they're trying to recall other parts of the relationship that didn't feel good. I'm completely open to hearing whatever complaints you have about me. And if you'd like to see a qualified family therapist to talk about any of your memories, I'm happy to do that as well." Just make sure they're someone who has expertise in this area.

For the many reasons discussed in this chapter, divorce can make the terrain of estrangement both more likely and more complicated to resolve. It can give you less influence over your child's perceptions of you and introduce people into your children's lives who are motivated to reduce your ability to reconcile. For all of these reasons, learning how to respond calmly, effectively, and fearlessly is critical to any future reconciliation.

Chapter 4

DEALING WITH MENTAL ILLNESS AND ADDICTION

Conversations, in a family, become linguistic archaeology.
They build the world we share, layer it in a palimpsest, give
meaning to our present and future. The question is, when
in the future, we dig into our intimate archive, replay our
family tape, will it amount to a story? A soundscape?
Or will it all be sound, rubble, noise, and debris?

Valeria Luiselli, *Lost Children Archive*

Shoshanna, twenty-five, has never had an easy time of it. Her prodigious intellectual gifts were no compensation for the ways that
her anxiety and learning disabilities dominated her day-to-day life
from childhood to adulthood. While she was growing up, her parents
provided her with an extensive team of supports that included therapists, psychiatrists, coaches, and learning specialists.

It wasn't until Shoshanna's sophomore year of high school that
her parents learned she had developed a problem with drinking. She
ended up in the ER for alcohol poisoning related to a school event.
The staff of the hospital informed them that she had a serious addiction to alcohol and recommended they send her to a thirty-day rehab
program in Napa, California. When she relapsed several weeks after
discharge, they sent her to a wilderness camp in Utah. When this
didn't help, her psychiatrist advised the parents to send her to a residential treatment program in Oregon with the hope that she could
transition from there to college. Her high literacy scores on the SAT,

in addition to her excellent writing skills, would ensure that she'd get into a decent college despite her significant learning disabilities. Assuming that she was psychologically able to succeed once she went to college.

She wasn't.

Shoshanna dropped out in the first semester of her second year, having barely passed her first, and moved in with a boyfriend she'd met at rehab. Far more upsetting to her parents was the way that she began blaming them for the difficulties she'd had in life—stating that she didn't want to see them ever again. She was especially angry at her mother for what she perceived as overinvolvement in her life: shepherding her to appointments with specialists, monitoring of her medications, involvement in her studies, and irritability when she would inevitably drop the ball on a school assignment.

When I spoke to Shoshanna, her contempt for her mother was palpable. "She likes to pretend that she was this superinvolved committed mother, but I really think it was all about her. I think she couldn't stand having a child who wasn't as successful as she was, who had problems in school, who—oh the shame—had to go to rehab. It just went against everything that she stands for, which is this lily-white picket fence, perfectly mowed grass lifestyle that she likes to show the world. 'See how perfect I am?' And my father just falls in line behind her and does whatever she says because he's weak—so I really don't have a lot of respect for him, either."

In the past few decades there has been a significant increase in mental illness in American children, teens, and young adults. While much has been written about the perils to children of being raised by difficult parents, comparatively little has been written about the way that a child with subtle or overt mental illness may increase the risk of a later estrangement. Mental illness creates many opportunities for mistakes and misunderstandings on the part of the parent.

Children with mental health struggles of any age can generate an ongoing debate in the household similar to those of Shoshanna's parents: *Is her problem primarily one of avoidance or motivation? Is she anxious or just making excuses? Are we being too involved or not involved enough? Should we respect her desire to stop therapy or insist that she continue? Should we defer to her wishes to not take medication or monitor her to make sure she stays on them? Should we push her to be more social or allow her to spend all of her time in her room? Should we test her for drugs or believe her that she's not abusing them? Should we follow up on her homework to make sure she's doing it or let her face the consequences of failing? Should we send her back to rehab, let her do AA, or let her hit bottom again?*

Every one of these questions brings with it a suite of potential arguments, misinterpretations, and conflicts. It increases the possibility of the child's feeling hurt or overly pathologized. It can cause children to doubt their parents' faith in them, which can make the parents doubt their own capacities.

Raising a child with some degree of mental illness also puts an additional level of strain on a family, as parents (married or not) often disagree about the best way to address the issues; they worry about the expense of therapists, psychiatrists, or residential programs (if affording such things is even possible); and they struggle with finding appropriate referrals for the child. In those homes, it's possible for the most conscientious of parents to be later viewed by the adult child as having been overly intrusive, critical, unsupportive, or otherwise inadequate in their parenting.

Which is tragic for everyone: for all the talk about the perils of helicopter parenting, some children require a whole fleet of helicopters as a result of their learning disabilities, attentional problems, anxieties, or difficulties regulating their moods. While some are grateful for the parent's extensive efforts, others perceive, as did Shoshanna, the parent's high level of involvement as emblematic of the parent's dysfunction or narcissism. Their later resentment of that participation imagines a less flawed self that could have achieved more without the parent's involvement. Or they imagine a parent who would have been more compassionate and patient in managing their challenges.

On the other hand, it's not difficult to sympathize with a young adult's perspective like Shoshanna's: while she may have genuinely needed her parents to do all that was done for her, she could have still felt diminished, smothered, or squashed by the process, especially as an only child. She could justifiably have been humiliated by her parent's extensive involvement, however necessary it was to her overcoming her challenges with education or addictions. The dynamic, however necessary, may have misshaped her subjective world in the same way that a miracle drug may leave someone with lifelong vulnerabilities.

While her parents felt like they had done a heroic, let alone expensive, job of providing her with every resource imaginable, Shoshanna had an entirely different portrait of her childhood, especially now that she was living on her own and reckoning with the ways that she felt unprepared to launch an adult life.

BUT WHY END THE RELATIONSHIP?

I've found in my clinical work that there is often a proportional relationship between how much an adult child may need to blame the parent for their issues and how much shame or feelings of defectiveness they carry into adulthood. For those young adults, later contact with the parent feels like a powerful tide to pull her off her own moorings, and a reminder of her earlier feelings of inadequacy or need.

Those who are born with any of the forms of what gets labeled as mental illness, in addition to those facing many other challenges such as learning disabilities, spectrum disorders, eating disorders, attentional issues, social awkwardness, or even lack of attractiveness, may feel defective or inadequate in ways that make it hard for them to feel hopeful about their lives, their ability to succeed, or their capacity to tender a romance.

After separate interviews with the parents and Shoshanna, I concluded that this was more a case of worried but conscientious parents rather than overly rigid, uncaring, self-centered parents. Given my assessment, I determined that Shoshanna needed to blame her parents as a way to feel less defective and that her parents shouldn't fight that impulse in her. I encouraged them to admit that they *had* been very worried about her growing up. It's understandable that she wished they could have found a better or different way to raise her that didn't feel so intrusive, dismissive, and undermining—whatever their intentions, or however unrealistic that desire.

I advised them to acknowledge some serious blind spots as parents (because every parent has them) and say that they could see how it could look self-centered on the part of the mother and enabling on the part of the father. They should add that they do trust her ability to run her own life, despite whatever messages they'd given to the contrary.

I encouraged them to avoid defending themselves, justifying their behavior, reminding Shoshanna of how much they did for her, or trying to use prior actions as a certification of their love and devotion.

As her parents showed their commitment to allowing Shoshanna to blame them, and empathize with its consequences, she was slowly able to gain more traction in her life. This was because the parents were willing to shoulder the debilitating feelings of shame that made her life much more difficult. And as she began to feel more confident about her ability to be on her own, she was better able to allow herself, slowly and over time, to allow her parents back into her life.

When I counsel empathy over confrontation, parents sometimes worry that I'm encouraging a position that is "enabling" the young adult's immaturity. This concern misunderstands the disabling influence of shame and the powerful need people have to direct it away from themselves. The need for parents to take more responsibility or show more empathy to an adult child is especially necessary in a highly individualistic culture like ours, where the myth of the meritocracy reads, "You have no one to blame but yourself if you don't succeed in life." When parents say, "Yes, we could see how you might be in a better place if we had done things differently," it allows the adult to feel less shame about whatever ways they feel inadequate.

IT'S UP TO YOU

While the US ranks next to last in social mobility, the majority in the US believe that what matters most is individual initiative. But what happens when individual initiative isn't enough to get you where you want to go in life? Psychologist Martin Seligman has shown that individualistic attributions of causality that focus on enduring personal traits can generate feelings of depression and pessimism when events turn out poorly. If individuals are presumed to have the power to become whomever they want, failing to become that person can engender tremendous feelings of self-blame.

In my clinical practice I have seen how commonly parents get shamed and then rejected by their adult children for not providing them with the economic, cultural, and psychological capital to succeed as adults. In this construction, it's parents, not large institutional forces, who are the cause of failure. If the adult child doesn't have the wherewithal to construct a happy and successful life, it's parents who are blamed by the child and society for their lack of initiative and success.

Which is incredibly unfair to those parents. As historian Stephanie Coontz notes, "There is this American tendency to transform social problems into individual problems and societal failures into personal failures." Law professor Linda Fentiman agrees: "Blaming the mother has long historical roots. Even in [court] cases about [a child's] lead poisoning, where it's clear it's the landlords and manufacturers of lead paint who are responsible, a defense strategy is to trash the mother—to say she has a poor IQ and she isn't a good parent. And often the jury will accept that."

MENTAL ILLNESS, CLASS, AND PARENTING

Shoshanna's parents were fortunate to be able to afford the kind of care that they provided, regardless of the outcome. In addition, they had friends or colleagues who were doctors, lawyers, therapists, or other professionals who could quickly put them in touch with the best of the best for their child.

Many middle-class parents also send their children to expensive therapists, psychiatrists, and residential programs but typically have to go into debt to do so or forgo their own plans for retirement. As for America's poor, few options exist. As sociologist Matthew Desmond wrote in *Evicted: Poverty and Profit in the American City*, parents without *any* financial means have to watch helplessly as their children get in or out of drugs, join or try to avoid gangs, drop out of school, and cope with the ongoing threats of violence.

And in contrast to wealthier families, poor families are also poor in terms of having friends or family members who can put them in touch with people who could be of potential help. This lack of social capital puts enormous strain on working-class and poverty-stricken parents because they not only don't know where to turn for help but also can't afford it when they do. Since the radical defunding of mental health services and legal aid to the poor during the Reagan administration, prison and homelessness are the most likely outcomes for working-class or poor children with mental health issues.

This was true for a family that I worked with. The mother described their situation to me in the following way:

In a car. A small car. They call them compacts for a reason. Small but reliable. That's a good thing. Reliable. You hear stories of people putting two hundred thousand miles on cars like that. Cars that end up on TV ads touting their reliability as evidence that all cars of that make can travel that kind of distance. Which is good. You want a car like that if your child is homeless and living in one somewhere. You want a car that can go the distance. Won't break down in the rain. You want one less thing to worry about, since worry has become the motif of your life since his first psychotic break. Worry and regret, regret and worry: the wrought-iron bookends of every thought and feeling. At least he's not on the street or under a bridge somewhere. So said the policeman who was kind enough to let you know when he last spotted him. Can't bring him in. He wasn't breaking any laws. As long as he moves his car regularly. And where would they take him? Best case, he'd be 5250'd as gravely disabled, stay on a psych unit for fourteen days, get started on an antipsychotic, then discharged. Except he hates meds and would stop taking them the minute he left. That's what happened with every other hospitalization since he was eighteen. Hospitalize, medicate, discharge. Hospitalize, medicate, discharge. No group, no follow-up, no therapy, no psychiatrist, no friends, no work, thank God for the SSI because he refuses any kind of help. He can get food and gas. He wasn't dead somewhere from cold or starvation. There is that. In the world of worst-case scenarios, there's that. A small fire to warm your hands while the snow and wind roar all around, threatening to suffocate or bury you.

Some days you're confused whether you hoped he had died or feared that he was alive. It was the not knowing that was so disorienting. Mrs. Greenburg? Yes? I'm sorry, ma'am. A call you imagined so many times you're surprised that it hadn't yet come true. We need you to come down to the station.

You had good friends. Very good friends. Dedicated, kind

friends. Friends who had been through everything with you and who you could call in the middle of the night if you needed to. They told you that and you believed them. And you still hated them. Hated the simplicity of their sufferings. Their distant husbands, and their critical daughters. Their financial woes and their physical ailments. The luxury of lives not engulfed in the constant flames of sorrow and regret.

And you hated your husband. Hated that he could put your son out of his mind. That he could simply not think about him. Hated him for believing everyone possesses a switch in their brains and all you have to do is reach over and flip it off. Just like that. Just don't think about it, that's what I do. Besides, your son wasn't dead. He wasn't dead yet. As far as you knew. He was still alive. He was alive and living in his car. That's a good thing.

Parents whose children are both estranged and suffer from mental illness live within layers upon layers of sadness, worry, guilt, regret, and grief. The mother whose son lived in a car and who had disappeared from contact with her for sometimes weeks at a time, sometimes years at a time. Is he dead? Is he alive? Is he lying in a ditch? Is he beat up and crying in an alley?

While all estranged parents blame themselves, parents with mentally ill children suffer with the knowledge that even if their child stops being estranged, they will probably never stop being mentally ill. Coming home or returning to their lives doesn't mean the end or the resolution of their pain or worry. Parents like this mother are caught in a devil's bargain in which allowing the troubled adult child to come home often means choosing between tolerating threats, verbal abuse, and irresponsible behavior and kicking them out and worrying that they'll become homeless or worse.

Naive parents, therapists, or friends are big on the counsel of tough love. Tough love imagines that everyone, no matter how troubled, has somewhere hidden deep inside them the psychological wherewithal to pull himself together after he hits bottom. In part, parents are offered this advice because it's easy to stand outside someone else's family and see the towering mistakes they're making and imagine if they did it differently, things would fall into place. And yet, this ignores the simple but painful truth that there isn't always a solution with deeply troubled kids.

Because what if the adult child doesn't have a well to draw upon? If so, the consequences are terrifying for parents to imagine. What if the bottom is suicide? What if the bottom is another psychotic or manic break? What if the bottom is homelessness? What if the bottom is another overdose that results in death? These are outcomes for which most parents can rarely forgive themselves or which they struggle their whole lives to comprehend.

While most of the time it is the adult child who initiates an estrangement, some parents of mentally ill or severely addicted children eventually estrange themselves from the child because of a fear of physical harm. This is because their child has already threatened to harm them or because of the implicit threat of violence as a result of delusions, auditory hallucinations, or simply emotions untethered to any feeling of empathy for the parent.

Others, because of addictions or criminal tendencies, can't be trusted to be at home because of the likelihood of their stealing from the parent or bullying them into giving more than the parent has to give, or wants to give, or thinks is in the best interest of the child to give.

It's difficult to accept how much we are under the throes of forces largely outside of our control. Even families who are well-resourced may find that there are limitations to what the best of professionals can offer. As Mark Twain famously quipped, "Everybody talks about the weather, but nobody does anything about it." Genes, environment, luck, and outside influences make charting a child's fate—especially a child such as Shoshanna or the son who was living in his car—challenging for even the smartest and most affluent.

This is in part because our genes are constantly influencing our children's emotional and intellectual lives, sometimes for better, sometimes for worse. According to geneticist Robert Plomin, "Genetic influence has been found not only for schizophrenia and autism, but for all types of psychopathology, including mood disorders, anxiety disorders, obsessive-compulsive personality disorder, antisocial personality disorders, and drug dependence."

Even traits such as lack of empathy and disregard for others, known as *callous-unemotional traits,* have a strong genetic influence. A child who is genetically prone to depression is also more likely to filter the parent's behavior through the lens of that predisposition and view the parent more negatively than a child with a more sunny, optimistic predisposition.

Some psychiatric illnesses have a kind of genetic detonation date, not switching until a certain age or until a significant stress occurs such as a loss or breakup. This disparity between the pre- and post-dates of symptom onset causes some adult children to review their childhood and assume that the signs were always there and that the parent failed to attend to them.

Believing that a parent neglected a child's obvious symptoms puts a large number of today's parents and adult children on a wild psychoanalytic goose chase that brings little clarity, resolution, or happiness to either. A common refrain I hear from estranged mothers is "I missed the signs when he was growing up. He's saying that he's been depressed his whole life and I didn't see it. I should've been paying more attention. I thought I was. I let him down." As the example of this guilt-ridden mother illustrates, not only are adult children reckoning with their anxieties, conflicts, and failures by looking back at their childhoods, but parents, too, are pulled into this pit of analysis where the present deficits in the adult are blamed on the parent's deficits in the past.

Genetic studies provide insight into the limits and limitations of parenting. They explain, at least in part, why reasonable parents may be later made to feel like they didn't do a good job because of the way the adult child understands and experiences the parent's behavior. The lens through which they view the world could cause them to misinterpret the parent or fail to understand the parent's motivation. As any parent knows who raises more than one child (and for those of us who also have twins), pretty similar parenting can produce kids who are pretty different from each other in terms of personality, temperament, intellect, and mood.

Obviously, this works the other way around. If a parent, for example, is predisposed to have callous-unemotional traits, it would be easy for a child to feel unseen, unloved, or neglected. In addition, a depressed parent may experience the child as more difficult, demanding, or burdensome than would a less depressed, more energetic parent. Perhaps more important, a parent could be objectively viewed as reasonable and an adult child could *still* wish that the parent had been different: more involved, less involved, more affectionate, less intrusive, or more empathic, whatever the reason for those desires.

Which is why getting into the weeds with your adult child about the exact causes of their behavior or the injustice of their wrongful accusations is a fool's errand. If your adult child says, "You should've been more x, y, or z [fill in the blank: available, patient, insightful]. As a result I'm b, c, or d [fill in the blank: too anxious, depressed, have intimacy issues, not successful, can't manage money]," you're far better off just accepting that as an unknown that you have no need to contest. "Yes, perhaps you're right. At the time I wasn't aware that you felt that way or needed something different from me. I'm so sorry I missed that. I could see how that would've been better for you." Put another way, it's almost impossible for any of us, parent or child, to know the exact influences of how we came to be, and so it's better for you and better for your adult child for you to bring as much humility to the table as you can.

DOES MY CHILD HAVE
A PERSONALITY DISORDER?

Dear Mom,

I just thought you should know that I am so done with you and everything you stand for. You only do things if they're going to make you seem like a good person, which we both know that you're not. You're actually a clueless self-centered, self-absorbed person. After our lunch on Sunday where all I did was ask you for a loan, a LOAN, Mom, to your SON so he could start a business, something which, if you were to ask a few questions, he happens to know a lot about! And all you cared about was when you were going to be paid back. Really? I thought you were my mother, not a banker!!!! So, yes, I'm copying in everyone in the family so they can see you for who you are because they really don't know you the way I do and unlike me, they've all bought into your bullshit. I'm so sick and tired of your judgment and criticism and putting me down every chance you get. Even though you always act like you don't, we both know that you do. So have fun with my siblings for now and everyone else in the family because they'll find out about you soon enough and be done with you just like I am.

Sincerely,
Ken (your son)

It's possible to read an email like this without knowing the family and feel confused. Perhaps this is a story of a kid who finally got fed up being humiliated by his mother, so he wrote an angry screw-you letter to her and copied everyone in the family, an action that he may or may not regret when he calms down.

But in reality this is a son who had successfully bullied his mother into giving him money and sympathy ever since his parents' divorce. Ken was eight when his father moved out of state. Like many parents, his mother, Becky, lived with chronic guilt over the divorce and erred on the side of giving too much rather than too little. While her daughters were able to show empathy for her struggles and stressors after their father left, Ken went in the opposite direction. He blamed her for driving their father away and seemed to take pleasure in finding small flaws in her character. "Raising Ken was like raising a wild dog," Becky told me. "If you constantly pet them and feed them and give them every single thing they want, they won't bite you. But as soon as you turn your back on them they tear right into you."

While it's clear that Becky made her share of mistakes with Ken—she didn't stand up to him early on, let guilt interfere with her ability to set limits, and tried to prove her love and dedication to him by being endlessly giving and endlessly forgiving—it's *not* correct to say that she is to blame for the fact that Ken has not become a responsible and respectful individual.

Even before the divorce, Ken had been difficult, defiant, and disrespectful. While he was also defiant with his father, he was sufficiently intimidated by him to keep his worst instincts in check. After the divorce, no such reins existed. In addition—as often happens to the custodial parent after a divorce—his mother became the stand-in for all of his feelings of loss and anger toward the dad who abandoned him. And as sometimes happens, his father was idealized as a way to protect him from Ken's angriest feelings.

Ken behaved in ways that psychologists might label a borderline or even narcissistic personality disorder because of his mood instability, his self-centered perspective, his black-and-white thinking, an inability to maintain long-term relationships or successful employment, and his abuse of alcohol and drugs. I don't love the term *personality disorder* for reasons I'll talk about in the next chapter. But since it's become part of the popular parlance—and because you may have been told that you have one by your adult child or their spouse, or because someone may have suggested that your child has one—it's worth talking through some of the ways that the challenging personalities of family members make reconciliation challenging, if not impossible.

Whatever the diagnosis, some adult children have the capacity to create incredible chaos and disruption in a family. Troubled adult children can not only sow doubt about the parent's character to friends and family, they can tempt those with their own gripes, vendettas, injuries, or pathologies to join in alliance with more troubled members. Those who are both disturbed and powerful either through wealth or charisma can draw weaker members into their sphere of influence to do their bidding and cause further bedlam.

In Ken's case, his father was an all-too-willing ally to validate Ken's character assault on his ex-wife. Rather than reining in Ken's worst instincts, his dad aided and abetted them as a way to reassure himself of the wisdom of his ending the marriage. This put Ken's sisters in the difficult position of trying to maintain a relationship with their father (they'd already given up on their brother) while strongly disliking the way he was allying with Ken to throw their mother under the bus.

WHAT'S A PARENT TO DO?

There is sometimes no straightforward strategy with troubled family members. Their inner lives are often so filled with anxiety, anger, or chaos that no matter how sensitive or exact the accommodations made in their direction, they're unable to feel happy or satisfied for long.

In a healthy relationship with an adult child, a parent has much greater freedom to state their perspective, clarify their intentions, or communicate feelings in a nuanced way. In a healthy relationship there's enough room for both people to exist as individuals, flaws and all.

Not so with a more troubled adult child or their spouse, whatever the diagnosis. In those cases, the parent necessarily has to be more careful. This has to do, in part, with the way our genetics constantly help or distort our view of the other: Is this person safe or dangerous? Generous or penurious? Conscientious or demanding? Kind or cruel? Research by Paul Costa and Robert McCrae shows that our genetics are constantly voting in ways that make us open or closed to new experiences, conscientious or impulsive, extroverted or introverted, agreeable or suspicious, secure or anxious. Sometimes when parents and their children don't "fit" well together, it's because these predispositions are too at odds with the other's.

Whatever the cause, parents with troubled adult children need to learn how to apply *love and limits*, since children like Ken are willing to create so much damage. They require love because the adult child's personality is geared to a kind of desperate survival mentality that ultimately isn't their fault, and limits because that personality can cause them to do some pretty awful things. As a general rule of thumb, the following can be helpful:

- Calmly state what you're willing to do or not willing to do, without blame, criticism, or guilt trips. For example, "I'm willing to help you under the following conditions," or "I understand why you feel like that, but I'm not able to do that." Instead of "All you do is take and you never give anything. You're such a manipulative and destructive person."
- Calmly let your child know that when they talk to you in a highly provocative or disrespectful way, they make it hard for you to listen or pay attention. Explain that you know they have something important to say and you want to hear it, but you're unable to do so when they use a tone of voice that is hostile or intimidating.
- Don't let yourself be blackmailed. But don't criticize the

child for trying. Simply say, "No, that won't work for me." Or "No, I'm not willing to do that. But I am willing to_____."

- Empathize with what they're feeling or saying. "I could see why you'd feel like that [or, how you *might* feel like that]. However . . ."
- Ask what they'd like from you specifically and make a determination about what you want to do separate from your feelings of guilt or intimidation.
- Model being in control of your own emotions without acting like you're trying to control theirs.

Whatever the label, an adult child or their spouse who struggles with powerful psychological issues can make a close relationship difficult, if not impossible. This is because it's the closeness that they find so challenging. They lack the internal resources that allow them to navigate the normal slings and arrows of parent–adult child relations. They're constantly feeling hijacked by their emotions and perceptions. Desperate feelings and thoughts require desperate actions to find relief. And in the same way that some seek the comfort of alcohol, drugs, or sex, those who live in constant pain and threat of dysregulation seek the comfort of control and the control of others, no matter how manipulative the ends.

Chapter 5

PSYCHOTHERAPY AND THE CURATED CHILDHOOD

"MY THERAPIST SAYS YOU'RE A NARCISSIST"

*The tendency is always strong to believe that whatever
receives a name must be an entity or being, having
an independent existence of its own.*

John Stuart Mill, 1869

Jeremy's parents divorced when he was three. For the first two years after the divorce Jeremy saw his father every Tuesday and every other weekend, but this decreased dramatically when his father remarried and moved to Nevada, where his new wife's family lived. At that point, the custody arrangement switched to one week during the holidays and one month over the summer. His mother, Sherry, didn't remarry because she didn't want to introduce more men into Jeremy's life. Her mother had done that when she divorced Sherry's father and she vowed never to repeat that behavior with any child of her own.

Sherry had struggled with depression much of her life, and suddenly being a single mother with a small child and little spousal support didn't help matters. She couldn't afford therapy to ease her depression, so she worked hard, read parenting books, and paid attention to the advice offered on shows like *Dr. Phil*, *Dr. Laura*, and *Oprah*. Plus, Jeremy was a quiet kid who kept his head down, did his studies, and didn't give her any trouble, even as a teen. And because he was a good student, he was able to get a full scholarship to a decent liberal arts college in the Midwest.

But their relationship started to change when he went to college. When he first arrived, Jeremy called or texted his mother once a week to let her know that he was doing okay and making friends, since he knew that she was a worrier. However, that very quickly tapered off to once a month, as he became involved in his schoolwork and new social life. He eventually stopped responding to his mother's calls and found himself feeling burdened by her complaining and personalizing his distance. The more that she complained about his unavailability, the less he wanted to talk to her.

His father had been reaching out to him again after years of little contact, and he found himself excited about the possibility of reestablishing their relationship. After a difficult breakup with a girl in his dorm, he started seeing a young psychologist, referred to him by the counseling center. As part of their work together, the psychologist told him that his mother suffered from narcissistic personality disorder. He also recommended that Jeremy take a break from his relationship with her and focus on himself.

By the time that Sherry contacted me, Jeremy hadn't spoken or written to her in almost two years. I emailed Jeremy to see if he'd be open to talking with me about his mother.

He responded right away and we spent a session talking about his mother on the phone.

I liked talking to him. He seemed thoughtful, insightful, interested in his own psychology. While he was critical of his mother, it was clear that he also cared about her and didn't want her to suffer. I also discovered that his therapist was a bigger obstacle than were the criticisms of his mother, as we'll see when we return to him later in the chapter.

———

Therapists can do a lot of damage. We can encourage a divorce from a spouse who's more amenable to change than we realize, harming the life of the client and her children. We can encourage someone to stay in a marriage that creates ongoing depression for him or his kids. We can support a parent who cuts an adult child out of a will, without confronting how much he has contributed to the child's negative behavior. We can support an adult child's decision to end a relationship with a parent without being sensitive to how that decision may affect the client, his children, and the parent who's being cut off.

Perhaps a more important problem than blind spots resulting from our inexperience, unexamined prejudices, or limited orientations, is that therapists' perspectives often uncritically reflect the biases, vogues, and fads of the culture in which we live. If you were a therapist in the 1950s and a woman showed up at your office claiming she was unfulfilled in her role as a mother and housewife, most likely your goal would *not* be to propel her into a career or into more meaningful activities outside of the house. Instead, you would investigate what prevented her from being happy with what made other women, ostensibly, so contented. Her boredom or lack of fulfillment with domesticity, an ideal at odds with the culture at the time, would be viewed as a neurosis to be treated with medication and psychoanalysis.

This example is just one in a long history where psychotherapy and the medical community labeled perfectly natural discontents with or reactions to prevailing social arrangements as "diseases" that must be treated rather than issues that must be addressed. Here's another: In 1850, Dr. Samuel Cartwright reported in *The New Orleans Medical and Surgical Journal* the discovery of a new disease, which he called *drapetomania*. Drapetomania was a condition that caused sulkiness, dissatisfaction, and a desire to avoid service. It was used to describe slaves who sought to run away from their servitude: *drapetes*, the ancient Greek word for "runaway slave," and *mania* for "excessive energy or activity."

These examples demonstrate how the failure of therapists to challenge the social, economic, racial, and gender norms of their time led them to translate adaptive behaviors, or at least understandable discontents, into illnesses. Today's therapists—as I'll show in this chapter—continue this tradition by failing to critically examine new cultural and societal trends that often serve to lessen well-being and increase family conflict and division.

One of the more profound ways that our culture has changed in the past century is in its embrace of the individual as separate from the family and the community at large. Today's culture of therapy both reflects and contributes to our nation's ever-growing embrace of individualism. While prior to the 1960s, the aims of psychotherapy were generally to encourage people to conform to the institutional dictates of the time, today's therapists and self-help authors want to help their clients become more resistant to the forces of guilt, shame, and worry about others that stand in the way of their developing their talents and pursuing their dreams. To that end, family members have increasingly come to be viewed as facilitators of (or obstacles to) a fully realized life, rather than necessary and forgivable features in an expectably imperfect existence. While the family was once where individuals located themselves in a chronological or social order, it now comprises the institution from which they must be liberated.

With the exception of parenting small children, encouraging individuals to feel some sense of obligation or care for other family members is not typically on the agendas of most therapists. As a result, an adult child's psychotherapy can sometimes increase family conflict and distance. Unless a client requests help in having a better relationship with the parent, sibling, grandparent, or in-laws, most therapists worry that too much emphasis on the needs or *feelings* of the person outside of the room will be antithetical to helping their client focus on their own needs—which is, after all, the point of much therapy today.

As therapists, we hold up the ideal parent or family experience as a way to shine a light on what an adult's life *might* have been if she'd had better parenting. This serves the purpose of helping our client to not blame herself for self-limiting and self-hating voices, and to allow her distance from parents and others whose contact tends to amplify that voice rather than diminish it. It also allows a creative space to imagine what she might feel or accomplish without the critical voices that may have brought her into therapy in the first place, whatever the origin.

Helping adult children see what they didn't get and what they should've ideally gotten from parents is one of the biggest tools in a therapist's tool chest, and one that I go to on a daily basis. An analysis of a client's childhood is useful because parents and siblings can powerfully shape identity, self-esteem, feelings of trust or safety in the world, and later, one's ability to parent. Psychotherapists can be efficacious teachers about the relationship between the adult child's functioning as an adult and the family's contribution to those inadequacies, deficits, or conflicts.

But there's a downside to that. In so doing, therapists tempt adult children to feel contempt or even hatred for their parents. They may encourage their anger because anger is powerful: it can carry anger away from the self; in blaming others we're relieved of the self-blame, the shame, and the guilt we feel about our defects and our failures. Anger is active: it can cause us to feel like we're pushing back rather than feeling victimized by the outcomes of our lives. But in the same way that hating the sin and not the sinner still involves hate, supporting anger or contempt for a parent doesn't necessarily free the adult child from that which they hope to be freed.

Therapists can inadvertently encourage a kind of victimized stance in relation to the parent as opposed to one that views the parent in a more three-dimensional way. As Illouz writes in *Cold Intimacies*: "Because the therapeutic narrative discusses, labels and explains predicaments of the self, the self is in turn invited to conceive of itself as ridden with emotional and psychological problems. Far from actually helping manage the contradictions and predicaments of modern identity, the psychological discourse may only deepen them."

In our culture of choice, self-expression, and—most important—rights, today's individual psychotherapists operate much like attorneys in a litigious divorce; we believe our job is to bring power and authority to our clients but aren't obligated to consider how those actions may affect the long-term well-being of the family members of our clients. We perpetuate a myth of self-actualization untethered to the obligations and benefits of family, community, and social institutions.

IF ONLY I'D HAD DIFFERENT PARENTS

In today's environment, where everyone has strong ideas about what constitutes good parenting, it's not unreasonable for an adult child to have beliefs about how their lives might have turned out with better, or at least different, parenting. However, this kind of social comparison, much like other status assessments, can lead to more unhappiness rather than less. It causes the assessor to view themselves in a one-down role in comparison to others. They think, "If only I'd had different parents, I'd be in a better place today."

And maybe they would. On the other hand, this kind of analysis may, quite wrongly, tempt adult children to conclude that:

- The mistakes that the parents made radically altered them and the trajectory of their lives.
- Their present state of mind and life condition were primarily formed by the parent or family environment rather than by genes, neighborhood, class, peers, economics, or culture.
- Estrangement is the best strategy to heal or alter that trajectory.
- Working on the relationship with the parent or choosing to

be in some limited form of contact is worse for them or, in other ways, not a worthwhile endeavor.

- Whatever consequences exist for the grandchildren or other family members are worth it, or at least balanced out by the concomitant increases in happiness that attend estrangement.
- They owe the parent nothing, despite the benefits incurred by the parent's sacrifice or investment of time, love, or finances.

On the other hand, when the parent is the client, many therapists fail to recognize the legitimacy of the adult children's complaints about the parent. They accept the client's narrative that the children are overentitled, disrespectful, self-centered. In so doing, they fail to help their clients address the valid needs and requests of the adult child. Instead, they encourage a kind of outdated and misguided form of assertiveness training: the parent is encouraged to set limits, insist on respect at all costs, and remind the adult child of everything they have done as parents. "This is what it feels like to be young now," wrote a young journalist. "Not only are we screwed but we have to listen to lectures about our laziness and participation trophies."

WHY IS IT JUST UP TO THE PARENT TO FIX IT?

As historian Steven Mintz told me, in the past, family conflicts were more likely around tangible resources like land, inheritance, or family property. While those quarrels can still exist, today's tensions are more psychological than material and thus harder to resolve.

I frequently hear the request from adult children that the parent "do more work" as a condition of reconciliation. On the one hand, fair enough: it's reasonable for an adult child to want the relationship to be a more hospitable environment to interact in. On the other, I have noticed that some of the adult children who take this position are not open to providing feedback about what specifically would constitute success, nor how progress could be evaluated in the absence of contact.

For parents on the receiving end of this request, the absence of feedback can be maddening. "When I asked him to tell me what he wanted me to work on," said one parent, "he said that wasn't his responsibility. Not his responsibility? Whose responsibility is it, then, if this is supposed to be a relationship? And how will he know I'm doing the work if he refuses to pick up the phone or answer a text?"

Diana, a young woman in my practice, told her parents that her marriage was suffering because of the poor role model provided by them. She felt that she needed to make a clean break from her parents in order to focus on her marriage. Seeing her parents triggered bad memories, she explained. "They probably should've broken up, but that's not really my decision. I have to do what's best for my children and my family, so I can't be around them. Whenever I talk to them, I end up having a fight with my husband the next day and I just don't need that kind of drama in my life."

While I counseled the parents to listen empathically to their daughter's complaints, I also understood the hurt and anger they felt after the session when we met without the daughter. "Yes, my wife and I used to fight a lot. I'm Italian, she's Greek, what do you expect? But we loved each other and still do. Nobody threw any punches, there weren't any windows broken. Grow the hell up. Since when is just ending a relationship with your parents the right thing to do? We gave our kids everything."

Another client explained the estrangement by saying that being around the parent made her depressed and unable to focus on her own feelings. "You were so worried and overinvolved growing up. It made me doubt myself. Whenever I'm around you, I can feel all those feelings start to surface. You'd have to do a lot more work on yourself for me to want to have contact again."

ASYMMETRICAL BALANCES OF POWER

In an ideal world, parents and adult children would enter negotiations about the problems in their relationship as equals; in the real world, they don't. The dynamic is more like a couple: the wife is ready to divorce her husband if he doesn't change and the husband really doesn't want to lose her. That she's ready to leave gives her more power to set the terms of the relationship.

In addition, the relative power of the adult child, if estranged, is heightened by the suffering faced by the parent as a result of the estrangement. This means that the parent will necessarily have to find a way to empathize with and comprehend the perspective of their adult child if they want to restore the relationship, while the adult child isn't necessarily under the same obligation. Unless initiated by the parent, estrangement is almost always a negative for the parent. However, as we saw in "How to 'Break Up' with a Narcissistic Parent," estrangement and the establishing of boundaries can be an expression of autonomy, authenticity, and strength for the adult child—however needed or justified by the parent's prior behavior. As the author in this article stated, "Ultimately, asserting low or no contact with a narcissist parent can be a healthy, even liberating choice." While estrangement offers a way for the adult child to feel proud or "liberated," it more generally offers only shame, humiliation, or grief for the parent.

This is not to say that most adult children choose estrangement lightly, or that they pay no social cost. In my experience, most adult children estrange themselves only after a long period of trying to have a better relationship with the parent. Communications professor Kristina Scharp found that most of the adult children in her studies said their estrangements occurred slowly over time. However liberating the final decision to estrange is, it still is often made on the foundation of prior extended periods of strain or turmoil.

British journalist and researcher Becca Bland was so affected by her estrangement from her parents that she formed a charity called

Stand Alone to provide support to other estranged adult children, and later to their parents. In an interview, she told me the following: "Today's young adults see contact with family as voluntary and based on displays of love and acceptance. Parents who feel like they have a right to demand contact based on obligation or duty rarely get their adult children to respond in the way that they think they should."

In addition, while most adult children do want to eventually understand their parent's perspective, their ability to do so may be limited or constrained by how much guilt or how many feelings of responsibility that such an understanding engenders. Given that, I often tell the estranged adult children who are considering family therapy that they are under no obligation to forgive, forget, or to reconcile; only to consider a dialogue with their parent and me. I say this because I know that, in most estrangements, the adult child believes that the estrangement is crucial to their psychological well-being, however much that reality is at odds with the parent's needs or perspective.

FAMILY THERAPY WITH JEREMY AND HIS MOM

After speaking with me on the phone, Jeremy agreed to do a few sessions with his mother and me. Sherry was right that Jeremy was a kind, quiet person. But a kind nature can sometimes be a burden; it may overly weigh you down with feelings of guilt and responsibility for those you love. In my experience, sometimes the nicest kids have to become the most aggressive to reassure themselves they're not responsible for another's well-being.

I had counseled Sherry before our first family therapy session, attempting to prepare her for what was to come. I'd advised: Listen in a nondefensive way to whatever Jeremy has to say. Try to find the kernel of truth in his assertions, however hurtful they may be. Even if his words are at odds with your memory and self-reflections, try to hear it as his perspective and not a matter of right or wrong.

In my solo session with him, I recommended that he directly tell his mother what bothered him. Jeremy didn't hold back. He didn't dilute his perceptions or try to shield her from being hurt. It seemed as though he was waiting for this moment to get all of this off his chest, which I supported because I wanted him to get as much on the table as soon as possible.

"You chose to stay in bed with your depression when I was young instead of deciding to get up and fix yourself," he began. "And as a result, I've had a much harder time knowing how to do basic things in life or prioritize my own needs in relationships. My therapist said that I was parentified by you and that you were emotionally incestuous with me growing up. That's why I haven't wanted to talk to you. I need to work on myself."

I had wanted him to be direct. But I also knew that I would need to translate his words—products of his own therapy—which, undeciphered, sound like the worst kind of character assaults: "emotional incest," "parentified," "narcissistic personality disorder." These, the flora and fauna of the *Diagnostic and Statistical Manual,* can sound pretty humiliating to those on the receiving end.

Softening the bite of psychiatric diagnoses is especially important, since they are now an active part of mainstream culture. We call someone "borderline" or "a total narcissist" when we used to say "jerks" or "assholes." We might still call them that, but putting it in the context of a diagnosis sounds so much more authoritative.

While diagnosing is perhaps an unavoidable part of living in a society obsessed with personal growth and development, labels have consequences and can affect the behavior of those doing the labeling as well as those being labeled. In the same way that a diagnosis of cancer or Alzheimer's may cause family members to increase or, in some cases, decrease, contact, so, too, can a psychiatric diagnosis affect people's attitudes toward those to whom they're related.

In this poignant example, Jeremy wasn't exactly wrong in his assessment about what he didn't get from his mother or how it may have shaped his life. There's ample evidence that being raised by a depressed parent (most of the research is on mothers) can have a negative effect on the child. And he very likely did grow up feeling more responsible for his mother's well-being than he might have preferred or that might have been useful to him—though there's other research that shows that the strengths learned from that role can also be a positive. But he was blaming his mother for behaviors she would've done differently if she knew how, or if she had had the psychological or economic resources when she was raising him.

DO PEOPLE CHOOSE TO BE BAD PARENTS?

There is often less free will when it comes to parenting than most realize. Parents are as much under the throes of their genetic dictates, partner provocations, childhood traumas, financial threats, and community deprivations as are the children being parented. Sherry's deficits in parenting stemmed not only from her own parents' deficits but also from her financial struggles, her genetic and environmental vulnerability to depression, and her lack of having another parent with whom to share responsibility raising her son.

Our current construction of causality in the family—where therapeutic discourses lead people to believe that choice is the organizing and guiding principle of life—often create more conflict in families than it solves. From Jeremy's perspective, his depressed mother should have or *could* have just pulled herself up by her bootstraps, gotten out of bed, and marched herself into a therapist's office.

Studies show that most adult children explain their estrangements based on the personal traits in the parent that caused their behavior rather than contextual, economic, or cultural mechanisms. However resonant that causal framework is with American ideals, it fails to describe how depression works, how decision-making works, or even how choice works.

For the child under a therapist's guidance to later look back and say that the parent should've known better or behaved differently—that they now deserve the distance, if not the contempt, they receive—is wrong. It suggests that the parent was handed a map for a geography that wasn't yet charted when they were raising their children and given resources that were beyond their reach.

This is not to in any way minimize the enormous amount of damage—sometimes permanent—that problematic parenting can cause. Children raised by those who were emotionally or physically abusive, or neglectful due to mental illness or alcohol or drug addiction, know firsthand the pain that can be caused by parents. That pain can radiate out into all aspects of his life. Telling an adult child "I did the best that I could" may be small consolation to someone who suffered for many years as a result of the parent's behavior. And it provides scarce motivation for the adult child to engage in a process of reconciliation. This is why I encourage parents to do due diligence on their children's complaints and work hard to repair whatever harm was done.

MISDIAGNOSING THE PARENT

Jeremy's therapist wasn't wrong that his mother needed more love, caretaking, and tenderness than he could reasonably be expected to provide. Nor that the incompatibility of their temperaments may have created genuine suffering in him. But in my experience, many therapists misdiagnose a mother's maternal depression as narcissism. Depressed mothers can be more needy, anxious, and sometimes disparaging. Therapists might interpret this depression as narcissism or some other personality disorder.

Did Jeremy's mother have narcissistic personality disorder, as he and his therapist believed? She did not. More important, that diagnosis foreclosed the possibility that they could together build a bridge of understanding where Jeremy—without guilt or regret—could accept the limitations of what he could or *should* provide his mother and his mother could accept—without bitterness or complaints to her son—that his care and attention would never be enough to make up for the difficult hand that life had dealt her before and after becoming a parent.

Psychiatric diagnoses are problematic because they reify a complex of emotions that in reality are ever-shifting and open for other inputs and revisions. Therapists, self-help authors, or well-meaning family members who try to be protective by labeling behavior in this way can do more harm than good.

Jeremy's mother *did* deserve a better life. It just wasn't necessarily her son who could provide it. And Jeremy deserved a better life, too. It just wasn't necessarily his mother's fault that he lacked it. Giving the mother a psychiatric diagnosis, especially one as outsize and definitive as narcissistic personality disorder, greatly oversimplifies her life and struggles; it devalues her years of love and dedication, however flawed; and it weakens the fabric of connection that could otherwise have existed. She deserved a different narrative, one that was deeper and more compassionate, that saw her less as a freewheeling agent, more as someone responding to what life offered her from what she had to offer in return.

Carl Jung wrote that nothing affects children more than the unlived lives of their parents. I sometimes discover, underneath the contempt a client feels for the parent she has rejected, a deep reservoir of sadness for that parent and a longing for them to be happy. The parent's sorrows, frustrations, feelings of inadequacy become so burdensome that the child doesn't know any other way to shed that weight other than to write her off. As author Andrew Solomon wrote in *Far from the Tree*, "There is no contradiction between loving someone and feeling burdened by that person; indeed, love tends to magnify the burden."

What some adult children find oppressive about their parent may not be the parent's personality disorder, as is so commonly highlighted in therapy offices and on forums, but the weight of their own feelings of empathy.

GOING WITH DAD

I have found in my practice that an adult child, as was the case with Jeremy, may later kick a single mom to the curb in favor of a less involved, less available dad. This happens not because she was such a terrible mother, more because he doesn't know any other way to feel separate from her—her worries, her fears, her guilt, even her love.

In this scenario, Dad's lower involvement becomes a more appealing engine of autonomy to the young adult. Dad has already demonstrated that, however much he may have also suffered in the separation or distance, he can live without the child. Given that, he is in less danger of being perceived as needy, dependent, or demanding by the child trying to pull away from his mother's orbit.

This later shift in loyalties can be especially galling for the mother who raised the child or children without the father's help. As one mother said in regard to her nineteen-year-old son rejecting her and idealizing the once-absent father, "I did all the heavy lifting raising him and now his dad gets to do a victory lap over how well my son is doing in life. What's fair about that?"

For the adult child, the decision to estrange the parent, however painful, is nonetheless tied to a narrative of liberation from oppressive forces and the pursuit of happiness. There is no equivalent upside for the parent. It's all downside: failing at life's most important task; being denied the valued reflection of oneself as a parent; feeling shame before one's peers and family; losing not only the adult child, but often a relationship to cherished grandchildren. And for those parents who are all too aware of their parental failures, they also lose the opportunity to do for grandchildren what they couldn't for their own children.

Jeremy's mother had a hard time with the first few sessions. Her chronic depression made her less able to hear her son's complaints as complaints and not as an attack on her fundamental worth. But, as often happens, her ability to just listen, reflect, and find the kernel of truth helped him to see that she was stronger than he had given her credit for. And it also helped when she was able to tell him that while she did miss him and would like to be in more contact, she didn't need him in the way that he thought she did—to give her life purpose— and that it wasn't selfish of him to be more focused on his own life and less focused on hers. They talked about a way to be in contact going forward. It would be less than she wanted, but so much more than she had before.

Reconciliation therapy between parents and adult children is similar to couples therapy where one member is willing to call it quits. For those who are open to consider a deep examination of the foundational problems in the relationship, a marriage can sometimes be saved and in many cases made better than ever. The same can be said for estranged parents and their adult children.

Chapter 6

FLASHPOINTS

GENDER IDENTITY, SEXUALITY, RELIGION, POLITICS, AND PERSONALITY CLASHES

Our prejudices lead us to tear nature where we want it to break.

Gary Greenberg, *The Book of Woe: The DSM and the Unmaking of Psychiatry*

Sometimes family members turn out to be very different from who we thought they would be. These differences can create rifts that grow and expand over time, leading to an eventual estrangement. For example, parents' reactions to a child's need to transition to a different gender or to declare a gender identity not understood by the parent, a child's choice of a romantic partner, same-sex or otherwise, the desire to maintain or abort a pregnancy, to vote for a political candidate or swear allegiance to a political party, to marry someone outside of their faith, to renounce their faith, to have a personality style incompatible with the parents', or to simply be far less available than the parent wants—any one of these can lead to ongoing conflict and tension that results in conflict, distance, or an eventual end to the relationship.

This chapter will look at some of these common areas of disagreement and make suggestions for how estranged parents can respond in ways that increase understanding, reduce tensions, and improve the chances of reconciliation.

———

Ariel is a sixty-two-year-old mother, estranged for the past two years from her twenty-two-year-old son, Robert. Robert is in the process of transitioning from being a female to a male and recently underwent "top surgery" to have his breasts removed. He began testosterone therapy when he turned seventeen, which resulted in a deepening of his voice and the appearance of facial hair. He became estranged as a result of feeling unsupported by his mother when he decided to transition.

Ariel describes Robert as a sensitive but precocious child. He excelled academically but struggled in early adolescence with depression, intense social anxiety, and low self-esteem. Despite these challenges, he completed his undergraduate degree in three years with a double major in math and philosophy. He is currently pursuing a doctoral degree at Penn in computer science, the same field as his mother.

When Robert told Ariel about his decision to transition at seventeen, she was both scared and surprised: "I never really saw that in Robert. You hear about those cases where the parents had their suspicions from a very young age in terms of how their children would play dress-up, want to act like the opposite sex, the kinds of toys they play with, their attitudes—he had none of that. He was more of what we used to call a 'girly-girl.' Loved playing with dolls, dressing up in a feminine way. So honestly I was completely caught off guard when he told me that he wanted to transition when he was seventeen." (Unlike some parents of children who have transitioned after puberty, Ariel was fluent in the proper use of pronouns and referred to her former daughter, Vanessa, as Robert, "he," and "him.")

A small but growing number of estrangements in my practice appear to be associated with a postpubescent teen's or young adult's desire to transition. The seemingly sudden appearance of *gender dysphoria* (the feeling that the sex assigned at birth doesn't align with one's gender identity) may present a greater challenge for parents than cases where parents have had years to consider their child's need or desire to transition.

For both child and parent, the stakes couldn't be higher: for adolescents or young adults who've known they wanted to transition, but couldn't because they feared parental rejection, social isolation, or violence—who have watched their peers be taunted, beaten, even killed—the stakes aren't just about identity, they're about survival. From this perspective, announcing their desire to transition is a profound act of courage and selfhood. It's entrusting the parent with a potential truth about the child that may be critical to their ultimate happiness. It's understandable that they might need a parent to quickly adopt a position of support, acceptance, even advocacy. It's also easy to see how a parent's failure to do so could signal, rightly or wrongly, the parent's inability to shield the child against potentially negative reactions from other family, friends, or strangers.

On the other hand, parents who haven't seen signs of gender dysphoria in their child—where the behaviors weren't *consistent, persistent, and insistent,* or where the parents weren't yet conversant in the culture's evolving concepts of gender—may need time to make sure they are endorsing a decision that is truly in their child's best interest. A need to transition may be especially confusing for parents of teens, since adolescence, as described by developmental psychologist Erik Erikson, is a period where identity is in the process of experimentation and consolidation. While parenting is in many ways a never-ending series of small mournings, a change in a child's gender is hardly the least consequential.

I asked Ariel about the sequence of events following Robert's announcement of a desire to transition.

"Initially I thought, I *thought* but didn't say, 'There's no way. All of a sudden you've decided you're a boy? No way!' But I didn't say that. I'm sure my face said it all."

"What were the kinds of things that he found the most upsetting when he told you?"

"I just said, 'Have you gotten therapy for this? Are you sure?' Because he was already talking about wanting me to help pay for surgery and hormones and I was like, 'Whoa, let's talk about it and make sure it's the right thing. Hormones? Surgery? Those aren't just things you rush into.' And he said he knew and didn't need therapy and why didn't I just trust him to make the right decision? And now it's become this whole thing about how I've never seen him; that the signs were there all along and I just didn't pay attention to them. It was always about what I wanted and never about what he wanted."

"You were taken completely off guard, it sounds like. This wasn't something you'd seen in him before?"

"Trust me, the signs were *not* there all along. I've asked everyone who knew him from childhood and they're all just as surprised as I was."

"That's so painful."

"Honestly, he has not been the most stable person in the world and I've just been worried that this is going to make life harder, not easier."

"How long was it between his telling you and your letting him know that you wanted to support him?"

"I don't know. Maybe a month? But he says that everything I said in that first month proved to him that I was 'transphobic.' I hate that word. I'm not transphobic. I'm just grieving the child's life that I had envisioned. Sometimes people are born into the wrong bodies or genders or whatever. So what? So now you're a boy. Okay. You still can't talk to me?"

How to Help Ariel?

There were many issues to be addressed in a potential reconciliation between Ariel and Robert:

1. His feeling, right or wrong, that she wasn't supportive of his decision to transition.
2. His accusation, correct or not, that she had never supported his other decisions in life and was more focused on herself.
3. His belief that she was acting out of some form of prejudice.
4. His long-standing issues with anxiety and depression that preceded the announcement to transition and may have existed independently of that desire.

Because Robert was refusing Ariel's attempts at reconciliation, I reached out to see if he would talk to me. He didn't respond, as is sometimes the case when I reach out to an estranged adult child. So I encouraged Ariel to write an amends letter to see if he'd be willing or able to open a dialogue with her. It went like this:

Dear Robert.

I love you and miss you. I am hoping that there's a way to bridge the gap between us. I know that you wouldn't have cut off contact with me unless it was the healthiest thing for you to do. That said, I want to try to address what has happened and see if we can make a new start. It's clear that when you announced your desire to transition that I responded poorly. I was scared and I could see how that caused you to feel unsupported, even unloved for a decision that was so monumental. I could also see how that could have looked like an expression of prejudice on my part. I don't consider myself transphobic, but in hindsight, I could see how you would've worried that I was. You're also right about your younger years— just because I didn't see any signs doesn't mean that there weren't

any. You've said that I've never supported your other decisions in
life. While I believe that I have, clearly I didn't in a way that caused
you to feel supported in a way that you needed. I have a lot to learn
about how to be a better mother to you, but I'm committed to doing
that if you'll let me. If you want to write and tell me more about
how you're feeling about me, our relationship, our past, or anything
else, I promise to read it from the perspective of learning and not in
any way to defend myself. Or, if you wanted to meet with a family
therapist, I'd be grateful to do that as well.

There is much in this letter that was hard for Ariel to write and
might be hard for any parent.

Ariel asked, "How can I say, 'I know that you wouldn't have cut off
contact with me unless it was the healthiest thing for you to do' when
I don't think it was the healthiest thing for him to do?"

"It's because you're speaking to *his* feelings, not your feelings. He
feels like it's the healthiest thing to do for himself, or he wouldn't be
doing it. You have to show that you can start from a place of alliance
with him, not opposition. It's not enough to just assert your love and
dedication. You have to be able to psychologically meet him where he
is right now."

"Won't he assume I'm agreeing with his decision?"

"It doesn't matter if he thinks you are or aren't agreeing with his
decision. He needs to know that you support his ability to chart his
own life, even when you think his map is wrong."

"But isn't my job as his mother to tell him his map is wrong? That
he's about to take his life over a cliff if he hasn't already?"

"You've already given your opinion on this. You can't stand in
front of him and wave him away from his choices. Yes, parents do
need to—at least once—give their opinion about something they
disagree with, especially if they think that decision will be harmful
to their child. But they also have to repair the hurt that sometimes
results from that and accept the possibility that they may be wrong."

"Well, also this thing about how I never supported his decisions is just revisionist history. I've always supported his decisions. Aren't I just playing into his mental illness by acting like there's any validity to that?"

"I understand why it feels like that. But the question is whether anything is served by your continuing to assert your version of the past once he's clearly rejected that version. In finding a way to ally with his perspective, you're not saying, *Yes you're right*; you're saying that he *might* be right, and if so, you were unable to see it at the time. That allows a bridge between your own reality and his. And nothing good will be exchanged between you until that bridge is built."

These are common questions from parents. My advice stems from three principles:

1. All parents have their blind spots. Just because a parent tells me that their version of the past is accurate doesn't mean that it is. From that vantage point, helping the parent write a letter that empathizes with the adult child's perspective creates a way to correct for the disparity in their memories or assessments.

2. There are separate realities in every family: A parent can reasonably feel like they provided their child with good, even ideal parenting—and their child could still reasonably wish their parent had made different parenting decisions.

3. Accepting the adult child's viewpoint encourages them to reduce their feelings of opposition or defensiveness. This creates a better opportunity for a more collaborative or nuanced version of the past to occur.

Ariel reluctantly emailed her son the letter that I helped her write. I never know who is going to respond positively to an amends letter and who won't. There are a number of reasons why an adult child might not respond to the most perfectly crafted letter, regardless of the cause of estrangement:

1. Their child isn't ready to forgive because they feel too hurt, mad, or harmed by the parent to be ready to reconcile.
2. They believe, rightly or wrongly, that the parent isn't sincere.
3. They need to blame the parent for their unhappiness, and forgiving the parent deprives them of this opportunity. This can occur when a troubled adult child needs to blame their failures in life on the parent as a way to protect themselves from feelings of shame or defect.
4. They're being negatively influenced by a romantic partner or some other influential person such as the other parent in the case of divorce.
5. They don't feel sufficiently individuated from the parent and need to be mad as a way to feel separate.

Fortunately, Robert did respond positively to Ariel's letter. He texted the following to her shortly after it was sent: "Thanks, Mom. I appreciate that. That's exactly what I needed to hear. Let's talk." He agreed to do a few family therapy sessions to talk about ground rules for going forward. Things don't always go as smoothly, but I'm always happy when they do.

While children who need to transition pose conceptual and communicative challenges for some parents, adolescent and adult children who eschew male and female labels also require parents to learn a new language and conceptual framework. As Columbia sociologist Tey Meadow notes in *Trans Kids: Being Gendered in the Twenty-First Century*, atypical gender was once considered a form of psychopathology and a failure of gender. Today it is considered a *form* of gender.

Many parents have not yet caught up to the radical reconstruction that has been under way in this arena, especially in the past decade. Consider, for example, that the dating app Tinder lists thirty-seven custom gender options, while Facebook offers fifty. According to a recent study by the Pew Research Center, more than one-third of Generation Z (those born after 1995) said they knew someone who preferred to be addressed using gender-neutral pronouns compared with 12 percent of baby boomers.

One of my clients became estranged from his gay son when he refused to refer to his son's new romantic partner with the requested pronoun of "they" instead of "he" or "him." "I'm sorry," the father told me. "My son's been out for three years, that's fine, it's always been fine that he's gay as long as he's happy. But now he's got a new boyfriend who says he's 'nonbinary' and if I say 'he' instead of 'they' my son hits the roof. I just can't go there. So now he refuses to talk to me which is like, wow, you're going to cut off contact over that? Be my guest."

I sometimes hear parents struggling to use the newer pronouns preferred by their adult children or their romantic partners. As psychologist Diane Ehrensaft writes, "No sooner do we think we have all the new terminology about gender clear in our heads than we discover we were all wrong and that today's words are already passé." Some parents resent feeling scolded, threatened with estrangement, or accused of prejudice by their children for failing to adopt these new ways of thinking about gender. That's understandable. But here, too, you're better off making room for your estranged adult child's request if reconciliation is your goal. This is true for several reasons:

1. Your child will experience you as more respectful of his or her wishes, and that willingness to change improves your chances of reconciliation.

2. Your child may feel more hurt or rejected by you than you realize. If you're willing to be more adoptive of their requests,

they will feel more cared about by you and less inclined to distance themselves.

While this father struggled with the relatively new concepts of the nonbinary identity, many parents still struggle with good old-fashioned homosexuality. For example, Samuel is a twenty-five-year-old man who reached out to me after one of my NPR interviews about estrangement. He was born and raised in Chillicothe, Ohio, a small town located along the Scioto River. I was familiar with the area, since it was a grade school destination to see the Shawnee burial mounds and an Underground Railroad stop when I was growing up in Dayton.

Samuel moved to San Francisco five years ago in his early twenties. He said that his father was a minister in Chillicothe and was deeply religious. His mother was a stay-at-home mother of four and was very involved in their congregation. Samuel came out to his parents when he was twenty-two and it went about like he expected—catastrophically.

"I really didn't expect my parents to suddenly become card-carrying members of PFLAG or something [the advocacy group for parents and friends of LGBT kids], but to this day, they still insist on telling me that I'm going to burn in hell every time I talk to them. I mean, *literally* every time. So, guess what? I don't talk to them. There is a reason that I moved to San Francisco and I'm no longer in Ohio, you know? I need to be around people who get it and don't make me feel like I'm a pervert just because I prefer men over women."

"Well, that makes sense. Was the conflict mostly over your coming out or were there other issues that led you to cutting off contact?"

"There are other issues. I'm just not like any of them. I'm the weird one who ran off to San Francisco."

While many adult children adopt similar religious and political values as their parents, some grow up to have interests, personalities, tastes, passions, hobbies, and desires far different from anything conceived of by their parents. And when that occurs, family members can sometimes become unrecognizable to each other. Researchers Becca Bland and Lucy Blake found that "clash of personality or values" was a common reason that participants gave to explain estrangement from their parents. Megan Gilligan, Jill Suitor, and Karl Pillemer found that adult children whose mothers reported that they were dissimilar to them were far more likely to become estranged than adult children whose mothers reported that they shared a similar outlook on life.

"It was hard enough growing up in an area that wasn't very supportive of my sexuality, without having my own family make me feel like crap," Samuel explains. "The confusing part is that my parents are basically good people if you can be close-minded, homophobic, and sometimes racist, and still be a good person. I think they believe what they believe and that's fine, just don't act like I'm on a fast track to hell every time you see me and expect me to want to race home for the holidays. I'm religious, too, just not like they are. I still believe in God. I found a nice church out here. So unless something changes, I'm done."

"You're saying that you wouldn't be estranged if they were able to keep their opinions to themselves about your sexuality?" In my initial interviews with estranged family members, I'm interested in which areas are nonnegotiable and which have some room to maneuver. It was his parents' need to constantly tell him that he was going to hell that caused the estrangement. If they could keep their disapproval to themselves, he could focus on what was good between them.

Samuel's parents were caught in a dilemma between their faith and their love of their son. While telling your gay son that he's going to burn in hell for his sexuality doesn't exactly sound like a loving act, it *is* a loving act if you believe that hell is what truly awaits him. From the parents' perspective, convincing him, seemingly by any means necessary, that he should renounce his sexuality was an expression of deeply held religious values. For the son, convincing his parents to accept him or at least discontinue their ongoing disapproval was the only road to a potential relationship.

In my meeting (there was only one) with the parents, I empathized with their dilemma of being caught between their desire to remain true to their religious beliefs and the potential loss of their son. I told them that the stakes were high because many people who feel rejected by their parents over sexuality or gender identity are much more at risk for depression, substance abuse, homelessness, and suicide.

I emphasized that Samuel had already struggled with some of those in adolescence and early adulthood (the parents didn't know this) and was at risk of relapse if they couldn't adopt a more supportive position. Sometimes letting parents know how much the child has suffered can cause them to soften their position.

"Samuel also told me that he knows you don't approve of his sexuality, he said he just needs you to stop talking about it. He knows you wish he weren't gay, so it's probably not productive to keep reminding him about it. You flew all the way out here to see me because you love your son and want him to be happy. Is that right?"

"That's right. And we want him back in our lives. We all miss him."

"I understand. It seems like he's in a lot of pain over the estrangement and so are you. Sexuality is not something anyone chooses in the same way you both didn't choose to be straight. Sometimes we show our love the most powerfully when we do the thing that is the hardest for us to do."

"What about those programs that convert people away from being homosexuals?"

"They don't work. And he isn't interested in converting. Wouldn't it feel better to have him back in your lives and agree to disagree about this, like other things parents have to do, rather than have this huge gap between you?"

"Well, yes, but we just worry about his soul if he continues down that path."

"I understand that that's something you're scared about, and I don't claim to have any authority when it comes to religion. But your position at this point just makes him feel rejected and unloved. He apparently joined a church out here, so it's not like he's given up his faith in God."

"Well . . ." the father said. The mother, recognizing where this was going, jumped in.

"No, we don't want him to feel unloved. We love him. We're just worried about him."

"I believe that. My role isn't to judge what's right or wrong. It's to help families see what's possible. Here it's possible that you could have your son back in your lives by focusing on the good between you and not on this area of disagreement. Lots of families have to find places where they agree to disagree, and you wouldn't be the first to do that around someone's sexual choices. Sometimes it's the parent who decides, after he or she has kids, that they're the ones who are gay."

They looked at each other to gauge the other's reaction to this surprising revelation.

"How does that go?" the father asked.

"It all depends on the family members. Some are very accepting, some have a really hard time with it but eventually come around, and others break apart over it and never see each other again."

"Well, that's sad," the mother said, looking down at her hands.

I suggested that not discussing it wasn't the same as endorsing it, and that families commonly choose to avoid topics that are potentially controversial in the interest of facilitating harmony. Samuel felt like he had already compromised enough by accepting them for who they were without anger and without trying to convince them to be otherwise. He needed his parents to agree to stop trying to persuade him to renounce his sexuality.

I couldn't tell where things would go when they left my office, but I was doubtful that they'd take my counsel. My only hope was based on the fact that they were both in obvious pain, they'd flown out from Ohio to consult with me (which shows a commitment to try to find a solution), and their son's terms were reasonable. That isn't always enough to produce an agreement, but it gave me some cause for optimism.

But it didn't work. I received a voice mail at the end of the day from the father, saying that they were heading back to Ohio. They appreciated my time and my perspective, but they couldn't be silent around something that was so much against their values.

In the same way that reconciliation requires recognizing that you won't get everything that you want, so, too, does remaining estranged. In this case, it meant that the promise of reconciliation for both Samuel and his parents didn't outweigh the costs of change. Their family illustrates the way that sometimes the family you're born into, or the child to whom you give birth, is too different from you for there to ever be a meeting of the minds. And when that happens, going your own way may be the only outcome, however much disappointment is created by that choice.

MICK AND LAURA

"If you vote for Trump in the next election, we are done." So began a letter to a couple in my practice. *"We can kind of forgive you for falling for his racist bullshit in the first election, but if you can't see how evil he is then we don't want you around our children and we don't want you around us. Love, Dale and Fran."*

Mick and Laura are the parents, Dale is the son; Fran is the daughter-in-law.

Politics is a much more common source of disagreement among family members today than at other times in our history. As with many estrangements, the stated complaint is sometimes code for or condensation of a variety of complaints held by the adult child. For example, political scientists Christopher Ojeda and Peter Hatemi found that children who felt supported and connected to their parents were more likely to adopt their parents' belief systems than those who didn't. As with differing ideas about the nature of gender or sexuality, political beliefs can occur at the tenuous and conflict-ridden junction of values and identity. Helping parents withstand the child's contempt or anger, regardless of which side of the political divide they fall on, is no small task.

How can a parent hold on to their own ideas and ideals while simultaneously working toward reconciliation? Marital researcher John Gottman found that helping couples deeply empathize with the underlying values motivating a spouse's decision or action was critical in containing the potentially destabilizing differences that commonly occur in marriages. From Gottman's perspective, incompatibilities are part of family life, even in the best of marriages.

I have found this model to be useful in helping parents address the complaints of their adult children. If we use Gottman's model, the task is to encourage a full and open discussion not only about the political differences but any other complaints that may be lurking underneath; to seek to understand why the adult child is so troubled by the parent's political orientation and to express empathy for that view, even if you don't agree with their conclusions. In addition, to avoid getting pulled into a right-or-wrong debate. Or any debate.

Mick and Laura reached out to their son, Dale, with this model in mind. Dale revealed that he was not only upset about their politics but by the "fact" that they'd always preferred his older and more successful brother. He said that he had also felt neglected by them growing up. The parents were very surprised by the idea that they preferred his older brother (they didn't) and also by the fact that he felt neglected. Rather than trying to reassure him or prove him wrong, they took my advice and simply empathized with how he felt as a child and as an adult. They empathized, expressed tenderness, and listened to how they could help him to feel more prioritized in the future. Over the course of a few family sessions, this allowed Dale to begin to lower his guard and move toward a reconciliation. That and an agreement to avoid future political discussions at all costs.

Psychologist Diane Ehrensaft has written about the importance of viewing gender as existing on a spectrum. She suggests we think of parental acceptance and support as also existing on a spectrum—whether it relates to gender, sexuality, politics, or other differences. I think this is a useful frame. We can do harm to our children and to our relationships with them by our unexamined prejudices, our off-the-cuff remarks, our strongly worded opinions. Our children can harm us in the same way, of course. But if a closer relationship to our children is the goal, we are required to see the world through their eyes, to live in their skin, and to exist in their reality, even temporarily.

Mary Catherine Bateson wrote that marriage requires *a constant rhythm of adaptation between two people who are changing.* The same is true for relationships with our adult children. They're changing. We're changing. There are things we may not like about them nor they about us. Our task is to find ways to let our love and support be the guiding lights of engagement. To illuminate ways to communicate that increase closeness and reduce hurt; and to hope for patience—theirs and ours—as we try to navigate these new and often uncharted territories of parent–adult child relationships.

Chapter 7

SONS-IN-LAW, DAUGHTERS-IN-LAW, AND THE CULT OF ONE

When she went to change, when she came back, dressed in her beautiful traveling clothes, when she handed out the wedding favors, when she had left, with her husband, then a huge fight would erupt, and it would be the start of hatreds lasting months, years, and offenses and insults that would involve husbands, sons, all with an obligation to prove to mothers and sisters and grandmothers that they knew how to be men.

Elena Ferrante, My Brilliant Friend

When Sam brought Maria home for the first time from college, she didn't make a good impression. She spent much of the evening on the couch texting on her phone, barely engaging any of the family members in conversation, including Sam's two sisters with whom he was very close. Sam seemed a little embarrassed by her behavior but was careful not to pressure her into involvement in the family interactions.

"She's just shy, I think," said Sam's mother to her husband and daughters after the first meeting. "We're kind of a loud and overwhelming family; she was an only child, isn't that what Sam said? I think we just need to give her time to get to know us. Sam seems happy with her and that's all that matters."

"I think she's a *bitch*," said Sam's younger sister, Sara, a high school senior.

"Seriously, I must've asked that girl ten questions about her college studies, her hobbies, her family, where she grew up. Whatever. I hope she makes Sam happy, but I'm just not willing to work that hard to get to know somebody. Did she even ask you one question, Mom?"

"No, but that's okay," Sam's mother said, ever optimistic. "She probably just needs time to settle in. I think if she makes him happy, then I'm fine. She doesn't have to be my best friend. Besides, she's his first serious girlfriend, so it's not like he's necessarily going to marry her or anything."

"Oh, Jesus God, I hope not," Sara said. "Because I know girls like that and this one is bad news. Trust me."

Sara was right and her mom was wrong.

Within one year of their dating, Sam had cut off all contact with his parents, sisters, and grandparents, as well as his childhood friends. Everyone. Like many of these cases, the deterioration in the family relationship occurred over a surprisingly short period of time; a trail of small misunderstandings and mystifying communications construed by Sam's girlfriend—and then Sam as her defender—as intentionally hurtful, hostile, and manipulative on the part of Sam's family. Visits with Sam and Maria always ended with a furious phone call the next day; Sam would yell at his parents or his sisters for disrespecting Maria and "just not getting it." When Sam's mother asked Maria if she planned to have children, Sam told her that Maria was incredibly insulted by that and found it intrusive. She also said that she didn't like Sam's mother's cooking, so she didn't want to have dinner there again.

What surprised Sam's family and later, friends, was the dramatic change in his personality. He had gone from someone who was friendly and outgoing to cold and hostile.

"It's like she's taken over his mind," his father told me in my first meeting. "And the more we plead, the more he moves away. We tried reaching out to her parents, but they had no interest in helping us and acted like we were being mean to their daughter. We said, 'Look, we're just trying to get our kid to talk to us. It seems like ever since they've been together, he wants nothing to do with us; we don't know what we've done.' But they just acted like it wasn't really any of their concern and like we had been mean to their daughter. We're happy to apologize to her if that's what it takes. But they didn't even seem willing to help us do that. It's apparent that they're in contact with them, though, because we still have access to his Facebook page and we see all of the activities they're all doing together."

This sequence is surprisingly common in my experience: the adult child couples with someone who is either troubled or highly insecure, and she feels threatened by his attachment to his family or friends. Slowly she encourages a dissolution of any and all prior relationships until the only attachment is to her and, not infrequently, her family.

In this chapter, I tackle one of the most intractable problems that can lead to estrangement: sons-in-law and daughters-in-law. I'll ask: Why does the adult child sometimes cut everyone off? What's in it for him or her to estrange? I'll ask: Is there any hope for the son-in-law or daughter-in-law—can they be changed? How should a parent understand them? I'll also tell the story of Rahel, who cut off her parents shortly after marrying Tom. Rahel and Sam will be our guiding lights in this story, as we try to figure out why this is such a common cause of estrangement and how it can be solved.

THE TROUBLED GATEKEEPER

Rahel is a thirty-three-year-old mother of two. While she had had a very uneven relationship with her parents, it wasn't until she married her current husband that the relationship completely ended. Tom, Rahel's husband, was an attorney who radiated an attitude of quiet contempt and dismissive superiority. Rahel's parents were both uncomfortable with Tom from early on. They didn't like, for instance, that he monitored what Rahel was eating and how often he would speak over her during conversations. "It felt like he was trying to obliterate her," her mother told me in our first meeting. "She was always a very verbal, intelligent, and outspoken person and suddenly she's this quiet, deferential shrinking violet. I really wanted to ask her what the hell she was doing with a guy like that, but I knew she would not like that. So I kept my mouth shut. But maybe I should've said something, because now she won't talk to me at all."

At the wedding, Tom's father spoke to Rahel's parents in a way they later took as a warning. "Tom was not the easiest kid to raise," he began, "and he's not the easiest person, period. We probably made a lot of mistakes with him growing up. I hope they're happy together." Thinking back, Rahel's parents realized that the wish for future happiness sounded more like an expression of skepticism than an actual wish.

Shortly after their marriage, Rahel began to reduce her contact with her parents. Even before the wedding, they noticed that Tom never came with her to family events, which she always blamed on his work. Contact with her parents dropped from every few weeks, to every six weeks, to every two months, to none at all. While the reasons initially given were prosaic—ranging from "I've been really busy" to "I've been meaning to but haven't gotten around to it"—they increased in negativity in correspondence with the parents' protests about her dwindling responsiveness or availability for potential visits.

Then the shoe dropped: Tom wrote a letter on his legal stationery demanding that all future contact go through him:

> *Mr. and Mrs. Wolcott,*
>
> *Please make all future communication through me. Rahel is upset every time you write. I don't think you have any idea how critical and negative you are and how much that affected her growing up and continues to affect her. You can continue to write her, but from now on, all correspondence should go through me. I*

will read what you write, and if I find it appropriate, I will pass it
on to her. You are both pretty clueless when it comes to parenting,
so this is how it has to be. In the meanwhile, I suggest you both get
some counseling for yourselves so you can figure out why it's better
for Rahel to not want anything to do with you.

Sincerely,
Tom
Tom Adams, Esq.

Rahel's parents were very troubled by the letter. Not only by the accusations about their parenting, but that Tom had appointed himself gatekeeper. Even more upsetting, he'd shown himself early on to be uninterested in their feelings. What could they possibly say or do to demonstrate that they weren't the people he assumed they were? And if Rahel was so unhappy with them, why wouldn't or couldn't she tell them herself? She had always expressed pride in her independence and in her identity as a strong woman. Had that changed? Why was she allowing her husband to be her voice if these really were her complaints? She'd never had a problem complaining before. What terrible things had they done that she needed to station her husband at the gate?

A CULT OF ONE

In my clinical experience, it's not uncommon for a daughter-in-law or son-in-law to act like a powerful cult leader, enforcing absolute obedience. One of the most potent methods of this brainwashing is persuading the adult child that his or her parents are bad, if not outright evil. While it's not hard to see how this kind of manipulation would be easily achieved in those homes where the parent was truly abusive or dysfunctional, this method can be remarkably successful even in functional homes, *especially* in those where the parent and child enjoyed a very close relationship.

Doesn't that mean that there were significant problems hidden in the relationship between the parent and adult child, ones that the new spouse is simply shining a light on or playing to their advantage? Sometimes. But I don't believe that hidden problems explain the majority of these kinds of estrangements. I would argue that almost any adult child is vulnerable to this kind of manipulation when he or she is faced with an extremely troubled spouse.

For example, a very troubled or manipulative spouse can persuade the adult child that:

- They have repressed memories of how bad their childhood was, including repressed memories of abuse.
- They are overly dependent on the parent and need to stand up more for themselves, or for the spouse who is supposedly being abused or mistreated by the parents. To that end, the manipulative spouse is likely to inflate any of the normal slings and arrows of family life into a severe and unacceptable character flaw of the parent that can't be tolerated.
- Any positive contact with the parent (or anyone related to the parent) has to be reinterpreted as negative to forestall their power to influence the adult child away from their troubled spouse.

It's interesting how similar these characteristics are to those commonly observed of members in a cult:

- Sudden or dramatic change in personality or belief system
- Rewriting childhood history as bad or abusive
- Use of language that seems coached or out of character

- Rejection of parents, siblings, and anyone close to them
- Rejection of anything related to the past, such as cherished childhood objects
- Black-and-white thinking
- Radical change in life plan
- Secrecy
- Dogmatic belief systems

As Stanford researcher Philip Zimbardo wrote, "A remarkable thing about cult mind control is that it's so ordinary in the tactics and strategies of social influence employed. They are variants of well-known social psychological principles of compliance, conformity, persuasion, dissonance, . . . emotional manipulation, and others that are used on all of us daily to entice us: to buy, to try, to donate, to vote, to join, to change, to believe, to love, to hate the enemy . . . Cult mind control is not different in kind from these everyday varieties, but in its greater intensity, persistence, duration, and scope." In other words, we're all vulnerable to being manipulated to behave in hurtful or problematic ways given the right set of circumstances.

One of the traits of highly manipulative people is the ability to both consciously and unconsciously know what people need in order to feel good. If their partner has insecurities about intelligence, for instance, they'll make him or her feel intelligent. If they're insecure about their potential for success, they'll make them feel like their potential for success is limitless. If they feel unattractive, they'll make them feel like they're highly attractive but can be even more so. On the one hand, they speak to the pain of those feelings of inadequacy while promising, subtly or overtly, to make all that pain go away. On the other hand, they can manipulate them by playing on those same insecurities.

WHEN YOUR CHILD'S SPOUSE IS AGAINST YOU

Let's return to Sam's family. When a new spouse or romantic partner is an active and highly empowered agent of estrangement, it's important that estranged family members accept that he or she is the new *alpha* and, therefore, the gatekeeper to any future contact with the estranged adult child or grandchildren.

"You can't go around her; you can only go through her," I told Sam's parents and sisters in my first meeting. "Therefore, you can't criticize his wife because he'll pass it on to her and that will dig you in even deeper. And you can't directly criticize her because she can and will use that against you in the court of your son, where you are currently guilty until proven innocent. You also can't establish an independent line of communication with him because she'll feel too threatened by it."

I encouraged Sam's parents to view his girlfriend as fragile, rather than intentionally divisive. Your attitude about her matters, I emphasized, because the suite of emotions generated by feelings of fear and loss are more likely to get you to overreact, get aggressive, or get all emotional on your child or Maria. This is exactly the opposite of where you want to be. Better to think of this troubled partner as having attached a bomb to your child; remember that she is all too willing to connect the detonation wires if you come at her hard or even fast. Some degree of caution, even compassion, will allow you to slow down and approach with the kind of respect and restraint that the situation requires.

As I heard more about Maria, it was clear that she suffered from acute social anxiety, the kind where interactions with almost everyone are excruciating because of the fear, self-doubt, and self-recrimination they can produce. Being brought into a loud, extroverted family like Sam's, where people are both intimate and opinionated, was nothing short of terrifying to her. While she may have appeared self-centered and uninvolved as she sat on the couch texting, she was likely trying to soothe the panic that welled up inside of her. Her later attempts to vilify Sam's family, however problematic, were attempts to justify her need to shield herself from situations that triggered her anxiety. Her desire to have him cut off contact with them was also a way to control her fears and ward off the family's potential, however unlikely, to influence Sam against her.

This isn't to say that she was any walk in the park. Sometimes the sequelae of defenses developed to reduce anxiety can make those who suffer with it intensely prickly, remote, or both. In addition, people with Maria's personality don't require a lot of evidence to conclude that someone has crossed a line with them and should therefore be rushed to the trash compactor. Also knowing the reasons that someone behaves in a difficult and provocative way doesn't necessarily mean that such understanding provides a path to reconciliation. Or as one estranged parent said of his son-in-law: "Just because he suffers from depression and anxiety doesn't mean that he's still not an asshole." However, failing to understand what motivates the negative and provocative behavior increases your risk of compounding your problem rather than solving it.

I encouraged Sam's parents to write a letter of amends to both Maria and their son—not because I thought she would relent, nor because I thought they had done anything particularly wrong. But rather, I hoped this would strengthen their son's ability to modify her intransigence. From my perspective, the primary cause of the estrangement was his loyalty to her and fear of her disapproval and rejection. The more the parents could acknowledge her power and centrality in his life, the more their son could say, "I think my parents get it and are really trying. Let's give them a chance." The more they could position themselves as unthreatening to her by respecting her boundaries, the safer she might feel to have contact. The more the parents criticized her, by contrast, the more empowered she would be to claim that his family was hurtful, toxic, and dangerous.

But Why the Change in Personality?

Many parents have told me that their once sweet child has now taken on the personality of their troubled romantic partner. Sometimes this observation reflects a need to blame the new husband or wife for changes that the adult child may have always wanted to make. For example, where their child has longed to be less available, more assertive, or more verbal with their complaints, and the spouse has freed him or her to do so.

However, it is also true that sometimes people are transformed by their marriages in negative and hostile ways. I think this occurs as an attempt to resolve what Leon Festinger in 1957 referred to as *cognitive dissonance*. Festinger writes that we're all powerfully driven to experience ourselves as consistent in our thought processes. As a result, if we become aware of an inconsistency in our beliefs, we'll change one or more of the beliefs to make them more internally consistent.

How might the theory of cognitive dissonance explain why Sam changed from being a kind and considerate family member to being critical and angry?

Here's how the shift in personality might work:

1. Belief: My parents and sisters are good people who deserve my love and respect.
2. Belief: Maria hates my family and thinks they brainwashed me into thinking that they were good to me when they really weren't.

Since Sam loves both his family *and* Maria, he's in a quandary. If he remains committed to Maria, he'll produce endless fights by disagreeing with her or pushing her into being more involved with his family; she has already said that she doesn't like them and doesn't feel comfortable being in their presence. He will also feel guilt toward Maria if he remains in contact with them, as she's made it clear that he needs to choose her over him and being close to them is therefore a betrayal of her.

Since Sam has to come home to Maria each night, his path of least cognitive dissonance is to accept her version of his parents as the correct one. In taking on her behavior, he further lessens the dissonance because he reduces the notion that her behavior is wrong. He also avoids having to deal with ongoing feelings of guilt, sadness, and regret toward his family. This is his way of saying: "Of course Maria is treating you terribly. I am, too. That's what you've created! Maria is right and you're wrong!"

COMMON MISTAKES MADE WITH SONS-IN-LAW OR DAUGHTERS-IN-LAW

Sometimes the parent drives the adult child into the arms of the troubled spouse by pointing out obvious problems in the future spouse's behavior or character. For example, when first dating, the adult child may ask the parent what he or she thinks. The parent might respond: "I think the fact that they have a criminal record is something you should maybe pay attention to, don't you?" Or: "Do you think the fact that they have no way to support themselves is important? Isn't that going to unfairly burden you when you become parents?" Regardless of whether the criticism is fair or unreasonable, the child may believe that the parent is questioning his or her taste and judgment. Rushing into the arms of the other is a way to express rebellious independence.

In other words, young adults may feel obligated to embrace the romantic partner more to assert their right to choose than because they're clear that they've just met Mr. or Mrs. Right. Consider the teenager who would rather shoot himself in the foot by getting bad grades simply to drive home the message that it's his foot to shoot. He does not see that in his rebellion he is doing something inherently self-destructive.

The family history of the daughter- or son-in-law is also hugely important. Whatever issues they may have with their own parents, a good chance exists that they're going to have them with you. If they felt overcontrolled by their own parents, they may be more likely to view you as being overly controlling. If they felt rejected, devalued, and abandoned by their parents, they may overreact to something that you do or say, and convince your child that you are much more critical and rejecting than your child realizes. If estranged from their own parents, they may be more likely to push your child in that direction.

When your child marries, he or she is not only marrying a particular person, but also the entire psychology of that person and the baggage of family relationships that have been built up over the years in that person's unconscious. Your child marries his or her sensitivities, vulnerabilities, and their still-unresolved issues. The more you understand these realities, the better you're able to navigate the often-treacherous terrain of having to deal with somebody who has a knife to your kid's throat: "Choose between your parents or me. You don't get to have both."

WHEN YOUR CHILD IS THE PROBLEM

It is also possible that your child's spouse may be reasonably healthy. It may, in fact, be your child who has psychological issues that make him or her unable to withstand the normal slings and arrows of adult life and family interaction. She may need to gang up with her spouse and her spouse's family against you as a way to feel more insulated from the problems that come from common parent-child interactions. He or she may be too sensitive, depressed, anxious, insecure, or troubled to be able to handle the conflicts that happen in every single family. His fragility may mean that he has to construct the world in an overly simplistic fashion: "People are either with me or against me." This is why sometimes the estranged child not only cuts off the parents, but anyone related to the parents, even revered grandparents, siblings, aunts, and uncles.

Why would this be the case? Likely his confidence is so low that he can't tolerate anybody challenging it. He can't accept, for instance, a non-estranged sibling who says: "Our mom and dad aren't so bad . . . They're good people. I don't think you're being fair to them. Give them another chance. What did they do that could justify not speaking to them?"

The avoidance of conflict is at the heart of many estrangements. Feeling guilt-ridden, overly responsible, too concerned about hurting another's feelings may cause some adult children to withdraw completely rather than risk discord with the parent. Understanding that may help you avoid pushing too hard on a child who can't tolerate it. Better in those cases to encourage complaints in one who is afraid of complaining.

Strategies Toward Reconciliation

1. As always, start with yourself. We all have our blind spots; even when we think we're behaving in the most upstanding, reasonable, and sympathetic way, we may be blind to how we have pushed our child further into the arms of their troubled spouse.

    How can you tell if it's more you than them? Here are some clues:

    a. The problems that you are having with your daughter-in-law or son-in-law mirror problems those that you have with friends, coworkers, spouse, or other family.

    b. You have gotten feedback from others that your behavior is more problematic than you believe it to be.

    c. You have made attempts to communicate more effectively with your daughter-in-law or son-in-law in the past and those attempts were well received.

2. Write an amends letter even if you didn't do anything wrong. Remember: the audience is not only your daughter-in-law or son-in-law, but your adult child. You want to strengthen his or her ability to say that you are trying and should be given a chance at reconciliation. And it's also a good way to see if your daughter-in-law or son-in-law is open to reestablishing contact.

3. Always include the troubled son-in-law or daughter-in-law in your communications with your child. If you give your adult child a birthday gift, make sure you give a gift to his or her spouse. Same with every other holiday. Always ask about how the spouse is doing. Send them love through your adult child even if you'd rather send them a letter laced with arsenic. The audience is your adult child, not their spouse. Don't try to develop a separate peace with your child unless that's what he or she wants.

4. Do not complain about his or her spouse. It will get passed on and your life will be made worse for it.

5. Respect their limits in your role as a grandparent, even if you don't like the limits.

6. If your child or his or her spouse claims that you haven't apologized enough, apologize again. It may not persuade, but it will show your adult child that you're turning over every stone to make things work.

ARE SONS MORE VULNERABLE TO ESTRANGEMENT AFTER MARRIAGE?

In my practice, I have found that men are more vulnerable to being negatively influenced by their spouses or girlfriends against their families for a variety of reasons: For most, their wives are their best friends, if not their only friends. In other words, men pay a higher price for opposing a wife or girlfriend seeking to cut him off from his family, because she is of singular importance to him: she is his primary source of support and nurturance.

In addition, supporting the wishes of his girlfriend can be an important expression of masculinity. Vulnerable to claims that he's a mama's boy or is failing to protect her happiness, he may be easier to manipulate. "I'm your new family now and you should be prioritizing me and my feelings" may be an assertion that is hard to resist, especially once children come onto the scene.

However common it may be today, allying with a wife against a mother to demonstrate male independence wasn't always considered good or necessary behavior for American men. According to family historian Rebecca Jo Plant, demonstrating masculinity was once thought to involve a prolongation of maternal love and involvement, rather than a repudiation of it. After the Civil War, men returned to the family home to be cared for by their mothers, not their wives. Victorian mothers might refer to a son as "lover boy" while a son would refer to her as his "best girl" without any fear of ridicule. Try that today.

Historian Stephanie Coontz writes that, by the 1920s, the Victorian portrayal of maternal love as welcome and necessary to a son throughout life began to give way to the view that such love was considered intrusive and infantilizing, and that a mark of masculine adulthood should be to distance oneself from the mother's influence and even affection. She cites the example of a popular 1926 play, *The Silver Cord*, which tells the story of a son triumphantly delivered by his young wife from his mother's meddling in his life. As Coontz notes, by the end of the 1920s, adult ties with parents had been firmly replaced by the primacy of marital ties and privacy.

But it didn't end there. By the 1940s and 1950s, *mother love* was thought to be a primary cause of pathology in sons, resulting in effeminacy, homosexuality, even political subversion. Over time, moms got blamed for schizophrenia, autism, and a whole host of psychological maladies. Pathologizing maternal love or attachment to the mother facilitated an ideology that encouraged developing a self, distinct from family relationships and obligations.

A further vulnerability in men is their tendency to shut down as a way to avoid feeling overwhelmed or "flooded" with emotion. According to marital researcher John Gottman, for most men, marital satisfaction is based not only on how sexually responsive their wives are, but how uncritical they are. Men are thus more likely to want to avoid conflict and criticism, even if it means having less contact with family or friends.

Women, in contrast, often have the role of being *kinkeepers* in families and can face more social censure for failing to attend to the needs of family. A kinkeeper is someone who keeps track of family members' birthdays, holidays, and graduations—makes sure that gifts are sent, cards are written, calls are made. They have a stake in preserving the family and suffer when family relations are strained. However, kinkeeping depends on who you define as kin. It's not uncommon that when the daughter-in-law is the primary cause of estrangement, she forms a powerful dyad with her own mother at the exclusion of the son's family.

Men are more typically excused from the role of kinkeeper and, as a result, may be less likely to feel guilty toward their parents when they cut off contact. Finally, for both men and women, supporting a spouse may be tied to their own goals of individuation and separation from a family of origin. They may feel stronger or more independent. In short, it can feel developmentally more in line with feeling like an adult.

WHEN THE SIBLINGS DON'T WANT TO RECONCILE AND THE PARENTS DO

Sam's parents were more than willing to follow my lead, but his sisters were not. They both strongly disliked Maria and the pain she had caused their parents. Moreover, they felt rejected: Sam had kicked them out of their lives when they'd once been close. While they wanted their brother back in their lives, there was only so much crow they were willing to eat. The parents, on the other hand, were willing to eat a whole murder of crows if it got them back their son.

The dynamics of conflict between parents and adult children are often quite different than they are with siblings. For the estranged child, rejection of the parent can be tied to expressions of autonomy, power, or even a healthy retribution for long-held and unexpressed feelings of hurt or anger. It can be a way to rebalance authority by making a greater claim to equality with the parents, a final step on the path to adulthood.

For estranged parents, there's not only the pain endured from the loss of contact, but also the loss of identity and self-esteem. They lose the capacity to see themselves as good, loving parents. They lose the pride in having raised a child who honors them with loyalty and affection.

Parents and siblings operate in different realms of suffering and influence. This is because siblings don't typically experience the same assault on their identity and self-esteem as do parents. The role of siblings does not carry as much obligation or symbolic authority as that of parents. When an adult child criticizes a parent for failing to be a good mother or father, it can be devastating. But the accusation of being a bad sister or brother, however hurtful, doesn't carry the same authority or moral sting: the role demanded of a sibling is much more vague. That's why sibling conflict can quickly deteriorate: the stakes aren't always high enough to motivate one of the members to take the high road. But a willingness to take the high road—that is, to take more responsibility than may be objectively reasonable—is often what's required to resolve estranged family dynamics. (I'll provide more guidance for parents about their non-estranged siblings when I discuss siblings in Chapter 8).

BUT WHY CUT OFF EVERYONE?

While estrangements may occur only with one parent, sibling, or other family member, sometimes the adult child cuts off all the family members—as did Sam. Why cut everyone off? The adult child may be attempting to reduce conflict with his or her demanding spouse or romantic partner, but that isn't the only cause: for some, estrangement offers a rare opportunity to define oneself anew. A disadvantage of contact with family is the way that the reflections of self may continue to reinforce a view that is at odds with our *desired* view of ourselves, what the French branch of psychoanalysis referred to as the *idéal du moi*, or "ego ideal."

Viewed in this light, cutting yourself off from everyone you used to know is like a spiritual quest, a kind of psychological wandering into the woods without provisions. Out there, you seek to prove that you can psychologically survive alone—and that you can do it with strength. This may be especially compelling to those who felt overly dependent on a parent, or who grew up feeling defective, shamed, or deeply misunderstood in a family. Contrary to popular belief, this can also occur in homes without obvious dysfunction or pathology.

There is a lot of power in cutting off a parent or family member— especially in a society like ours where cultural rites of passage or other markers of adulthood and mastery elude us. Thus it's critically important for those who are trying to reconcile with an estranged family member to acknowledge/recognize the kernel of health, strength, or desire for mastery in the decision, however mystifying and painful it is to be on the receiving end. It's tempting to say: "I can't believe that you're doing this to me." Yet far better to restrain oneself, and say, "I know that you wouldn't do this unless you felt like it was the healthiest thing for you to do." Because that is exactly how it feels to the person who's doing the estranging.

Sam's parents were able to eventually reconcile with him, but it didn't happen quickly. They needed to show him that they could tolerate his independence of them for a considerable period of time while expressing empathy and not criticizing his distance. They also needed to patiently continue to reach out to Maria and not get pulled into defensiveness when she was critical or hostile. No small task. But one that eventually resulted in a reconciliation.

No such happy ending occurred for Rahel's parents. As sometimes happens, even her husband stopped responding to her parents' heroic efforts of amends, empathy, and taking of responsibility. How can a parent survive emotionally when reconciliation seems hopeless? How can they cope with the pain? How do they stop thinking about all of the things that they could've done differently? These are critical questions that I'll address throughout the upcoming chapters. For now, I'll end this chapter with a poem by Melanie Gause Harris.

THE ART OF LOSING MY DAUGHTER

You try forgetting one thing at a time
Her first steps and words spoken
When you tamed her curls every day
with detangler and a wide tooth comb.
Months before you carried her
In your belly, then spent days content
With her toddling about the house
Banging on the piano,
watching Mr. Rogers.
The nights your husband let you sleep

and held her in the steamy bathroom
when she had the croup. You could
never bear her troubled breathing.

When you bathed her
You sang "I give her all my love."
Then wrapped her in a pink baby towel
Still singing, "That's all I do."

The day you left her
in the church nursery you cried.
The night you left her with friends
everyone said she didn't make a sound.
Then she saw you and cried fiercely.
Why had you left her anyway?
You know she was confused.

Then in preschool placed in a corner
face to the wall she rubbed her eyes
until they were bruised.
All to keep from admitting
to something she didn't do.

In kindergarten she is busy
directing other children
as if in a play. In first grade
She's a star doing her work.
This is the way it goes
For years.
Then boyfriends.
A man asks.
You give him your blessing.

He hurts you once.
Then he hurts you every day
By keeping her away.

So it's time to start the
Forgetting. She is forced to choose.
She chooses him. And you know
It's too painful to keep remembering.
All the growing up you did together
Is over. So you must practice losing her
Every day. You know it will take forever.

You see how far she's gone
In her white Buster Brown shoes.
She moves on, toddling,
Towards her destiny
She is good, doing well
They say.

Chapter 8

WHEN SIBLINGS ESTRANGE

THE IMPACT ON THEIR LIVES AND
THOSE AROUND THEM

Sally and Carla needed help with their chronic differences. The two sisters had been estranged on and off for the past ten years. Carla lived with their mother, Joan, and Sally was estranged from their mother. Both recognized that their mother was a very difficult person, easily given to mood swings and angry accusations. But the daughters had adopted lifelong diverging strategies for how to manage their mother that were still active in their present conflicts. The latest fight concerned Carla's demand that she be reimbursed for the amount of time and effort spent taking care of their mom and Sally's refusal to agree. The sisters sought my help as a last-ditch effort at mediation before taking their conflicts to court.

When I met them, I was struck by how different and unrelated they appeared. Carla was two years younger but looked much more youthful. She was attractive, quick to engage, and self-deprecating in a humorous way. Sally was almost a foot taller and looked like someone who expected a fight. Her attitude was defiant when she sat down, as though she expected me to side with her sister just like everyone else.

After hearing about their goals, I asked about their lives growing up in the same house.

Watching them recount their childhoods, I was reminded how the shifting tides of genes and environment often create more variations than similarities in siblings. Where Carla was quiet, sensitive, and accommodating as a child, Sally was direct, defiant, and intense. Where Carla could ride out her emotions from a remove of silent resolve, Sally felt constantly under siege.

As Sally described their younger years, it was clear that she envied Carla's ability to move in and out of their mother's moods, dancing in to cheer her up and darting away when the shadow of her impatience moved toward anger. Until the eventual estrangement, Sally said she and her mother were like prizefighters in the ninth round, verbally slugging it out, toe-to-toe, neither giving an inch.

I resisted the urge to side with Carla, the more charming and reasonable of the siblings. I could see how Sally's limited ability to govern her emotions made her a poor fit for their mother's overwhelmed parenting when she was growing up. The combustible volatility of Sally's moods probably made her draw more fire and elicit less support from their mother. Carla, in contrast, possessed a prodigious ability to understand her mother's temperament, which kept her out of harm's way and enabled her to disentangle herself if conflict started to develop.

Parents often tell their children "We love you all the same," but most children know that it's a lie. I knew that my mother favored me over my older brother. I was the baby for a full eight years and occupied that niche with all of the charm, innocence, and radiance that my conniving little heart could muster. My older brother, whose temperament was more suited to a warrior clan than to a tribe in the Midwestern suburbs, created a superabundance of opportunities to endear me to my mother by being the easygoing son.

So I could see why Sally hated Carla—for the same reason I could see why my older brother punched me or twisted my arm behind my back when my parents left a room. Being the Oedipal victor has its costs.

Sally struggled in childhood, struggled in adolescence, and struggled in adulthood. She reminded me of other clients who seem to come into the world with a third-degree burn—every human encounter makes them hurt and vulnerable. But Sally was gifted with a formidable intelligence that got her into a competitive graduate program in biology at Dartmouth. It was there that she met and fell in love with Sean, a fellow graduate student from Ireland.

Sean was that rare reparation that sometimes happens to those who have been otherwise unlucky in life: he was a great guy. Sean was also the parent Sally needed and never had: affectionate, hard to rattle, and able to set limits from a place of love before it morphed into something unmanageable and destructive. It was Sean who encouraged Sally to try family therapy rather than go to court.

It was clear that Carla and Sally needed help to understand what they were fighting over. From Sally's perspective, no amount of money could replace the fact that Carla received more love and attention from their mother. She had done so by being more winning, more lovable. It was because of those qualities that she'd received much more from Mom than Sally ever could or would.

From Carla's view, Sally didn't acknowledge the amount of sacrifice required by her to care for their mother. Nor did Sally acknowledge how that sacrifice interfered with other meaningful things in her life such as dating or having time to herself. In addition, because Sally had occupied the "difficult daughter" role, Carla felt more obligated to maintain the "perfect daughter" role in which she didn't want to burden their parents with worry. While their mother grieved her estrangement from Sally, her obvious preference for Carla throughout her life contributed to Sally's unhappiness and eventual estrangement.

ARE PARENTS TO BLAME IF THEIR GROWN SIBLINGS ARE ESTRANGED?

In my practice, I often meet individual clients who want to explore the ways they felt treated differently from their siblings and to understand how those differences affected their confidence or self-perception. Because siblings typically enjoy the longest family relationships, their ability to influence the other—positively or negatively—over the course of their lives is significant. Studies show that differential treatment—where parents behave more positively toward one of their children—can affect the overall well-being of children even after they're grown and also increase their later risk for depression or lower self-esteem.

And yet sibling relationships are not influenced by parents as much as we believe. Brothers and sisters can engage in a range of behaviors that are well beyond the control or influence of parents by choosing friends, activities, or romantic partners that pull them in unpredictable directions. This is especially true for parents in poverty or who otherwise have limited means. These sibling differences can result in a later sibling estrangement despite being raised with psychologically sophisticated and conscientious parents. While there are an infinite number of things parents can do to worsen sibling relationships, there are often real limitations to what they can do to make them better.

Rather than a straightforward cause and effect, sibling relationships are constantly mediated through the ways that genetic predispositions interact with culture, neighborhood, online sources of influence, economic security or insecurity, and good or bad luck. Children who are oppositional, aggressive, overly reactive, unempathetic—or those with ADHD, learning disabilities, autistic spectrum disorders, even vulnerabilities to depression and anxiety—may create obstacles for parents *and* siblings. And to complicate matters further, a child who is easy to parent (like Carla) may invite more envy, anger, even abuse from a sibling who is less winning or less temperamentally matched with the parent (like Sally).

Many parents, moms especially, feel they've failed their children if the siblings are estranged or distant from each other. Which is tragic because, if anything, today's parents have less influence than ever over the quality of their children's relationships. As with marriage and relationships between parents and their adult children, very little bonds siblings to each other today beyond ties of affection. As family historian Steven Mintz notes, while siblings once competed over material resources, today's siblings compete over emotional resources, which are harder to quantify. "Mom loved you best" is a more difficult thing to measure than "Dad gave you a hundred acres and all I got was this lousy cow." Misperceptions and hostilities can abound when love and attention are the aspects being measured.

While sibling conflict and antipathy may sometimes seem inevitable, it wasn't always the case in our nation's history. In the early national period, Euro-American siblings often played a more critical supporting role in each other's lives. In African American, Native American, and Euro-American households, the relationships between siblings provided a much-needed counterbalance to inequalities around wealth, status, and power. Sibling loyalty and affection, rather than rivalry and conflict, were far more common prior to the twentieth century. Open rivalry was anathema. In wealthier families such as the Browns of New Hampshire, the Sedgwicks of Massachusetts, the Reynoldses of Pennsylvania, and the Izards of South Carolina, "siblings commonly professed their loyalty and consulted each other in every decision," notes historian C. Dallett Hemphill, in *Siblings: Brothers and Sisters in American History*.

Historian Peter Stearns observed that as family sizes shrank from an average of four to five children per family in 1900 to an average of two to three children by 1925, experts suddenly became alarmed about sibling conflict for the first time. Educational reformer Dorothy Canfield Fisher (named after the idealistic character Dorothea Brooke of George Eliot's *Middlemarch*) warned in 1932 that parents needed to work hard to staunch sibling competition and jealousy. "In inciting their children to rivalry . . . parents may be wrecking their chance of present and future happiness." Stearns argues that, unlike larger families where children often saw themselves as part of a group with shared responsibilities, smaller families likely led to a decrease in sibling bonds and increased rivalry. And, as the example of Carla and Sally illustrates, loosened bonds can sometimes mean greater conflict.

FAMILY THERAPY WITH SIBLINGS

Research on couples shows that deeply understanding the other's perspective can often help move couples from gridlock to compromise and negotiation. My experience is that helping siblings understand each other's perspective can also help in resolving an impasse.

But getting anyone to understand another is no small feat. Siblings can carry some pretty big baggage. While parents are often willing to do whatever it takes to bring an estranged adult child back into their lives, brothers or sisters may be less motivated to show the kind of dedication, empathy, and responsibility required to move a conflict off the shoals upon which it's stuck.

As with parent–adult child therapy, success often hinges on who has the most power. Power doesn't necessarily mean wealth or status, but rather who has more of what each wants. The person with less power may be more motivated to accommodate the terms of the more powerful because of the positive or negative influence held by the other. For example, if a parent's goal is reconciliation with an estranged adult child, the child has more clout because his position is driven by compelling narratives of strength, growth, and liberation from oppressive figures. For the child, walking away has significant advantages; reconciling, in contrast, poses significant disadvantages. For the parent, there is rarely any upside to a continued estrangement and compelling disadvantages to its continuance. This reality lessens the parent's power in the negotiations.

Siblings, however, typically come into the therapy office as equals, each possessing something desired by the other. One sibling may want, for instance, to feel less guilty about the estrangement. Another sibling might want to have more time with the other. Developmental psychologist Lucy Blake observed that sisters commonly have more frequent and more positive interactions with each other than with brothers. And while feeling burdened with responsibility for a parent or other family members isn't unusual, taking responsibility may also provide ways to feel a sense of status or meaning in the family.

Sally wanted Carla to accept that Sally had gotten a poorer hand in the family and that Carla was still benefiting from her position as the favored child. She also wanted to thwart Carla's request for money from her mother, since that would affect her eventual inheritance.

They had very different goals, and I wondered about the best way to help them. Many assume that family therapists are like judges: they listen impartially, gavel in hand, and declare one person right and the other wrong. *Case dismissed. Please see the bailiff before leaving the courtroom.* But it is rare that I invoke the authority often conferred upon me. More commonly, I try to help each person talk about his or her experiences and desires in a way that feels clear and direct.

Which carries its own perils. For the client, talking openly about his feelings, needs, or perceptions risks replacing a familiar narrative—one that he has been telling himself all his life—with one that may invite more self-criticism, guilt, or sorrow. These are emotions most of us will gladly avoid if we can. For those unwilling to change their narrative, there is also the temptation to experience feelings better left unfelt. Which is why some avoid therapy: not only because of a common misperception that getting help is weak, but because they don't want to unearth painful emotions or memories they have worked hard to bury.

The risk of revealing too much—either to others or to oneself—is particularly true in family therapy, where family members in the room can shape, counter, or refute the long-standing image held by oneself. Their story line risks being reduced from an autobiographical fact to a contested opinion. For the same reason, some avoid visiting their family at the holidays: it's not only the conflict they want to circumvent, but also the reflection of a self they have worked hard to change or rewrite.

Carla and Sally: A Rocky Beginning in Family Therapy

Carla was more willing to take the first step toward reconciliation.

"Sally," she began, "I know that I've had things easier than you have. I know Mom wasn't nice to you growing up and that you paid a big price for that. I also know that Dad staying out of everything must have felt like he sided with her."

"Yep, sure did," Sally said, looking at her phone.

"So I get why you feel like I've already gotten everything from them. Why should I get more money?"

"You got it." Sally was unmoved.

"I get that, Sally. I do."

I hadn't prepped Carla to lead in this way, but I was glad that she did. Even though we hadn't made much movement in the joint session, it was still a start at changing their dynamic.

I asked Sally to also reflect Carla's position, which turned out to be a bigger ask. She was unable to get halfway through a sentence about Carla's perspective before tearing it apart. "Yes," she said condescendingly, "you feel like you have a really hard life because you get to live at Mom's house rent-free and now you want to be paid for it." I tried modeling it for her, but she couldn't do it. It became clear that in my request to simply repeat Carla's position, Sally felt like she was being asked to endorse it. Ideally she would say something like "So, it sounds, Carla, like you feel like I'm not taking into account all of the ways that you currently have to give to Mom, things that we would have to pay someone else to do, so you deserve to be compensated. And that it also means that you can't do other things in your life that you'd like to that I'm free to do. Do I have that right?" And once Sally could say that, then I'd want her to go one step further, which is to find the kernel of truth in that telling. To be able to say, "Yeah, I could see how you'd feel like that. Even though you're closer to Mom than I am, it interferes with other things that you do want to do." This doesn't mean that she agrees with Carla or that she will change her mind. Just that she can see that Carla isn't crazy to have the stance she has. It didn't go that way and the initial session ended without a resolution.

THE FREEDOM TO SAY THE UNSPEAKABLE

Why was it so hard for Sally to articulate Carla's position? Sally came into family therapy already weakened as a negotiator. Like many who have suffered in their lives, she felt as if any relaxation in her stance would crumble her much-needed walls. She felt, rightly or wrongly, that whatever gains she made in life were those she fought to achieve; that Carla's lovability and favored position in the family were already ingrained in her consciousness; that her own perspective would be drowned out by Carla's; and that I, as therapist, would be charmed into siding with Carla in the same way her mother and everyone else was.

I decided to change strategies: instead of getting her to reflect on Carla's position, I would focus more on where she was in the moment.

"Sally, it must feel like repeating back what Carla has said is giving her more than she deserves. You must feel something like 'Why does she get to occupy the role of the favored child all of her life—and then get paid for it? Why should I have to repeat an unfair pattern?'" I glanced at Carla to see if she was objecting to where I was going. She wasn't.

"Mmm," Sally said, eyeing me warily, waiting for the other shoe to drop.

"So maybe that's your position. I can understand. From Carla's perspective she feels like she's owed more. But from yours, you're under no obligation to accept those terms at all. That may be a bridge too far. Your position may simply be 'Sorry. I guess we have to go to court over this, because I just don't feel like you deserve to get any more than you've already gotten. If that feels unfair to you, so be it.'"

"Well, I'm here, aren't I?" Sally said to me with a small sneer. "I guess if I felt that way, we wouldn't need to pay you all of the money we're paying you, would we?"

"That's true," I said, unsurprised that she was now turning her anger onto me. "And I agree that resolving it here would probably be a less costly move than going to court. I'm just saying that one option is that we all decide that this isn't fixable and stop working on it."

I often find it helpful in family work to lay out the most extreme position, one even more extreme than that stated by the participants. This is a way to make all possibilities open for discussion. I do the same in marriage therapy if one or both of the members keeps threatening divorce as a means of intimidation or as a way to refuse to accommodate the other's requests for change. While I'm not a fan of divorce, especially where children are involved, I don't think that the prospect should be so forbidden that it disempowers the therapist. So I'll sometimes bring the unspeakable out into the open by saying, "I'm always the last one standing when it comes to divorce with children, but maybe we should discuss it." Then I pause, look to see if the faces reveal relief or horror, and press on: "Have the two of you thought about who would stay in the house, what shared custody arrangements you prefer, how you would tell your children if you were to divorce?"

In offering to end therapy and accept the prospect of separation, I am forcing the couple to examine their feelings of what that decision would entail. This neutralizes separation as a weapon of manipulation. And it frees them to have a direct conversation with the feelings that underlie the threat. *Is this what you want? Let's seriously consider it.*

I had my own experience with walking up to that abyss. When my twins were young, my wife and I went into couples therapy to try to save our marriage. I fondly refer to it as the *dark years*. More than once in the decade after they were born, my wife and I seemed to take turns saying, "Maybe we should just split up. This is definitely not working." Not as a threat to scare the other into changing, but more to express that we might have made a serious mistake in getting married. We were completely overwhelmed balancing the needs of our twin boys with my desire to have my daughter feel secure and loved in a blended family. My wife felt frustrated that I was unable to adapt to domestic life in a way that would feel fair and intimate to her. I felt like she was too preoccupied with parenting and not focused on having fun in the ways we did before the twins arrived. We both imagined someone more companionable to our temperaments and aspirations—someone we might have overlooked in the years ramping up to marriage.

Fortunately, we had a good couples therapist and we were able to weather the storm, or at least to buy us enough time to grow up. But I learned firsthand that there is something clarifying about asserting your freedom to hold a position, even an extreme one. It can help you to perceive the future more clearly. Otherwise, you might view that position as too dangerous to explore. It's the upside to our culture's complicated emphasis on assertiveness and rights in family relations: *You don't like it? You're free to go.* Sometimes just affirming that truth to yourself or to the other gives you power. And once a position is clarified, it's easier to know whether you want to act on it or not.

Saying the forbidden is useful in parent–adult child therapy as well. I will sometimes advocate the adult child's perspective even more aggressively than the one they're currently taking with a parent: If I feel like they're beating around the bush, I might say, "You feel like your father failed you growing up. So why should you be there for him now?" It provides a kind of a "He said it, I didn't" cover that sanctions them to explore what they might be afraid to vocalize. My stating it even more boldly than the adult child allows them to see their position more objectively and with less conflict than if it comes out of their own mouths. If the adult child actually feels that way, now the feelings are out in the open and can be discussed. However, if my account doesn't represent their feelings, it gives them the opportunity to refine my statement.

This is why I always tell parents to start by just empathizing. Reflect back what your adult child says and speak to the kernel of truth in their complaints. The more you can show yourself to be a co-investigator of their complaints, rather than a defendant, the more quickly you can learn what they're feeling about you, and more important, *they* can learn what they feel about you.

Don't they already know? No, not always. What stays in the dark grows in the dark. If it's too forbidden to say, it might become too forbidden to understand. Saying it out loud—and seeing that you both survive—provides an opportunity for you both to see how you feel and, once stated, to see if that's how you *really* feel.

IN PURSUIT OF EMPATHY

While I wasn't sure I would be successful at getting the two sisters to compromise, I sensed a wary affection between them. Given the difficulty of a first session, I will typically wrap up by asking each person to say what they like, love, admire, or appreciate about the other. This not only provides an opportunity to repair the damage done by the complaints aired during the session, but to move the relationship toward more trust, positivity, and openness.

In their response to this question, it became clear that Carla admired Sally's strength, assertiveness, and fearless ability to fight for herself whatever the consequences. Sally, despite her jealousy, felt proud of Carla's effortless capacity to bring positive experiences and people into her life. And they both voiced their appreciation for the other's sense of humor. Yet the session ended without my having any idea whether it made matters better or worse. Whether it's with a sibling, couple, or parent–adult child, family therapy is not for the faint of heart. It's not unusual for people to leave the first session more raw than when they came in. Sometimes things fester between meetings because someone feels misunderstood by the other family member or me and I hear about it the following week. (Unless, of course, they don't show up.)

On the other hand, sometimes the space between sessions allows people to tie together all of the loose threads that got snagged during the meeting. I am often surprised by people's ability to acquire insights and perspectives that just weeks before seemed out of their reach. The days that pass between sessions allow some to more calmly and objectively consider what was being said by either the therapist or the other family member. In these cases, they come in ready to engage in a new way.

There is a truism in family work that therapy can proceed only as quickly as the least healthy member. In the next session, I found Sally a little softer. She still looked ready for battle but appeared to have stopped assuming that I would automatically side with her sister. She considered my statements with less obvious cynicism and more curiosity.

Sally's newer disposition gave me hope. It meant that she might be able to empathize with Carla without surrendering any of her goals, which in itself is a psychological achievement. Over the course of the following month, they were able to come to a compromise: Sally agreed that Carla would be paid something out of their mother's assets for her living with her. The amount was less than she asked, but more than she had received before the therapy started. Carla also offered to show Sally monthly statements and receipts of her spending; this would help reassure Carla that Sally wasn't taking more than her due. More important, the time they spent together in the sessions allowed them to begin to move toward ending their estrangement and toward a different relationship—a change that both clearly wanted but hadn't known how to achieve.

Chapter 9

THE RULES OF MONEY AND ESTRANGEMENT

SHOULD I CUT MY CHILD OUT OF MY WILL?

Sheldon and Bonnie wanted to know the best way to cut their child out of their will. They'd been attending my webinars for the past year and decided they needed more individual advice given the importance of the decision. Sheldon was eighty-two and Bonnie was seventy-two. They both looked ten years younger than their ages. He reminded me a little of my own father: rail-thin, eager to find humor, sanguine about life's difficulties—estrangement only being the latest. Bonnie was petite, fit, wearing a blond wig that was probably expensive at one time. She indulged in the playful banter between her husband and me, understanding that we exchanged humor as a kind of male ritual—a talisman against weakness and humiliation. But her eyes reflected a more urgent distress.

Money likely holds more meanings than almost any material object. It can be used to express love, commitment, value, protection, and security. At the same time, it can be used to control, punish, manipulate, and express disappointment. In the parent–adult child environment, money may cause a child to want to be closer, to push away, to feel competitive with other siblings, to grow up, or to forever remain tied to the apron strings of the parent. In this chapter we'll examine the many problematic ways that money can worsen an estrangement, complicate a parent–adult child or sibling relationship, and cause parents to consider cutting children out of their wills.

DENYING AN INHERITANCE

I typically ask parents to bring in any communication prior to the estrangement. This gives me a window into how the adult child thinks and constructs causality. It's not unusual for parents (always mothers) to bring in not only hostilities and ultimatums, but also a thick file of photos and loving letters from a better time. These once-loving messages serve as a kind of evidence to counter the blame or criticism that they expect from outsiders.

Seeing the history of communications can also help me answer such questions as:

- How reasonable are the parent's requests?
- To what extent does the adult child appear stable?
- Are others more involved in the estrangement than the adult child is acknowledging (e.g., a spouse, the other parent's ex, or other family members)?

Reviewing the correspondence also gives me a window into the extent to which a parent has contributed to the estrangement. For example,

- To what extent are the parent's responses or requests of the adult child respectful?
- Are they accepting of their child's requests for boundaries or too demanding?
- Are they supportive of their marriage or too disparaging?
- Are they supportive of their religion, sexuality, or values or too critical?

In reviewing Sheldon and Bonnie's communication with their son, it seemed clear that he wasn't really estranged—he just wasn't as available as they wanted, especially since he got married. But in hearing their history I understood why his distance was so painful: Early in their marriage, they had given up on being parents because of a series of miscarriages. Then, at the age of forty-one, Bonnie became pregnant and was able to carry a son to full term. Saul was born healthy and strong. More important, Saul was the child they always hoped for: loving, kind, and empathetic.

Before Saul's marriage, they felt like they'd hit the lottery, especially when their friends complained about their relationships with their adult children. But after Saul got married, especially once he became a parent, he started being less and less available: fewer phone calls, fewer visits. More frustration when they'd complain they never got to see him.

"So how do we cut him out of our will?" Bonnie asked me. "We want to leave the money to our grandchildren. We don't want to punish Saul, but we just don't feel like we can give him an inheritance given how we're being treated."

I stifled the impulse to say what I was thinking: "Do you have any idea how many of the truly estranged parents in my practice would kill to have as much contact as you're having with your son?" But I held back. He was their only child, and they were older parents. For them, time was more precious, the opportunity to watch their granddaughter more limited, the ability to resolve the conflict more pressing. And like most people, they judged their situation not in light of what others had but in terms of what they once had with him.

"I could see why you'd be upset. That's a huge change. He used to be so available, and now he's much less so."

"Do you think it's his wife?" Sheldon asked. "I have a feeling it is."

"Oh, she's always been really nice to our face," Bonnie said. "I don't think it's her, but Sheldon does."

Beyond the normal pressures to be available as a husband and father, it didn't sound to me like their daughter-in-law was a significant cause. His distance seemed more like a normal and predictable lessening of availability: he had transitioned from being a loving and available son to a loving and available husband and father.

"So about the will?" Bonnie persisted.

I asked what they hoped to achieve in constructing it in the way they suggested.

"Well, we don't want to punish him, we just don't feel like he deserves it after all that he's putting us through."

"You feel like you're being a hypocrite for rewarding bad behavior?"

"Exactly," Bonnie said, imagining that I agreed with her conclusion. "So what do you think?"

"I'm of two minds," I said. It never hurts to spend a lot more time empathizing before telling people what they don't want to hear. "On the one hand, I totally get it. He's gone from being a great son to someone whom you feel you never see. And he hasn't been that willing to be more available even after you've told him how hurt you feel."

"That's it," Sheldon said, with the finality of feeling proven right.

"But," I said gently, "Saul's behavior isn't that unusual, and I certainly wouldn't consider him estranged. He's definitely less available than he used to be, and maybe we can see if that can be changed at all. But based on everything I've read in his correspondence, and everything you've told me, it sounds like this is truly all the time that he has. And it sounds like he does care, even though it doesn't feel that way. It sounds like he feels really sad and guilty that he's causing you both so much distress."

"If he feels so guilty, why doesn't he do something about it? He's a grown man," Sheldon said.

"I understand what you're saying. But we can feel guilty because we know our choices are hurtful to those we love, even if we feel like they're the best ones we can make at the time."

I continued cautiously because parents always hate my next piece of advice.

"I'm also not a huge fan of cutting kids out of wills or even skipping generations," I said, "unless there are really good reasons for doing so. Here, I'm not so sure there is. There isn't any way to do it in a non-punitive way if that's your goal. It's going to feel like a punishment to him."

"There's not a way to write it up that doesn't seem that way?" Bonnie asked.

"I don't know what it would be," I said. "No matter how you word it, you're still making a strong statement of complaint and rejection. I think the will goes to what you want your legacy to be, doesn't it? As you know from the passing of your own parents, we're still parents after we die because we live on in the hearts and minds of our children. He already feels guilty about not being able to give you more, so constructing your will this way will only make him feel even worse. I assume that's not the goal?"

"No, we don't want him to feel worse. We just don't want to reward bad behavior," Sheldon said, thoughtful but annoyed—I couldn't tell whether at me or his son.

"I just don't think we can call this bad behavior. You can say you feel sad, disappointed, hurt, wish it were otherwise. But Saul's conduct is too normal to be considered bad. And more important, the more you complain about his lack of availability, the less he's going to want to spend time with you."

Sheldon looked across to Bonnie with an expression I recognize from years of practice, one that says: "I told you therapy is a waste of time." But they agreed to come back for a few more sessions. While they assented to stop guilt-tripping their son and prioritize the times that he was available, they didn't take my counsel to leave him in their will.

SHOULD I SKIP A GENERATION?

Some estranged parents feel like giving their kid an inheritance feels unreasonable given their feelings of hurt or neglect, so they leave it to their grandchildren. Here are the positive and the negatives of doing so:

Positives
- You're indirectly giving to your child by giving to their children.
- You're acknowledging that the grandchildren are a casualty of the estrangement rather than the primary agents of it.
- You're providing a gift to your grandkids that has meaning and value to you and, presumably, to them.

Negatives
- Your message to your child is still punitive, however carefully worded.
- Doing so complicates your grandchildren's relationship with their parents by making them feel guilty toward their parents. Such guilt may lessen or erase the positive intention of your gift to them; put them in a caretaker role with their parent; and/or become burdensome rather than welcomed.

AN ABUSIVE CHILD

Katherine felt used. Her son was once again off the medication prescribed for his bipolar disorder. He was once again yelling at her on the phone. He was once again telling her what a terrible mother she was, saying she had ruined his life, that everyone in the family hated her, and that she's a self-centered bitch. He wishes she would just curl up and die. She hung up the phone feeling angry, hurt, and humiliated. Meet Alan, aged thirty-seven, single, unemployed, and living off his mother's money.

Like Bonnie and Sheldon, Katherine wasn't exactly estranged, if estranged means out of touch. Rather, she was locked into a horrible dynamic with her son and unable to make good financial decisions because of it. "I just feel like I've created this *monster*," she told me. "I know I shouldn't refer to my own son as a monster, but he kind of is one. I keep feeling like it must be my fault that he turned out this way. His father and I split up when he was young, and his dad's a decent guy. But my son basically wants nothing to do with either one of us. The only time I hear from him is when he needs money. And I keep giving it to him because I feel so guilty."

I took a thorough history of Katherine, including a developmental history of her son. Part of what's useful to parents is learning how to distinguish between decisions that may have been detrimental to the child's development—and those that weren't. While her parenting was far from perfect (is anyone's *not* far from perfect?), it didn't seem likely her behavior had caused Alan to treat her in an out-of-control and abusive way. It's one thing for an adult child to say, "I resent that you weren't there for me more, that you were critical, self-absorbed, whatever." But it's another to scream insults and tell them that they should die.

Most of the time when I get estranged adult children in my office with a parent, it's only after the parent has written a letter of amends demonstrating an awareness of the damage they caused and a desire to repair. It is understandable that a formerly abused child would need some period of time to talk in a not-too-censored way about how much suffering the parent had visited upon them as a result of their child abuse, if child abuse had occurred. Given that, I will allow a session or two of venting, with the agreed-upon purpose of helping the parent listen, learn, and empathize.

However, many adult children feel like it's okay to forever engage in what psychologist Terry Real refers to as *offending from the victim position*: You hurt me, so that justifies my being as contemptuous and as disrespectful for as long as I want. I sometimes hear—especially from adult sons of single mothers—something like this: "Now that I have children, I can't imagine treating my kids the way that you treated me. What were you thinking, being so abusive to a small child?" I could imagine a grown but still hurt child asking that question from a genuine desire to understand. "What were you thinking, Mom? Why did you have so little control over your emotions that you would strike a small child?"

Whether it's incest, neglect, or emotional or physical abuse, I have seen how an adult child who seeks to understand—and a parent who seeks to make amends—can create profound opportunities for repair in both parent and child. For the adult child, it helps him to understand at a deeper level that he didn't deserve the trauma that was visited upon him. For the parent, it provides the opportunity to repair the damage she caused and permission to begin the long uncertain journey toward self-compassion.

However, for an adult child to ask that question and not care about the answer—to raise it only to shame the parent and justify the estrangement—is to imagine themselves somehow purer, more insulated from the random and terrible forces that cause hurtful parental behavior. In addition, it ties them to a narrative of victimhood, however empowered they may feel in the moment of shaming the parent.

Alan had never been verbally abusive to his mother until his first manic episode at the age of twenty-seven. The radical change in him caught his mother completely by surprise. He eventually saw a psychiatrist, got stabilized on lithium, and resumed contact with Katherine. Normalcy was temporarily restored: he was again calm, again respectful. But he hated how the medications made him feel and so he didn't stay on them for long. When he was off the meds, he would tirade against his mother until he hit enough of a bottom to force him back on them. And, as often happens to those with bipolar, his manic episodes would leave a trail of overspending and other problems that were expensive to solve.

Despite being coached by a string of therapists to stop rescuing Alan, Katherine always stepped in to bail him out. "I just feel like it's my fault that he gets into these positions. Clearly I didn't teach him enough about managing his life or he wouldn't keep getting into trouble in the ways that he does." (I rarely hear fathers blame themselves in this way. They may think it. But they rarely say it.)

"I think I have to help you with your out-of-control guilt," I said, stating what I thought was the obvious.

"Is that what it is?" She looked surprised. "He says I made him this way."

"He either genuinely believes that or he uses it to manipulate you into doing what he wants."

"But what if I *did* make him this way?" She smiled through tears.

"He's been diagnosed with bipolar and has been treated for it. He's mentally ill. You didn't cause him to be bipolar," I said softly.

"He says I did."

"Sounds like he says a lot of irrational things when he's in a manic phase. The problem is that you buy into it. That's not good for you or him. It's not good for you because it makes you feel like you were a terrible mother, and you weren't. And it's not good for him because you end up rewarding his mistreatment by giving into his demands. Even if you had been a terrible mother, it's not good for either one of you to continue in this way."

I wasn't surprised to learn that Katherine had grown up in a household with an abusive father. When she was young, she swore to herself that if she ever became a parent, she wouldn't make a child ever feel as scared and lonely as she felt as a child. And she succeeded magnificently in that goal. However, her preoccupation with not being abusive made her scared, guilt-ridden, and confused when her son accused her of the thing she never wanted to be. Alan was aware of this vulnerability in her and, consciously or unconsciously, used it to pry more from her than she wanted to give.

Our children know these things about us. They are perceptive. They observe how we respond to our spouses; they observe how we react to their siblings and to our friends.

"My counsel is that you don't give him money unless he agrees to go back on meds when he's in a manic phase and he speaks to you respectfully. If he can't meet both of those conditions, then you should not respond to his abusive emails or phone calls."

She agreed to try, which meant that she wouldn't. Nonetheless I helped her write the following email to him:

Dear Alan,

I love you and I'm sorry you're struggling right now. Regarding your request for financial help, I'm open to considering it but not unless you're back on meds. I know you think you're not in a manic phase, but you never do while you're in one. And from what I understand from the professionals that I talked to, that's not unusual. However, that's condition #1. Condition #2 is that I no longer am willing to have you talk to me or write to me in the disrespectful way that you've been doing up to this point. You can calmly tell me that you're mad at me, you don't respect me, like me, love me, that you don't think I was a good parent, whatever— but you can't call me a bitch and you can't tell me I should kill myself. That's abusive and I don't want to hear that ever again from you. I won't be responding to any emails that contain that kind of language in them, and if you go there when I'm on the phone with you, I'm going to hang up. I'm happy to go into family therapy with

you to address whatever complaints you have about me, once you're
back on your medication. I love you very much.

Mom.

A complicating factor was that several times in the past ten years
he stopped talking to her completely. Katherine was keen to avoid
that. His ability to cut her off also weakened her ability to set appropriate limits.

"What if he refuses to agree to my conditions?"

"He probably won't agree to them," I said with a smile to convey
We both know that.

"Then what do I do?"

"You have to decide which is worse: continuing to have this kind
of contact with him, which makes you feel terrible about yourself and
contributes to his not dealing with his problems? Or continuing as
you've been doing so you can have the contact that you have? I don't
think there's a third option. Some parents feel like abusive contact is
better than no contact and other parents don't. My counsel is to hold
to the limits that I've outlined, but he's not my kid, so I don't have to
live with the pain if he goes to no contact with you."

When I tell a parent, "He's not my kid," it's not to absolve myself
of responsibility: I stand by my claim of what I think is the healthy
choice. I just want to acknowledge to the parent that doing the right
thing is often really, really hard when it's your child. You're being
pulled in so many different directions by so many different therapists,
family members, and friends—I don't want you to feel guilty if you
can't take my advice.

Katherine couldn't. At least not for a very long time. She struggled over the next six months, mostly giving in to Alan's demands for
money. Her fear of losing him, combined with an insufficient immunity to his accusations that she ruined him, caused her to give him
money even when she knew it was wrong. She always had an explanation that sounded reasonable when she embarrassedly explained

it to me the following week: "Well, he's not doing well and I felt like this might move him in the right direction." "He said this was the last time he was going to ask for money and I believe him." "He had a really good reason for the money this time."

I asked her each time whether she gave into him because he had changed his behavior in the more positive direction that we'd discussed. Each time she said no, he was as abusive as ever. Over time she was able to understand that, in fearing becoming abusive like her father, she had started believing herself to be similar to him. Through therapy, she was able to see that there were no grounds for her fears: she and her father were clearly different people in how they approached parenting. She also learned to tolerate her worries based on the belief that setting more limits could result in a possible estrangement from Alan. Finally, she was able to set more limits because she slowly accepted that her guilt toward Alan was irrational. He continued to torment her for the next year but, last I heard, agreed to go back on meds and was doing better.

With a child like Alan, guilt makes everything worse. In the realm of money, it can:

- Make you give more than is good for your adult child.
- Make you feel like you have to forever make up to him for whatever ways you hold yourself responsible for how his life turned out.
- Make you feel like you have to make up for whatever ways *he* holds you responsible for how his life turned out.
- Perpetuate your feelings of hopelessness, impotence, and a sense that nothing you do is good enough.
- Make you feel more resentful and taken for granted after your gifts are belittled or shown insufficient appreciation.

CUTTING A CHILD OUT OF YOUR WILL

For some parents—especially those who have been verbally abused by their child, had the police called on them, or been cussed out by their son-in-law or daughter-in-law, or who have simply had to live with the heartbreak of not seeing their son, daughter, or grandchildren year after year after year—writing a child out of a will feels like the only empowered response. "Why should this kid get so much of what I've worked so hard to get, when they've only made me miserable? In what universe does that equation make sense?"

I understand how a good person wouldn't be able to keep their estranged child in their wills. If my daughter had never reconciled with me, I don't know for sure if I could have. I want to think that I could. But I might have been too hurt.

However, I believe that as parents, we need to think of how our decisions will play out well after we're gone. I have heard plenty of stories in my office of adult children who regretted their inability to reconcile with their parent while they were alive. Perhaps your adult child is one of those who can't make peace with you now but may think differently of you when you're gone. Having your last message be one of love—not anger but rather regret that you are not closer—may be your last chance to show them that their view of you was a flawed and limited one. It may also carry your legacy with your grandchildren forward in a more positive light, rather than a negative one.

I worry that cutting a child out of an inheritance may only prove his or her worst feelings correct about the parent. This is not to say that such harsh feelings on the part of the adult child are justified. Rather, our own feelings and perceptions as parents aren't always the best measure of who our children are.

In the same way that parents do the best they can raising their children, adult children do the best they can to have a relationship with the parent. It's not fair to blame your child if:

- They're too mentally ill or unstable to know how to be close to you or have a relationship with you.
- They've been too poisoned against you by your ex.
- They've been controlled or dominated by a spouse.
- They feel too enmeshed with you and don't know any other way to feel separate than to be negative or distant.
- They're unable to resolve how hurt they feel by the choices, decisions, or actions you made when they were young. This can be true even if you think you're deserving of more forgiveness. It can also be true if you have made significant attempts at amends or feel like their conclusions are wrong.
- Their therapist has successfully persuaded them that you were abusive even if you know that you weren't.
- Your values are so at odds that they don't know any way to be happy except to not be in contact.

I also do not believe parents should even consider cutting their children out of their wills unless they have done the following:

- Reached out and tried to reconcile for several years.
- Clearly told their child what they would like from them in order to have a better relationship.
- Empathized with whatever complaints the child has lodged against them.
- Accepted the adult child's requests about boundaries, availability, etc.
- Made amends.

If you are satisfied that you have done all of the items listed above, and you still feel too hurt, angry, or betrayed to leave your child in your will, then I would consider writing something like the following:

Dear __

 I have tried to reach out to you for many years and it has become clear that you don't want a relationship with me. I hope you know that I am sorry for the ways that I hurt you, failed you, or let you down. That is a source of pain and regret that I will carry to my grave. I assume that you have good reasons for not wanting a relationship with me.

 As you know, I'm getting older and am planning my estate. I have to admit that it is hard for me to leave you your inheritance when I feel so shut out by you. I know you have your reasons for cutting me out, but it doesn't feel good for me to leave you money when I feel that you have been unwilling or unable to work on our relationship. We don't have to have a great relationship, but I would like some relationship with you. If you're willing to go to family therapy so we can have the help of a neutral party, I think that I would feel differently about all of this. Let me know what you think.

Love,

Mom, Dad, etc.

Your child might write you back and accuse you of blackmailing them into having a relationship with you. If they do, you can write back something like the following: "I could see how it would feel like that. I'm trying to find a way to heal our relationship. I acknowledge that I might have some pretty big blind spots that interfere with my fully understanding why we can't have any kind of a relationship. So my goal isn't to persuade you that I'm a great person or a great parent. It's to have some kind of forum to work on our relationship before I'm no longer here. And to give you the opportunity to see if there's a better solution to our differences than the one that currently exists between us."

If you're not willing to write a letter like the one I've shown here, then I would recommend that you write something like the following in your will:

It is with deep regret that I am not leaving you an inheritance. I have tried for much of my life to reach out to you, to make amends for the ways that I caused you pain either when you were young or grown. But I have not felt that you were willing or able to reach back to me. Whatever my limitations were as a parent, and they were many, I don't believe that I deserved to have a life without you or my grandchildren. It is not my wish that you suffer, nor is it my wish to pay you back. However, it would feel false to me to leave you so much of what I would've wanted to give you if you had let me have a relationship with you.

Love,
Mom, Dad, etc.

I confess, I don't like this letter as much. No matter how it's shaded, it sounds punitive. I don't think the punitive spirit is a great parting message. But if it feels too difficult to leave them in your inheritance, this letter would probably be the best way to do it.

Why Should My Estranged Child Get as Much as My Non-Estranged Children Who Have Been Nice or Helpful to Me?

My advice is based on the premise that parents and adult children don't have as much free will as we think they do. All of us are constantly guided by a confluence of forces that operate largely outside of our awareness. These include genetics, peer group, good luck, bad luck, the people whom we marry or divorce, the liabilities and challenges brought to us by our own parents, our siblings, our children, and our place in time. So in the same way that it's wrong for adult children to believe that their parents were able to make better decisions—and simply chose not to—it's wrong for parents to think that their adult children are able to do it any better. We can be mad at them for not being kinder, more forgiving, more accepting, more grateful, less harsh and rejecting. But that's different from thinking that they're able to become anybody other than who they already are.

In addition, leaving a different amount to each sibling creates lifelong unresolvable problems among the siblings. If a troubled and angry estranged adult child decides to create a problem for the siblings in court, he or she could easily cost them thousands of dollars in court fees. In addition, any chance that the estranged child would or could reconcile with the siblings is diminished, if not eradicated, because of the rivalry or bitterness that will ensue.

But isn't it unfair, parents often ask me, to give the same amount to children who haven't been involved in their lives—especially when their siblings have given more? Some children, for instance, may have helped by taking the parent to doctors' appointments, fixing things around the house, or simply being kind in a steady way. Why shouldn't they get more than the estranged child? I empathize, and I also believe there are plenty of ways to reward more involved children while they are alive—ways that lack the finality of the inheritance. This might include gifts or loans that would not necessarily fall within the realm of their estate.

I Don't Want My Daughter-in-Law Getting a Dime After I'm Gone!

Benjamin and Barb were worried about the person to whom their son was engaged. Shortly after sitting down, Barb got right to the point: "We don't like the rude disrespectful woman our son has moved in with and said he wants to marry. I let him know that I didn't like her. I think she had bad manners and I don't think she's going to make a very good mother."

Oh, I thought. *Bet that went well.*

"He apparently told her what I said. Since then, we haven't seen him or heard from him. We want to let him know, in no uncertain terms, that we are not leaving him any of his inheritance if he stays with her or marries her."

I nodded. It was not an unusual threat in situations where the parents don't like the son-in-law or daughter-in-law.

"We also don't want her having any control of us when we get older. She's the type of person to let us rot in an old-age home if she gets her way." Then Barb proceeded to ask the question that brought her to my office: "So how do we get him to see that he's marrying the wrong person who could ruin his life?"

"Yeah, that is a tough one," I said. "You believe he's about to make a decision that could not only ruin his life but harm his relationship with you as well."

"That's what we're worried about," Benjamin said.

"I get that. The problem is that telling him you're cutting him out of your will won't motivate him to think of *her* more negatively. It will make him think of *you* more negatively. I could see why you'd be concerned; I probably would be, too. But whether she's right or wrong for him is for him to discover on his own. The more you take a position against her, the more he will feel obligated to embrace her as a way to prove his independence. If she *is* troubled, there's nothing she'd like more than to have an excuse to estrange you."

"We're not trying to control him. He's a grown man and can do whatever he wants. We just don't want him to ruin his life—because that is definitely where this is headed."

"You may well be right."

"We *are* right," Barb said playfully.

"Okay," I said, following her lead to lighten the tone. "You *are* right. Absolutely! The question is whether you can do anything to get this train to slow down. This may well be the mother of your grandchildren. If she's truly troubled, he's going to need you as an ally for when things get difficult."

Psychologist Mike Riera advises that parents shift out of the role of being managers and into the role of consultant when children become teens. I think the same advice holds for parenting adult children. We can't protect our offspring from making terrible choices any more than our parents could've protected us. But our role isn't to provide warnings or even advice unless the adult child has made it clear that's what he or she wants. This is true even in situations when we think advice is what they need—and even when their ability to ruin their lives is strong.

With the above framework in mind, I advised Barb and Benjamin in the following way: "I would retract what you have said about taking him out of the will if he marries her. I would also try opening a new avenue of communication by reaching out to her. Even if you don't like her, he will respect you for trying in spite of your reservations."

Benjamin and Barb responded with the same thought: "But we don't want her getting any of our money once we're gone."

This is a common concern. While a psychologist is useful on the emotional side of things, the legal side is better addressed by a lawyer. According to Peter Myers, an estate attorney in San Francisco, a will can be written in a way that stipulates that the inheritance be solely administered by your adult child. In addition, it can stipulate that if your child divorces, the money follows him or her out of the marriage.

Other common conflicts, according to Myers, occur when children who aren't part of the family business resent the siblings who have been a part and, as a result, inherit a greater share of the estate. He also sees conflicts occur when the parent has lost capacity and one of the siblings or a new spouse tries to take advantage of the parent's infirmity. Yet another typical problem takes place when one of the siblings has a psychological issue that makes him or her more likely to abuse or misuse the funds. "In all of those situations," Myers advises, "feelings are important but not the decider. Parents have to be careful and get legal consultation, because those with the most influence will be able to manipulate the situation in the direction they desire.

And that direction may be very different from that intended by the parent."

"In these instances, parents often consider using a third-party trustee (a private professional fiduciary, a licensed role in some states, or a bank or trust company) with crafted guidelines for distribution or access of the funds to the child. For example, tuition, medical expenses (or health insurance), treatment expense, therapy, room and board at college or other school, and a vocational degree program are often required distributions. Because no parent-child relationship is identical, it is important to customize your guidance and instructions with a qualified professional (typically a trusts and estates lawyer)."

After a few more sessions, I recommended that Benjamin and Barb consult with an attorney; this way, they could have the peace of mind of knowing their options in the event that their son marries his fiancée.

WHY DO MY KIDS ONLY CALL ME WHEN THEY WANT SOMETHING?

This is a question that I commonly hear from parents of adult children, and in it is embedded many more questions:

- Do my children really care about me?
- Are they just using me for my money?
- If I give it to them, am I rewarding all the ways I feel manipulated, hurt, or abused by them?
- If I don't give it to them, will they become even more rejecting than they already are?
- If I do give it to them, am I reinforcing their inability or failure to grow up?

These questions also raise questions about how to respond:

- Do I tell them that I feel manipulated?
- Do I use their request for money as an opportunity to talk about the relationship?
- Should I use money as a way to open the door to more time together, or should I refuse the request as a way to set a limit?

So let's return to your question: Why do your kids only call you when they want something? There are a number of ways to look at this. To start, I want to remind you that things are not always what they appear with adult children. Just because it *feels* like they only call when they want something doesn't necessarily mean that is true. If there is a big income disparity between you and your adult child—and there may well be—it is not unrealistic or absurd for them to want to benefit from your largesse. Their demand might make you feel used or unappreciated, especially if they generally act unappreciative or seem unavailable. But their desire or request may reflect a reality that you have more than they do, and as your children, they want you to share.

In addition, if you've been parenting in the past three or four decades, you have probably contributed to a certain degree of entitlement from your adult child. Parents can only be so mad at their children for feeling like they should be assertive, self-interested, and demanding in what they want from the parent—when they have largely been socialized to expect more from the rest of the world. For most parents, especially those who are middle and upper class, raising children who went after what they wanted was part of the parenting pedagogy.

There is also a generational culture clash about the value of money. Many of today's parents were raised with less wealth or a greater value around conserving money than were today's adult children. But therein is the rub, and a key part of this discussion: exchanges around money and resources often require some measure of discussion in them about your goals, your intentions, and where appropriate, your feelings.

And how do you know when you should or shouldn't say no? In the current environment, which suggests that parents should *give, give, give* no matter what, it can be pretty confusing for parents to know when it's okay to say or to give a good old-fashioned *nyet*.

The following are guidelines:

- Say no if you can't afford it. "Can't afford it" doesn't mean you don't have that much in your checking or savings. "Can't afford it" means that it will take away money from savings that you need for other important parts of your life such as travel or meaningful hobbies.
- Say no if the request is made in an overly demanding or entitled way. This doesn't mean that you wouldn't eventually say yes to the request. It just means that you would provide a little education in the process. For example, if your adult child rudely tells you that you need to give him money for his car, kids, house, etc., without a hint of affection or humility, you should say something like "Well, I have to say, when you ask like that it really doesn't make me want to. Which is a shame because I like giving to you. But it has to be a request, not a demand. I don't do very well with demands. I'm sure you can understand. Want to try again?"
- Say no if you're going to feel too resentful. This advice holds true even if you can afford to give. If you have tried setting limits or tying the request to a visit and it hasn't worked, then you should say no for the simple reason that you really don't feel like it.

This dialogue might go something like this:

You: No, I'd rather not.
Adult Child (AC): Why not?
You: Not sure. I've given you a fair amount of money over the
    past year and that's as much as I feel like giving right now.
AC: Well, it's not like you can't afford it.
You: That's true.

Note: If it's not true, then you may need to explain further. You might say, "Actually, I need to be saving for my retirement and really have to watch my pennies." You can invoke the advice of a financial adviser, if you have one, or cite the many articles that exist on the topic of savings for retirement and aging. This puts the blame a few degrees away from you, if they're inclined to blame.

AC: Then why won't you?
You: I guess, honey, ultimately there's only so much of it I want
    to give away each year.

If the demand for money comes from an abusive adult child, then this might be a good time for a moral lesson. So here you might add something like the following:

You: I also don't feel like you're that nice to me.
AC: Oh, I'm not? In what way?
You: You're pretty aggressive, you're impatient. You know the old
    saying *You can attract a lot more flies with honey than vinegar?*
    That also applies to family.
AC: Well, I don't think I'm that mean to you.
You: Well, I don't know whether you're mean, either. But you're
    not that nice and it doesn't leave me feeling like I want to

be as generous to you as I otherwise might. Try it sometime and see what happens.

Say Yes or No Without a Guilt Trip

It's hard for us to say no to our kids. We want to give to them and we want to be liked by them. These desires can tie us up in knots and make us say yes when we don't want to or say no with a guilt trip. If you're going to say yes, then do it with love and affection. If you say yes with a guilt trip, complaint, or accusation, you dilute the strength of the gift.

Moreover, if you say yes with a guilt trip, you place yourself in a worse position when you decide to say no in the future. This is because if you've shown yourself as a reasonable, giving parent, then your adult child has less cause to complain or accuse you of being mean or withholding. This doesn't mean that some kids won't anyway; it's just that you can feel more confident that your guilt is irrational. The only exceptions to this are the examples that I gave above, in cases where you provide a moral lesson before you say yes or no. If you are going to do that, do it only sparingly, such as once or twice a year, at most. Otherwise it will lose its meaning.

If you're going to say no and you don't want to provide a moral lesson, then do it in an affectionate, friendly way. It might go something like the following:

AC: I was wondering if you could help me pay for your
   granddaughter's piano lessons.
You: I'm sorry, honey. I can't.
AC: Why's that?
You: I've just given as much as I can give this year and don't
   have more to give. I'm sorry.
AC: Why, are you having a hard time financially?

Here, say yes if you are. If you're not having a hard time, say no—but go on to explain. You might say: I have a rough figure in my mind of how much I want to give each year to my kids or grandkids, and I'm at about that point right now. I'm sure you understand.

AC: Not really, but whatever.
You: Okay, well, I have paid for a number of things this year,
    which I'm happy to do, but that feels like about right for now
    for this year.

In other words, you reserve the right to say: "It's ultimately my money and I get to decide when enough is enough." You might not say that, but realizing it should help move a sufficient amount of guilt out of the way to make a clearheaded decision.

It's hard to be an estranged parent and still be expected to provide financial resources to someone who isn't giving anything in return. More to the point, to give to someone who is being so hurtful, disrespectful, or rejecting. However, as with so many other aspects where reconciliation is the goal, your task is to think about what's strategic more than what is fair. This framework may mean giving more or giving less and setting more limits. Either way, thinking about your ultimate goals will help you to avoid the pitfalls of responding out of whatever hurt or pain you feel in the moment. That's better for you and increases your chance at reconciliation.

Chapter 10

ABANDONED GRANDPARENTS AND THE WEAPONIZING OF GRANDCHILDREN

Suzanne wanted help setting limits on her mother, Joanna. Her mother had been bugging her to help her reconcile with Suzanne's brother, Ronald. In particular, she wanted Suzanne to help her regain contact with Ronald's young children, whom she hadn't seen in three years. Suzanne was reluctant to intervene because she worried she'd worsen her relationship with her brother and had already spoken to him about it. But she felt bad for her mom and knew that her mom was suffering with the loss of her son and grandsons.

Thousands of grandparents today have been cut off from contact with their grandchildren. While this sometimes results from the grandparent's problematic behavior with the grandchild, my clinical experience shows me that it more typically stems from conflict between the parent and the adult child or the adult child's spouse. Estranged grandparents suffer a double burden: the loss of a relationship with their offspring and the loss of contact with grandchildren. In this chapter we'll examine several families where this has happened and make suggestions for steps toward reconciliation.

HOW CAN I GET MY GRANDCHILDREN BACK?

In my initial consultation with Joanna I learned that she had struggled with anxiety all her life. She spent the early part of her life in Krebs, Oklahoma, in a household with two alcoholic parents and five siblings. Her parents owned a small farm they had to abandon when the sand started piling up in their living room during the 1936 Dust Bowl. Unlike her uncle, her father was unable to get hired with the Works Progress Administration, so they, along with thousands of others, packed up the truck and drove west. They landed in Holtville, California, where they pulled carrots for less than a dollar a day. Eventually, they made it to Oakland. Her father found work as a pipefitter at the shipyard and that's where they stayed.

Joanna had the same kind of faraway "I've seen it all" coral blue eyes of a Dorothea Lange photograph. She sensed that I was the only person who might help her see her estranged child again—and so she didn't flinch when I told her that, if she wanted to see her grandkids again, she needed to try a new strategy with her son. In addition, I advised, she shouldn't have Suzanne advocate for her because that almost never works.

"I'll do whatever you say, but screw my son, I want to see them grandkids."

"Kids or grandkids," I said. "I don't think anyone's offering you a separate deal, are they?"

"Nope, they're sure not."

I smiled. "I don't think you're going to be able to see your grandkids unless you make peace with their parents."

"Do I have to? Even my daughter-in-law?"

"*Especially* your daughter-in-law."

"Oh, goody," she said, looking out the window.

I asked when she noticed the first signs of trouble in her relationship with her son. She jumped in, as though she was waiting for the opportunity to answer:

"A lot of this started with the wedding. Her family's got money. Lots of money. She's one of those that thinks it makes you better than everyone. Her and her little prissy mother. They wanted one of these Princess Di, Barbie doll, *Keeping Up with the Kardashians*–type weddings. It cost more than my house in Rockridge, and her mom wants me to split it down the middle. I'm like, Helen, if you want to spend a hundred thousand dollars on their wedding, you go right ahead. I'm not stopping you, but no way I've got that kind of money. 'But that's what they *want*,' she said, as if that decided it. Well, I want a jet airplane, but that don't mean I'm gonna run out and get one, and that was that. I offered to pay for the rehearsal dinner, which still cost more than my wedding, honeymoon, and first car all rolled into one, and they said, no, never mind.

"And that's when I noticed my daughter-in-law—well, she wasn't my daughter-in-law yet—but that's when I noticed her first getting more distant from me. Then, after a while, things seemed like they were getting better and I thought we had all of that behind us. I used to watch my two grandsons two to three days during the week and sometimes on the weekend when they had their little date night." She handed me her phone with two grinning boys on her screen.

"Those are some cute boys," I said.

"Oh my goodness, yes. Sweet, too. They were always, 'Gammy this' and 'Gammy that'—that was what they called me. 'Gammy, when do we get to see you again?'" She paused; her eyes got wet, but she didn't cry. "I mean, what are they telling them happened? How are a three- and four-year-old little boy supposed to make sense out of a grandmother who's been in their lives every single week since they were born suddenly disappearing off the face of the earth? Did they tell them that I died? That I don't love them? I just don't understand this at all."

For most estranged grandparents, not knowing how the estrangement is affecting the grandchildren is a source of enormous worry. They also fear that the parents are telling the grandchildren that the grandparent doesn't want to see them or is in some other way toxic to them.

I asked Joanna if she had other ideas about what might have caused or contributed to the estrangement. I liked her edgy, cut-to-the-chase manner, but I could see how that might not play too well with a daughter-in-law who had her own ideas about children or family. I also know that, however objective we try to be in the reckoning of our lives, everyone has their blind spots. So I assumed she did as well.

"Oh, I don't know," she said, rolling her eyes. "It was all about boundaries. *Boundaries.*" She emphasized the word like it was from a language she couldn't get the shape of. "My son says, 'We don't want you letting them watch TV and all that crap you feed them when they stay with you.' 'Lord,' I told him, 'I'm their grandmother—that's what we do! I'm *supposed* to spoil them. Besides, it's the same crap you were raised on, and you don't seem to have turned out so bad.' 'Well, we're not raising them that way,' is what he said.

"Of course, then I really put my foot in it and blamed it on his wife, because that's where this all comes from. What am I supposed to do, lie?"

Something like that, I thought. So many relationships—especially with family—end because of a misguided notion about the importance of expressing everything you think or feel. Better to be strategic and restrained than vocal. Especially in the often-fragile arena of parent–adult child relations. Especially with a daughter-in-law or son-in-law.

She went on. "I told him, 'That don't sound like you, Ronald. I think you need to put a collar on that wife of yours. She's changing you.'" Looked up at me with a conspiratorial smile. "Probably shouldn't have said that, either."

I returned the smile. "Probably not."

"Well, that's just not who I am. That's the problem these days. Everything has to be shrink-wrapped and tied up with a pretty little bow on top of it. He's so nervous around that woman. Watches her every move to make sure she's okay with whatever he's doing. He says, "Mom, *both* Lorene and I feel that way. Don't blame it on Lorene! In fact, don't say anything bad about her to me. She's a *great* mother.' I knew that was a slam at me, like he was saying she was a great mother and I'm not."

Her voice got louder. "If the parents don't want to see me, fine—don't see me! But to tell me that I can't see my own grandsons just 'cause I give them Sugar Pops instead of some farm-raised, Napa Valley–certified granola from a recycled organic box with pictures of sunshine and rainbows on the cover. What the hell is that?"

I often hear this kind of complaint from estranged grandparents.

"And the way that his wife talked to me before they decided to make me persona non grata? She called me a bitch to my face. For what? If I would've talked to my mother-in-law like that, I would've had the taste slapped out of my mouth. My husband's mother was ninety-three pounds wet, but if she was mad at you, you knew it before you even walked into the kitchen and you stayed away till the coast was clear. But if I so much as pushed back an inch against whatever new rule my son's wife made, she'd always push back hard. 'Oh, don't say that word to the children. We don't like the word *no*, we like to give them choices. That's better for their self-esteem. It makes them feel like they're more in charge of their lives.' Of course, how much in charge you're supposed to feel when you're a toddler has always been a mystery to me." She imitated her daughter-in-law in a singsongy voice: "'You can do this or you can do that. You can have the cereal or you can have the eggs. You can wear your jeans, or you can wear your corduroys. You can play in the backyard or you can play upstairs in your room.' I worry about those boys; I really do. If they were my parents, I'd run away from home as soon as I got the chance, I really would."

I was very familiar with this sequence of events from other families in my practice.

Bringing together two families in marriage or long-term commitment is like bringing together two cultures, even when the families are from the same ethnic and social class. This is probably why arranged marriages are less vulnerable to divorce or unhappiness; marriage is held together with the many links of extended family relations rather than through the single link of romantic love. In contemporary marriage, there are no such guarantees. If anything, parents who express their distaste or disapproval of their child's spouse or family may forever pay the price of that unsolicited advice, especially if that opinion gets passed along by the adult child to his or her spouse as—mystifyingly—it often does.

MOTHER KNOWS BEST

Joanna was caught in a struggle faced by many daughters, mothers, mothers-in-law, and grandmothers. Studies show how men's and women's different ideas about family can cause some alliances to become more likely and others more problematic when couples marry and become parents. In general, wives have much clearer ideas about what constitutes reasonable or healthy family relations, and that clarity often causes husbands to defer to their wishes. Contrary to the title of the 1950s sitcom, in most homes it's *Mother Knows Best* when it comes to decisions about family relations.

Wives are also more likely to import their husbands into their own families rather than join those of the husband's. Men typically describe feeling less close to their mothers than wives feel to theirs and, as a result, more commonly defer to the wife's preferences. These include how often and how long the in-laws can visit; whether in-laws can babysit, go on vacation with them; and other mundane family decisions.

The prioritizing of the daughter-in-law's family can become an ongoing problem for parents or grandparents who find themselves on the B-list of access to their son and grandkids. Worse, the volatile suite of emotions generated by this new and diminished place in the pecking order causes many parents to express those hurt or angry feelings in sometimes the not-most-productive ways against their son, their daughter-in-law, and their daughter-in-law's family. Larger family wars can start with small conflicts that later engulf the extended family of grandparents, aunts, uncles, and siblings.

And like wars fought over territories, family battles don't always follow neat bloodlines of affiliation. Conflict can create niches where new alliances can thrive and dominate in environments where they once were hidden or contained. Daughters-in-law can ally together to take down or limit the influence of a powerful mother-in-law; a grandfather sides with a grandchild against his own son in expressing long-standing feelings of rejection or disapproval; an adult sibling with unresolved sibling rivalry and resentment allies with a niece or nephew against his brother or sister. An ex-husband supports his daughter in her estrangement from her mother. Different scenarios, but all joined by a common refrain: "Now you know what I had to put up with."

I knew what Joanna was going to need to change in herself if she had a prayer of seeing her grandkids again. And I didn't know if she was up for it: it would mean accepting her daughter-in-law as the new alpha, grieving her own diminished role in her son's life, and acknowledging that she had disrespected their limits. She also needed to back away from the confrontational approach she had been using. As the Chinese sage of early antiquity Sun Tzu said, "The side that knows when to fight and when not will take the victory. There are roadways not to be traveled, armies not to be attacked, walled cities not to be assaulted." Here Joanna needed to see that attacking her daughter-in-law or son would only result in her being further walled off from the lives of her grandsons.

And as often exists in these situations, the fight wasn't only between mother-in-law and daughter-in-law. Her son was using the intensity of his wife's position to lodge his own complaints against his mother—in ways that he might not have had the strength or even *inclination* to do without her backing. Standing up to his mother not only made his wife happy—it also gave him the opportunity to become less psychologically enmeshed with her. This was another reason why there was little upside to Joanna's adopting a position in her interactions that was contentious. For her daughter-in-law, Joanna's contentious attitude signaled her being possessive of her husband and unwilling to accept the daughter-in-law's authority in the household. For her son, it meant, rightly or wrongly, that his mother couldn't tolerate his being or feeling separate from her.

While conflict between mothers-in-law and daughters-in-law is nothing new, the enormous pressure experienced by today's mothers exacerbates those pressures, and that may also increase a young mother's anxiety about the involvement of other people, especially her mother-in-law. According to Oxford sociologist Oriel Sullivan, working mothers today spend more time with their children than did stay-at-home mothers in the supposedly halcyon days of the 1960s. They create that extra time by giving up time for sleep, leisure, and time with their spouses.

I knew that Joanna may have been unduly blaming her daughter-in-law because it was less painful to view the cutoff as coming from her than from her own son. But I also knew that she could be right—that her son was deferring to his wife in order to make things easier in his marriage. Many sons go along with estrangements they might not otherwise choose.

I helped Joanna write a letter of amends to both her son and daughter-in-law. I told her that the goal is to show that you're willing to accept their rules of engagement—that you recognize that you had violated their boundaries and are committed to doing a better job going forward. Often the daughter-in-law or son-in-law is the gate-keeper to the grandchildren; nothing will happen without his or her approval. Without this kind of effort on the part of the parent, the motivated son-in-law or daughter-in-law can keep the door closed. "See, they didn't even apologize to me," he or she might say. "They haven't changed. They just want to keep doing whatever they want no matter how I feel." Even if the estranged child's spouse is disinterested in a reconciliation (or highly motivated to perpetuate the distance), a letter of amends provides the adult son or daughter with the ability to say, "I think my parents are trying. The letter seems sincere. Let's give them a chance."

Joanna's pathway to estrangement from her grandchildren was very different from that of another estranged family I worked with, Yu Yan and Zhang Wei. Yu Yan and Zhang Wei were Chinese immigrants from Chongqing, one of the largest municipalities in western China. Yu Yan was a geneticist trained at Peking University, and Wei was a microbiologist who received his training at Tsinghua University. They had only one daughter, Wang Xiu Ying, whom everyone called Jennifer.

Like many first-generation Asian parents, Yu Yan and Zhang Wei invested mightily in Jennifer's education and development. She was a gifted pianist who was encouraged to apply to Juilliard but opted to study science like her parents. Jennifer was accepted to Harvard as an undergrad and then received her MD from Johns Hopkins University. Prior to her having a child, her parents described her as a dutiful and respectful daughter who rarely caused them problems.

Jennifer experienced a bout of postpartum depression after her first child and was referred to a psychiatrist by one of her mentors at

Johns Hopkins. In her sessions she was encouraged to talk about the ways that her parents might have contributed to her vulnerability to depression. When her son turned two, she told her parents that she "needed to take some space from the relationship" and that she didn't know when she would be in contact again. Her parents had been in almost daily contact with their grandson until that point. Suddenly Jennifer told them they couldn't see him again until their relationship was fixed.

Jennifer's parents were raised in a time and culture where estrangement from a child was rare and estrangement from grandchildren almost unheard of. The estrangement seemed to begin when her therapist, one of the few Chinese psychiatrists in her area, encouraged her to read the book *The Country of "Giant Babies"* by Wu Zhihong. The book—a huge hit with millennials in China—argues that the intensive family culture in China has caused a stunting of individual psychological growth in the youth there. The themes discussed in the book resonated with Jennifer's experiences with her strict parents.

Jennifer's psychiatrist encouraged her to get in touch with her feelings of anger toward her parents and suggested that her depression was likely related to her parents' strictness and high expectations of success. A year into her therapy, Jennifer finally confronted them. She told her parents that they had been too controlling, too involved; and she wanted them to accept more responsibility for why she was struggling with anxiety and depression. Her parents were stunned, frightened, and angry. Their reaction caused a rapid escalation of conflict, resulting in an eventual complete cutoff.

"We don't understand this in her," said Yu Yan, apologizing for her accent, which was almost undetectable. "In our country, parents work very hard for their children's success and they assume that the child will also be equally invested in the parents' well-being and happiness. We always knew that she would take on American values, since this is where she was born and raised. But we also thought that with Chinese parents, she would retain some of the values that are important in our culture. We don't understand what we have done that was so terrible to make her do this to us. Yes, we were very strict because a child doesn't learn how to become a musician or a scientist with parents who just say, 'Oh, you go do whatever you want. You want to learn how to play piano, but you'd rather go outside and play? No problem, you go outside and play. Oh, you want to be a medical doctor and go to a good college, but you don't want to study? Oh, no problem, you don't have to study. You decide.' No."

Yu Yan's beliefs parallel those described in Amy Chua's controversial book, *Battle Hymn of the Tiger Mother*. "What Chinese parents understand," Chua wrote, "is that nothing is fun until you're good at it. To get good at anything you have to work, and children on their own never want to work, which is why it is crucial to override their preferences. This often requires fortitude on the part of the parents because the child will resist; things are always hardest at the beginning, which is where Western parents tend to give up."

Jennifer's experience in some ways mirrors that of described by other second- and third-generation Asian Americans. In "The Last of the Tiger Parents," attorney Ryan Park notes how his parents' behavior caused him to be successful, but also provided him with a parenting style he wanted to avoid emulating. "I was absolutely sure of one thing: The childhood I devise for my two young daughters will look nothing like mine. They will feel valued and supported. They will know home as a place of joy and fun. They will never wonder whether their father's love is conditioned on an unblemished report card."

It's reasonable that today's adult children would want to parent their children in ways more in line with their values, and to parent in ways that avoid the mistakes they believe were made with them. The question is how those differences are handled in conversations with the parent.

Writer Michelle Kuo provides a way to acknowledge the parent's dedication while addressing the ways that it may have felt intrusive or hurtful to the now-grown child. "Tiger mom has become a shorthand to describe parents, usually Asian, with rigorous discipline. For me the term fails absolutely," she writes in her book *Reading with Patrick: A Teacher, a Student, and a Life-Changing Friendship.* "It mistakes a person's fragility for her power. My mother was authoritarian about learning because she didn't know how else to be. It was not a choice among pedagogies; it was desperation." In her *New York Times* article "How to Disobey Your Tiger Parents, in 14 Easy Steps," Kuo writes about navigating the tension between her own aspirations and the way they were at odds with those of her immigrant parents. Compassion, not contempt or overt psychologizing, lies at the heart of her advice. "In theory, parents know you most intimately. In practice, they often have no idea how much they hurt you. They feel, rather, that it is you who have hurt them. And this impasse is painful, because in a battle where both feel betrayed, victory is Pyrrhic."

Of course, it's not only Asian American families who have to navigate the tensions between their native culture and the culture of American-style Western individualism. Sometimes generational differences can be as profound in creating gulfs of understanding as those generated by culture. Parents who provided their children with far more sensitive, involved, and costly parenting than they themselves had received are shocked and betrayed when the adult child complains about how they were raised. "What more could you possibly have wanted?" is the refrain of the parent. "I gave you everything. And now you want to take away my grandchildren?"

"For centuries in the Western world elders reigned and were assumed to possess knowledge and wisdom as well as power," writes historian Paula Fass in *The End of American Childhood: A History of Parenting from Life on the Frontier to the Managed Child.* "Their welfare and needs were primary and their dictates unquestioned." While grandparents once held positions of authority in a family system, today their presence is held in place only by their ability to make their adult child or their spouse happy. In addition, changing generational attitudes about the show of respect to elders create fault lines where miscommunications and misread intentions are common.

Which is tragic, since studies show that the relationship between grandparents and grandchildren is not only good for the well-being of the grandparent but also for children's development: grandparents can provide the grandchild with an important feeling of attachment, resulting in the grandchild's feeling more secure and loved. They can serve as a corrective to problematic or even traumatizing behavior from the parents. For example, if the parents of the grandchild are critical, difficult, or simply too overwhelmed to give positive input to the grandchild, the grandparent can give them a different experience of themselves. In a non-estranged environment, grandparents can keep an eye on problematic or dysfunctional family behavior in the family and, where possible, intervene on behalf of the grandchild.

Grandparents also can serve as a rich resource of identity, history, and stories of family members. Because they are more invested in perpetuating the family lineage, they contain emigration stories, family recipes, clothing, or culture. Grandparents also provide a different role model of behavior for the child. They might have artistic or intellectual interests that speak to the grandchild that are different from those of the parent. In short, grandparents can create a foundation of safety, security, and identity whose removal may be deeply hurtful and disorienting to the grandchild.

Joanna, Yu Yan, and Zhang Wei are like so many of the estranged grandparents I work with: bereft, confused, cut loose from the insulating meanings of family. They are surveying a world where they have no place in the greater order of things. And like so many, they want to know, What can they do to get their grandchildren back? What can they do to reduce their pain?

THE ABANDONMENT OF GRANDPARENTS

Our culture's disdain of aging reveals itself in the little regard that is accorded the role of grandparents when conflict occurs. Grandparents are viewed as one more relationship to be disposed of when they don't satisfy the criteria required to sustain parent–adult child relationships. I have worked with far too many families where the grandparent is cast off because of conflict between the child or their spouse and the parent. This is true even when the adult child acknowledges that the grandparent was beloved by the grandchildren.

It is curious to me that a generation who has redefined what should be considered abusive child-rearing behavior is so casual when it comes to casting a grandparent out of their own children's lives. For a generation obsessed with closely hewing to theories on attachment between themselves and their children, it is remarkable how many seem to disregard the profound attachment that their children have to their grandparents.

And while this is often framed as healthy limit setting on the grandparents, one has to wonder, How healthy could it be? Is it good modeling to so prize your feelings that you'll sacrifice your children's relationship on the altar of that aspiration? Is it a strength to not be able to separate your child's needs from your own? Does it model healthy separation to assume that your children's mental well-being is so tied to yours, you can't imagine that your children are benefited by a relationship with your parents, even if you find that relationship upsetting or difficult? What does that teach children about the value of older people and what they might contribute to a life or to society?

I helped Yu Yan and Zhang Wei address their daughter's complaints purely from her perspective and without any expressions that would induce feelings of guilt or obligation. It was a struggle for them to think in those terms, where words like *duty*, *obligation*, or *respect* were completely removed from the discussion, but they were able to do it. Fortunately, their daughter responded and they were able to reconcile with her and their grandson.

Joanna wasn't as fortunate. While her son was willing to reconcile with her, her daughter-in-law remained skeptical—refusing to allow her contact with her grandsons for four more years. I encouraged Joanna to be patient, not to criticize her daughter-in-law to her son, and to continue to reach out to her in a consistent and friendly way. Eventually, slowly, she was able to be back in the lives of her grandsons. She was grateful for the contact. But she also had to grieve the loss of the years spent without them.

STRATEGIES FOR CHANGE

I often get letters from grandparents who complain that while they are allowed to occasionally see their grandchildren, they are so closely monitored and supervised that they have to walk on eggshells. In addition, the standards for how they're supposed to act around their grandchildren makes them feel like they're being treated like criminals.

Today's parents of younger children do sometimes have more strict standards around diet, exposure to television, and communication style than were common in the past. In other cases, some adults don't trust their parents to spend time alone with their children because they worry that they'll make them feel as bad as they made the child feel when they were growing up. This is difficult both for those parents who made real mistakes with their children and for those whose mistakes are more within normal limits.

What if My Parenting Was Normal but I'm Being Treated Like a Criminal in Regard to My Grandchildren?

This arena can be especially confusing for grandparents. Many have told me that their adult child won't let them spend time with the grandchildren on the grounds that they are going to make the grandchild feel bad about themselves in some way, or that they are going to abuse or neglect the child. If your adult child is in contact with you and has taken that position, then your best strategy is to do the following:

1. Ask a lot of questions: What do you worry that I'll do? Why are you worried about that? When was the last time that I did that? How did you feel when I did? Did my grandchild complain about that? What did you conclude about me as a result?

Note that the purpose of the questions is *not* to get into a debate with your adult child so you can prove them wrong. Rather, you're trying to gather more information so you can get a deeper understanding of what's going on.

2. Ask what a good visit would look like. *How would you like me to be around them?* Overall, your children get to say what the rules are in terms of the grandparenting. You might not like it, but unfortunately you don't get a lot of say about that.

Another common question from grandparents: *How do I know what my estranged child is telling my grandchild about me?* And second: *How do I protect myself from those lies?*

In general, you have relatively little say over what your child or their spouse tells your grandchildren about you. While some adult children and their spouses lie about the grandparents or blame them, some are healthy enough to preserve the possibility of a later relationship with the grandparent and therefore are more neutral in what they tell the grandchildren.

The model that I recommend to parents is based on the model used with parental alienation. It is straightforward: keep reaching out to your grandchildren. I do make two exceptions to this rule:

1. You've been served with restraining orders or threatened to have the police called on you if you try to maintain contact; or
2. Your grandchildren's gifts are sent back unopened. In those scenarios, it means that the relationship with your adult child or their spouse is too inflamed, and you should back off for a set period of time. In general, I recommend at least a year if those conditions are in existence.

Otherwise, continue to reach out. Sometimes—in particular if your grandchild has other memories of you—he or she may be able to maintain a perspective separate from the one offered by their parents. Some grandchildren may later cut off their parents, and they may turn to you for guidance and an alternative view of themselves from the one provided by their parents. The more you've stayed in their lives—even if only with gifts or cards—the more chances you have of staying alive in their minds.

What if Your Grandchild Repeats Something That They Heard from Your Estranged Adult Child or Their Spouse?

How you respond may depend on the age of the grandchild. In general, you want to make the response more about how they feel than how you feel. For example, I worked with a mother whose six-year-old granddaughter said, "Mommy said you were really mean to her when she was little." In this case, the mother didn't agree with her daughter's assessment.

I coached the grandmother to respond in the following way:

Grandmother (GM): Really? What did you think or feel when Mommy said that?

Grandchild (GC): I didn't like it.

GM: How come?

GC: I didn't like that you were mean to my mommy.

GM: I wouldn't like it if someone was mean to my mommy, too!

GC: Then why were you?

GM: Honey, I don't remember that in exactly the same way as your mommy. But you know that it often happens that we sometimes remember things differently that happened a long time ago.

The main recommendations here are:

- Don't be defensive.
- Don't put your grandchild in a loyalty bind between you and her parent by criticizing her parent.
- Show that you can take the criticism and still keep your poise. This makes you more trustworthy and appealing to confide in.
- Educate your grandchild on the confusing, contradictory, separate realities in the nature of family life. Loving family members can have very different perspectives on behavior and motivations.

This scenario might go quite differently with an older grandchild:

Teen: So, Mom said you used to smack her around a lot when she was young.

GM: She said that?

Teen: Yeah, why'd you beat on her?

GM: Sweetheart, your mom and I have different memories of
    her childhood. How did you feel when she said that?

Teen: I thought it sucked.

GM: You were upset.

Teen: Wouldn't you be?

GM: If I thought my grandma beat my mother, absolutely.

Teen: Oh, you're saying she's lying?

GM: I'm saying that children sometimes have different
    memories of their childhoods than their parents do. I have
    no memory of ever hitting your mom and I don't think that's
    the kind of thing I'd forget. But we clearly remember things
    differently. At this point I'm more concerned with what it's
    like for you to feel like your grandmother used to beat your
    mother. That must have been awful.

The main principle here is that you try not to get pulled into a
he said/she said. Keep the interaction focused on how your grandchild
felt, not on your innocence.

What if There Is Truth to the Accusations?

In that case, the interaction might go something like this:

Teen: So, Mom said you used to smack her around a lot when
    she was young.

GM: How did you feel when she said that?

Teen: I thought it sucked.

GM: You were upset.

Teen: Wouldn't you be?

GM: If I thought my grandma beat my mother. Absolutely.

Teen: Oh, you're saying she's lying?

GM: No, I did spank your mother on more than one occasion

and there were times that I lost control. I will carry that regret to my grave. I have tried to make amends to your mom.

Teen: Yeah, she says you don't mean it.

GM: Well, that makes me feel sad to hear that, because I do. And I'm sorry that you had to hear about that. I'm sure that was very difficult. I've grown a lot since then and it's not something I would ever do again, but I know that she still feels upset about that and I understand.

Here you're communicating not only *to* your grandchild, but potentially *through* her. Always assume that what you say will be repeated. In general, you're better off getting in and out of the conversation with a straightforward, nondefensive admission of your mistakes than to lie or completely avoid the topic.

What if My Mistakes Make My Child Mistrust My Grandparenting?

For those parents, an adult child's mistrust of their grandparenting can feel doubly painful. Not only do they have to be reminded of whatever ongoing regrets they have about their parenting, they're made to feel like pariahs in regard to their own grandchildren. This is often true even of parents who have made amends and who would never dream of harming their grandchildren. It's especially painful for these parents because many of them see that being a grandparent offers them the possibility of healing whatever damage they made as parents and restoring their own sense of self-esteem and identity as good people.

If you did make serious mistakes as a parent and your adult child is refusing or limiting contact with your grandchildren, it's important that you continually remind yourself of the following:

- I have tried to make amends to my child and am deserving of forgiveness.
- I did make mistakes with my children growing up. There were things that explain this, and I have tried to do my best since then.

Remember, the goal of this isn't to just let yourself off the hook, but rather to find a loving and compassionate way to be in relationship with yourself.

If I'm Completely Blocked from My Grandkids, What Can I Do?

Pat Hanson, author of *Invisible Grandparenting*, recommends that grandparents keep an ongoing journal or diary that they leave for the grandchild in their will. It contains all of the things they wish that they could've said while they were alive. Be careful not to use this as an opportunity to blame your adult child for not having contact with your grandchildren. If your adult child is refusing your gifts to them as well, you could keep a box and put the gifts in the box; leave that for them as part of your will. Or you could open a savings account and fund it for them to receive in your will. It may still have meaning to a grandchild even if they never met you. And it allows you the opportunity to give them a perspective on you that they may never have gotten from their parent, your estranged child.

Some grandchildren are more open to contact with the grandparent once they move out of their parents' home and don't feel as disloyal to the parent for being close to the grandparent. This is another reason why continuing to send gifts, even in the absence of contact, can be a worthwhile endeavor.

Competition from the Other Grandparents

Many parents complain that their counterparts—the parents of the daughter-in-law or son-in-law—get treated like royalty while they get kicked to the curb. It's hard enough to deal with the estrangement or distance from their own child; add to that pain the natural envy and jealousy of knowing that the other parents are getting more time with the adult child and the grandchildren, while they're getting crumbs.

What Can You Do?

- Avoid complaining. Right or wrong, complaining about the in-laws' getting more time with the grandkids will only make your adult child defensive, and that will likely make them shut down and pull away even more.
- Say what you want, not what you don't want.
- If you're in communication with your child, try to be as direct as possible with your requests while being careful to avoid making them feel guilty.

Do not criticize your adult child's spouse or blame them, even if you have good evidence that he or she is the cause.

Should I Sue to See My Grandchildren?

In response to the increasing number of unmarried or divorced parents, the existence of stepfamilies, the estrangement of extended families, the decrease in the number of grandchildren, and the increased longevity of grandparents, all fifty states (except the District of Columbia) have enacted statutes giving grandparents visitation rights. These statutes are due largely to the well-organized efforts of grandparents and their supporters such as Alienated Grandparents Anonymous in Naples, Florida, who have joined together to ensure that the law preserves the "special" relationship between grandparents and grandchildren.

However, these laws don't guarantee visitation—they simply give grandparents the right to *ask* for a visitation order. The Supreme Court gives a lot of privacy and protection to the parents and very little to the grandparents. In particular, the 2000 ruling in *Troxel v. Granville* dealt a heavy blow to grandparents' rights. That decision came down in favor of parental rights. What makes this situation even more difficult is that the federal courts give states the power to decide for themselves. Whether a grandparent has a tough legal battle depends heavily on the state in which he or she lives. Some states clearly come out in favor of parental decisions—even in cases where grandparents produce proof of love and attachment and demonstrate that visitation rights are in the best interests of the child.

In the vast majority of cases, visitation rights are granted only if the family is not intact. In some states, one of the parents must actually be deceased before a court will even consider awarding visitation to a grandparent. In many states, grandparent visitation won't be considered unless visitation has been denied by a parent. And in those rare cases where the law may be on the side of the grandparents, they are faced with a Sophie's Choice: Should they take their adult child to court, risking further estrangement, or hold back, hoping that one day they'll get access to the grandchildren?

I spoke with James Karl, a family law attorney who serves on the board of Alienated Grandparents Anonymous: "You should always exhaust your non-legal options first," Karl told me. "You're still on the frontier, which means that there's a great deal of uncertainty about outcomes. Get educated about your local state statutes and understand the political climate that exists for grandparent rights. If you're going to pursue legal action, then you better get ready to dig deep into your pocketbook and dig in your heels, because it's likely to be a long and bloody fight."

———

I often hear estranged grandparents describe the loss of their grandchildren as even more painful than the loss of their adult children. They describe the love for a grandchild as more raw and pure, its disappearance more disorienting and bewildering, the need to reconnect with the grandchild more desperate and vital. If you have been cut off from your grandchildren, I hope this chapter provided you with a potential path back to them.

Chapter 11

COPING STRATEGIES, INTERVENTIONS, AND YOUR NEW NORMAL

There are few relationships where there is an absolute right and wrong way to apologize. In most, it is typical enough to have good intentions, to offer an explanation for why we did something hurtful, and to say we're sorry. However, as you may already know, there are many pitfalls in making amends to an adult child. Among other things, you may be accused of being insincere, have your apology thrown back in your face, or be told that you're not taking enough responsibility.

Many parents also get caught up with the idea that they don't have anything to apologize for or any amends to make. Others get caught up in the rightness or wrongness of their child's accusations without trying to understand the underlying emotion that is being expressed. So I'd like to offer some guidance and clarification on this topic:

Why Are Letters of Amends Often Helpful in Reconciliation?

1. It shows that you care. "Of course I care. They know I care! Haven't I shown it in about a million ways?" I assume

you have. But estrangement requires a different kind of approach from a parent, one that you may not have ever tried.

2. Amends take courage. You know the saying that it takes a strong person to say they're sorry? Our children respect us more if we can fearlessly take responsibility for whatever ways our choices or behavior were hurtful to them.

3. It contributes to clarifying what we're responsible for and what we're not. Ironically, the longer and the louder we protest that we were great parents, the harder they will have to raise their voices to prove us wrong. That's why parents are often surprised by how distorted their child's memories are. Children may have to exaggerate them to feel like they're getting on our radar. "You were ALWAYS gone." "You were ALWAYS SO SELF-CENTERED!" The healthy response is to simply acknowledge that when you were gone it was a problem, and whatever ways you were focused on yourself were problematic to your child.

4. Separate realities: It's helpful to children to eventually see that we understand the separate-realities nature of family life: that parents can miss things that their children needed or wanted and be strong enough to simply accept that and not act like they should've been perfect.

5. It will help you in your self-forgiveness and self-compassion. Part of forgiving ourselves for whatever mistakes we made comes from feeling that we have done everything possible to repair the effect of our mistakes. If we believe that we've wronged our children, then we may believe that we're supposed to suffer for the rest of our lives. Knowing that we have done everything possible to reach out to our children and have tried to make amends for whatever mistakes we have made is one of the most powerful ways to heal, not only our relationships with our children but also our

relationship with ourselves. Real parenting is a minefield of mistakes. No one gets out without making tons of them.

6. It's good role modeling: being strong enough to face our flaws is part of being a good parent. It shows that we don't need to be perfect, that we can accept our inadequacies.

7. A letter of amends helps the child to feel more separate and adult. It is a powerful way to show that you want a relationship of equals with your child, one where he or she gets to make demands for how they would like to be treated in the future and to address how they were treated in the past.

The five most common beliefs that interfere with making amends:

1. I didn't do anything wrong. Many parents get stuck between the belief that they didn't do anything wrong and the belief that they didn't do anything wrong enough to deserve an estrangement. So to make it easier on yourself, go with the latter.

2. It makes me feel too bad about myself to think about my mistakes. Most estranged parents struggle against intense feelings of self-regret, guilt, and even self-loathing. Thinking about their mistakes, real or imagined, right or wrong, can trigger those feelings. Therefore, writing the amends letter can feel like an exercise in self-torture. However, as I noted above, it will help you with your self-compassion in the long run.

3. I worry it will be used against me. Many parents worry that if they admit to their mistakes, they'll be beaten over the head with them by their adult child. While it's easy to understand that concern, I have rarely seen it happen. Most of the time children respect that their parents are willing to take responsibility.

4. I worry that it will reinforce or enable their immaturity. If a child is estranged, they have drawn a very strong line in the sand. They're demonstrating that they need something different from you than your version of the past. Making amends may make them grow up faster.

5. I worry it will reinforce the ways that my ex has poisoned them against me. A letter of amends is actually a powerful way to show your strength and love and may be the best proof that your ex is wrong about you.

THE FIVE MOST COMMON MISTAKES IN WRITING LETTERS OF AMENDS

1) Not going far enough: The most common mistake that I see parents making in their letters is not simply admitting to their mistakes in a very straightforward way. Instead of saying, "Yes, I can be a pretty controlling person. I could see how that might have been hard on you" or "Yes, you did suffer a lot as a result of the divorce and were put through a lot that you wouldn't have been if we had been able to stay married. And I have to take responsibility for my part in that." Or "Yes, I should've protected you more from your stepfather. You have a right to feel disappointed that I didn't do a better job." Parents more commonly say it in a way that sounds like a simple misperception on the part of the adult child: "I'm sorry you felt that I was a controlling person" or "I'm sorry that you felt like I should've been more protective of you." Why is this wrong? It doesn't really take any responsibility.

I would rather you face head on the ways that it's not a misperception. Rather than trying to protect yourself, have more of a "bring it on" attitude: "Hell, yes, I am a flawed-assed human being. I could really see why that was hard on you."

2) Defensiveness: It's very hard for parents to hear their children's complaints and not get defensive. Heck, it's hard to hear anyone's

complaints and not get defensive. None of us like to feel like we've disappointed someone, especially someone we love, especially our own children. So it's human nature to want to prove them wrong. However, especially with an estrangement, this always backfires.

3) Explanation: Explanation, however human, misses the point. You can always try explaining your way back into your child's good graces, but it likely isn't going to work during an estrangement. "I was a single mother. We didn't have much money. I was working two jobs. We didn't know as much about what kids needed back then." They don't really want our explanations. They want our acknowledgment that we understand how they feel. Don't get into the right or wrong. The right thing to do is to empathize. To seek to understand.

4) Blaming the child: Many parents respond to being blamed by blaming back. "Well, you had a lot of issues. You were difficult, you were rebellious. You had ADD." The important point isn't how difficult they were, however reasonable your desire to not take all of the blame. The important point is their desire to feel like you understand.

5) Blaming others: It was your dad's fault, your mom's fault, your grandparent's fault. Again, empathize and reflect back what the child is saying. Blaming others, however accurate, just makes it look like you can't or won't take any responsibility.

Making amends can sometimes be done the most effectively by writing a letter. I think email is more effective since it's more informal, and that can work more in your favor. A letter or email provides us the time and space to collect our thoughts and carefully think about what we want to say. In addition, we're not pulled off course by trying to respond to our child's reactions or defensiveness in the moment.

Sample Letter: Wrong Way

Dear Monica,

I'm sorry that you think I wasn't a good mother. I really tried to be the best one that I could and given what I grew up with, always felt like I did a pretty good job. It was very hard raising you as a single mother with very little money and no support from your father. I guess I should have tried harder. I'm not saying that I was always the most patient person in the world, but I did try and I did love you and hopefully that counts for something.

So, what's wrong with that? Let's look at it step by step based on the statements that were made:

#1 "I'm sorry that you think I wasn't a good mother."

PROBLEM: Saying "that you think I wasn't a good mother" sounds defensive. We all let our children down in one way or another. It's better to say, "I'm sorry for the ways that I wasn't a good mother," or "I'm sorry for the pain that I have caused you."

#2 "I really tried to be the best one that I could."

PROBLEM: It's true, but again, the goal of the letter is to help your child believe that your goal isn't to defend yourself but to see the world from their perspective. Remember that what you tell yourself is different from what you tell your child. You tell yourself that you tried to be the best parent that you could. You tell your child that you're sorry for the ways that you weren't.

#3 "I always felt like I did a pretty good job."

PROBLEM: For the purposes of the letter, this isn't relevant. The goal of the letter isn't self-expression per se; it's to communicate a willingness and desire to see things from your child's perspective. Right or wrong, they are currently fixated on the ways that they believe that you didn't do a good job; so defending yourself will be counterproductive.

#4 "It was very hard raising you as a single mother with very little money and no support from your father."

PROBLEM: The most problematic part of this is the criticism of the father. Again, while the parent is stating a real fact, it tempts the child to defend the other parent and distracts him or her from your positive intention.

#5 "I did try and I did love you and hopefully that counts for something."

PROBLEM: Saying that it "hopefully counts for something" sounds critical, as though the child has no right to the perspective that she has. Therefore, it will make her feel defensive.

Sample Good Letter

Dear Monica,

I'm so sorry for the ways that I let you down as a parent. I know that I was harsh in many ways and that that was hurtful to you. I could understand why that might make it harder to spend time with me. It is true that I was preoccupied in many ways when you were young and that it prevented me from being as involved with you as would have been good for you. I'm glad that you let me know how you feel about that and I hope there are ways that I can make it up to you in the future.

What's right about this letter? Let's take it line by line.

#1 "I'm so sorry for the ways that I let you down as a parent."

STRENGTH: The mother doesn't try to sugarcoat it; instead she goes straight to the heart of the complaint. Her child is saying the mother let her down as a parent and the mother is saying she's sorry that she did.

#2 "I know that I was harsh in many ways"

STRENGTH: Admits to being harsh. Again, makes it clear that she's not there to prove the child wrong or overly sensitive. She's straightforwardly admitting to her character flaws.

#3 "and that that was hurtful to you"

STRENGTH: Addresses how the mistake or flaw resulted in the child feeling hurt.

#4 "I could understand why that might make it harder to spend time with me."

STRENGTH: Empathizes with the child's decision to be distant. Shows strength that she's willing to both admit to her mistakes as a parent and respect the child's choice however painful it is to the mother.

#5 "I'm glad that you let me know how you feel"

STRENGTH: The mother's willingness to put the daughter's criticisms in the perspective of health rather than selfishness or hurtfulness is an act of selfless love on the part of the mother that is rarely missed by adult children, even when they don't verbally acknowledge it.

HOW LONG DO I KEEP TRYING TO MAKE AMENDS?

I typically recommend that parents write one letter of amends using my guidelines and then do a follow-up six to eight weeks later if there was no response. In the follow-up letter write something like: "Just following up to see if you've had a chance to read my letter. I'm sure I left out some details that would have been good to address but just wanted to try to get the conversation started. Let me know if you have any thoughts or reactions, positive or negative. Love, Mom, Dad, etc."

COPING WITH HOLIDAYS, BIRTHDAYS, AND WEDDINGS

Speaking of pain, what are you doing for the holidays, your birthday, your child's wedding, the birth of your new grandchild, your child's graduation? These are all events that you never in your wildest dreams thought you'd be excluded from. If you're like almost every estranged parent, you feel a sense of morbid dread when these days approach. Some common questions are:

- What do I tell people when they ask me what I'm going to do with my kids over the holidays or my birthday?
- How do I manage my feelings of sadness, jealousy, or anger at my friends or children?
- Are there any activities that are better or worse to do on those days?
- Will I ever be able to get through a holiday and feel sane and whole again?
- I just found out that my child is getting married and I wasn't told. How am I supposed to deal with that?

WHAT SHOULD YOU SAY TO OTHERS WHEN THEY ASK ABOUT YOUR CHILDREN OR GRANDCHILDREN?

My short answer is, Whatever you damn well please. In other words, you don't owe anyone anything, so you shouldn't feel obligated to say more than you want. If it's an acquaintance or someone to whom you're not close, you can say something breezy and change the subject: "Oh, she's off in her own world. I don't see her or the kids as much as I'd like. Kids these days." If you want, you could give an update based on the last time you saw your child, grandchild, or something that you heard through the grapevine. And then change the subject.

In other words, you are not ethically obligated to say more than you'd like about your situation to anyone. Your main goal is to get in and out of the conversation and steer it to safer waters. If they insist on showing you pictures of their children and grandchildren, take a deep breath, say something appropriately complimentary, and then suddenly be overcome by a powerful desire to go to the bathroom or get something to eat or drink.

Here are a few responses you can use with friends and family:

- So if you could just say that you still think I was a good parent, that would really help me (only ask this when you trust them to give you the answer that will feel the most supportive).
- I just need to talk about it and need to feel like someone understands what a nightmare this is for me. If you could just empathize, that would be great.
- I need to be reassured that it's okay to talk about this at least for a little bit whenever you and I talk. I feel like I'm a big drag, but I don't feel like I'm being very honest about my life if I don't talk to you about it.
- When I say I don't want advice and you keep giving it to me, I don't feel very understood. I know it's not your intention, but you make it seem like this is all my fault or there's some easy answer here.

WON'T I BURDEN MY FRIENDS?

Many estranged parents worry about burning out their friends by always being sad or needing so much support. But in the context of friendship, talking about estrangement should be treated like any other chronically painful or difficult problem such as being married to a troubled or difficult spouse, dealing with a parent's chronic or dwindling health or a death, or having a painful or worrisome illness. If they're a good friend, they'll assume that you'll want to spend at least some time talking about it whenever they see you and that you'll then probably want to talk about something else.

It is true that we can burn out our friends or others who care about us if we talk only about our suffering. That's because no one has endless empathy. People rightly want us to focus on other aspects of our lives such as what we're grateful for, what's working in our lives, and of course, what's going on in their lives. But that's why I provide the examples of being married to a difficult spouse, or of dealing with an aging parent, a death, or a chronic illness—because those are experiences that a lot of people go through, or they know plenty of others who do. So think about how much support you might ask for or offer if it was one of those problems, and use that as a reference point in getting help for your estrangement.

As is true with any other aspect of friendship, some people will be better able to support you than others. Some are constitutionally unable to offer the right kind of comfort to a friend or family member suffering with estrangement. This can occur if they haven't had to wrestle with deeply painful, unsolvable issues and thus have a smaller experiential vocabulary. For others, their anxiety about knowing how to best respond can cause them to avoid raising the topic, to quickly get off it once it is raised, or to offer bromides best reserved for a Hallmark card.

However, if you're not getting support from any of your friends, it may be more a reflection of your worry about burdening them than a reality of having unsupportive friends. My experience is that most estranged parents err on the side of not talking to their friends enough about their situation. We're so worried about overwhelming people with our ongoing, unrelenting, tragic tale that we don't say anything. We assume that our friends are sick of our problems, feel guilty that they don't know how to help us, worry that their empathy isn't enough, or are frustrated that we haven't fixed it already.

This creates one of the most problematic aspects of estrangement: social withdrawal. It's problematic because you need a community of people to keep you strong and help you feel good about yourself. We need others to hold up a mirror because the one held up by our children is so powerful and compelling. We're wired to believe our children's opinions of us: who better to judge whether or not we were good parents than the people we parented? And yet part of the task of healing from an estrangement is reclaiming that authority. That doesn't mean whitewashing or ignoring our mistakes. It means removing our children from the role of being the ultimate arbiter of our value as parents.

We need community because we're not powerful enough to go up against our children alone. The message of estrangement is that you can have your most treasured person torn from you and there's nothing—or seemingly nothing—that you can do about it. That experience makes most people feel scared, impotent, and enraged. It has the potential, especially if you've had other traumas, to cause you to believe that this is a kind of validation of your fundamental lack of worth.

Since contact with others is one of the most powerful reminders of estrangement, you need a plan for how you're going to handle social events. The following are some recommendations:

Give yourself permission to say no. So many parents, mothers in particular, have a hard time prioritizing their own well-being because they're socialized to put themselves last. They worry so much about hurting other people's feelings that it shuts down their ability to actively think through what is in their best interest.

My advice regarding high-risk days like holidays, birthdays,
     etc., is to be selfish. If you think you're going to feel too sad,
     jealous, angry, or upset by seeing your friends or other family
     members with their adult children and grandchildren, then
     you shouldn't go. No, this isn't a strategy for everything—we
     can't hole up forever. But high-risk days have the potential
     to pack a much bigger wallop because of all of the memories
     that are evoked and because we get inundated with
     commercials, media reminders about family, and pictures
     and invitations from friends and families.

WHEN YOU HAVE TO SAY YES

But sometimes we have to say yes, whether it's because it will create
too many questions if we don't, or because there are people at the
event that we want to see despite the risk of feeling bad. And even if
we say no, there is still the possibility of running into people we can't
avoid. If you do decide to go to an event, write out a script for yourself.
The script should:

- Include what you'll say when you're asked about your
  children or grandchildren (see above).
- Include what you'll say when they show you pictures of their
  children or grandchildren, or start to tell you about them.
- Include an exit strategy from the event. Let your host or
  others know in advance that you may have to leave early
  because you haven't been feeling very well. Which you
  haven't. It's just more a mood issue than a bacterial one.

IS ESTRANGEMENT HURTING YOUR MARRIAGE OR ROMANTIC RELATIONSHIPS?

Psychological trauma has the potential to negatively impact your romantic relationship. Not only will the ongoing pain and frustration cause you to feel less fulfilled by the relationship (and life in general), but couples may also blame each other for the estrangement or believe that the other's stance is perpetuating the estrangement. You may have very different ideas about the best next steps, including whether or not to continue reaching out to your child, to cut your child out of your will, or to reconcile with a problematic daughter- or son-in-law.

Studies show that almost any stress outside of a couple has the ability to reduce that couple's marital satisfaction. This can be a conflict at work or dissatisfaction with some other part of one's life that doesn't directly stem from the behavior of the spouse. This is because good communication in romantic relationships requires a degree of energy and resourcefulness. It takes energy to be patient and thoughtful in considering your partner's feelings, to pull your equal weight with housework or other household matters, and to be happy enough with your life to bring that energy into the marriage.

In addition, it's easy to scapegoat our spouses. Emotions often need an outlet, and not infrequently, our spouses are an easy target. Sad but true—people often reserve their worst behavior for their spouses. I sometimes hear people say in couples therapy, "It must be you, because none of my friends ever complain about this." And I say that's because you wouldn't dream of treating your friends the way that you treat your spouse. We're often less careful with our spouses and expect them to forgive behaviors in us that we would never expect our friends to forgive in us.

There's also an idea, especially in our soulmate culture, that our partners should be endlessly giving, available, and interested, no matter how poorly we're behaving. Unfortunately, estrangement may cause us to be more depressed, short-tempered, and self-centered—

qualities that may not be so appealing when viewed from the other's perspective. That's why taking care of yourself is important: your partner doesn't have endless resources to support you, and you need to be able to give something back to the relationship.

Couples Sometimes Blame Each Other for the Estrangement

It's not uncommon for an estranged child to be angrier with one parent than the other. Children may feel closer to or identify with one parent over the other, even in non-estranged families. There may also be temperamental or personality differences between parent and child that make them more compatible with one parent.

This doesn't mean that the parent who is less of the issue for the child was a better parent per se. In some cases, they might choose the stronger parent to complain about because they know that he or she can take it. Either way, ongoing blame or feelings of blame can erode the overall strength and well-being of the couple. In addition, one member of the couple may blame the other more for the estrangement when that partner:

- Refuses to make amends.
- Won't reconcile with the daughter-in-law or son-in-law.
- Won't change behavior that is reasonable for the estranged child to request, such as working more on their anger, getting into a recovery program, or learning how to communicate in a way that is less alienating or hurtful to the estranged child.

In this instance, I recommend that you set aside a time to talk about the estrangement that is regular and predictable, but time limited. That way, the person who needs to talk knows that there will be time and the other knows that there will be limits to it. For example, daily sessions of five to ten minutes or once weekly for twenty minutes. Be respectful of each other's style. Express empathy for their position, even if you disagree with their perspective.

During discussions about the estrangement, do the following:

- Tell your partner what you're feeling and rank that on a scale of 1 to 10 in terms of the strength of that feeling.
- Ask for what you'd like in response. For example, "I'd just like you to listen and feed back what I say without comment. No advice, criticism, or complaining about me." Or "I'd like you to hear me out in terms of how I'd like us to work on this issue. Please listen, and then let me know what you think."
- Use "I statements" such as "When you cut me off every time I talk about our son, I feel hurt and misunderstood" or "When I tell you that I don't want to talk about our daughter for the rest of the day and you ignore me, I feel resentful." Not "You're such a pain about this stuff. Just get over it." Or "It's all your fault we have the problems that we do with our child."

Avoid what marital researcher John Gottman refers to as the Four Horsemen of the Apocalypse: defensiveness, criticism, stonewalling, and contempt. Studies show that no marriage can survive a steady diet of those emotions.

What If the Child Wants Contact with One Parent and Not the Other?

It's better to have only one parent estranged than both. Many parents believe that if they're allowing the child to just see one parent that they're enabling the power of the adult child to divide and conquer. It can cause the parent who's being kept out of the equation to feel jealous, resentful, and humiliated—as though the non-estranged parent is endorsing the estrangement.

However, if both parents are cut off, no one knows what's going on with their child. At least not from a parental perspective. In addition, if the non-estranged parent agrees to the request of the estranged parent not to be in contact, the estranged child will be mad at both parents instead of just one. The estranged child will view the non-estranged parent as too weak to stand up to the estranged parent and believe that they're unable to prioritize the child's happiness over that of the parent.

However, while it's important that the non-estranged parent show some degree of empathy about the estranged child's complaints for the other parent, they should, with rare exceptions, be careful to avoid endorsing an estrangement. They can do this by saying something like "For now, I'm okay with our meeting without your mother. And she supports my being here because she wants at least one of us to be able to see you and the grandchildren. I do feel a little in the middle, though, since I know that she'd love to see you, too. I also know that she's willing to do whatever it takes to have a better relationship with you when you're ready [assuming she is]." And that's about as much as you can say. It also shouldn't be said more than every few months or it will turn the adult child away.

If the arrangement of only one parent being estranged has been going on for a year or more, then the position of the non-estranged parent should become a little more firm. You might say: "So it's been a year and I haven't wanted to bug you about this, but is there any reason why you wouldn't agree to do a few family sessions with your mother at this point? I understand your complaints, but she's also been a good mother to you in many ways as well, so it seems like she deserves an opportunity to work on the relationship with you."

In general, pressuring an adult child rarely causes them to reconcile. Some estranged parents try to involve revered grandparents, family friends, siblings, or others to advocate for the parent, and I've never seen it work. The adult child typically just feels pressured and misunderstood. And it causes them to withdraw even further.

My Estranged Child Is Back: Now What Do I Do?

Using the strategies that I've recommended in this book will hopefully result in a reconciliation. That is my wish for you. But you may discover that even if you reconcile, your work isn't over yet. The reality is that if you were estranged, the reason for that estrangement may still exist and could get retriggered. I don't say this to increase your anxiety—more to validate that your anxiety warns you of a real risk. It's a risk because:

- Someone who is capable of estranging themselves once is probably more at risk to do it again than someone who would never consider it.
- The causes of estrangement are rarely completely resolved even after a reconciliation occurs.
- The parent's anger or hurt over the estrangement may cause them to react or respond in ways that create more conflict with the adult child.

How Do I Stop Walking on Eggshells?

You should start by acknowledging that it's reasonable for you to feel cautious. Don't shame yourself for feeling anxious or even scared of your kid: they have just put you through a major trauma, so feeling scared, sad, or even angry is somewhat normal and predictable.

For most parents, their greatest fear is another estrangement. This is particularly true for those who believe the cause of the estrangement was relatively small or incidental. But even if it was big and obvious, most parents feel some degree of terror that it might happen again.

Radically accept that reality. Say to yourself, "Yes, it's true they may estrange themselves again from me, and if they do, that will be deeply upsetting. But that's not a hundred percent under my control." Remind yourself that, however painful, you survived it the first time and you'd survive it again if you had to.

Another common emotion is anger. For many parents, the hardest part of taking my advice around early reconciliation is that they don't get to say how awful it was for them. Many parents, fathers in particular, have enormous amounts of anger at the child for creating so much suffering in their lives and the lives of their spouses.

"Why can't I tell them how awful it's been for me?" is a common question of the newly reconciled. The answer is, because you will move the ball closer to another estrangement. Of course you're always free to yell at your kid if you want to, but it may not feel very good if it only results in the door slamming shut again.

"Okay, so what am I supposed to do with all this anger?" Your goal, overall, is to get it handled before you see your son or daughter. Call a friend and rail at them about how poorly your child has behaved in your eyes; write them a furious letter and then burn it; work out; meditate. Just don't get into it with them. Not until you're very secure that your relationship is back on solid ground—which is often more a matter of years than of months. And if you get provoked in the moment, go outside, go to the bathroom, or leave.

Expect It to Be Awkward for a While

There's no way that a parent and child can come back together after a long estrangement and return to some earlier version of innocence right away. That said, I have worked with a number of parents whose kids acted like nothing ever happened. "Hey, how ya been? Good to see you. What have you been up to?" as though the most painful event in the parent's life was just some little thing to be shrugged off.

Take Them Where They Are

Overall, if they're upbeat and want to be lighthearted, I encourage you to join them there. If they're cautious and checking you out, then you can be cautious in response by not getting too far ahead of them in your mood or what you discuss. That said, you should do whatever you can to let them know that you're fine, you're happy, you're not damaged, you're not holding a grudge, you're not going to punish them. An early reconciliation is not a model for the rest of your relationship. It's a way to get a conversation started and open the door back into your child's life.

Welcome to the New Normal

I often talk with my adult friends about their relationships with their non-estranged adult children, because many of them experience some degree of conflict and disappointment with them, even if never estranged. So part of what I'd like to prepare you for is the new normal: Just because your child is back in your life doesn't mean you're going to hear from them as much as you'd like, see them as much as you'd like, or have them be as responsive as you'd like. It is still on their terms, and realistically, sorry to say, may always be. Maybe you're lucky enough to have other kids who are more available and responsive and you can be grateful for that. But don't expect your formerly estranged child to fall in line quite the same way. Maybe one day, but certainly not anytime soon.

STEPS IN EARLY RECONCILIATION

Ask for Guidance

Whether you do or don't understand the reasons for the estrangement, it may be helpful to ask for direction from your adult child about how to avoid conflict in the future. That conversation might go something like this (in person or over email): "I'm very happy that we've been able to spend time together again. Since I clearly did some things in the past that were upsetting to you, I'm wondering if we could make the agreement that going forward, we'll try to stay current on things that bug either one of us so they don't build up." (Here I say "either one of us" but you might not be able to say what bugs you, because it might not be worth it.) The main point is that you're encouraging them to tell you what's bothering them, and that alone will gain you credibility and increase the chances of their communicating more with you.

"What if I think I did something that's bothering them but they never admit it?"

Some adult children estrange because they're conflict avoidant. They don't know how to handle the normal, expectable slings and arrows of family life, so they shut down, withdraw, and build up resentment until they don't know any other path than to cut off the parent. Overall, this kind of child needs the parent to be a little more thoughtful about which issues create conflict and to ask about situations where there was an unexpected reaction.

Let's say you spent time with your son and noticed he looked resentful when you were playing with your grandson. While it might be hard to say in the moment, the next day you could say, "You looked kind of annoyed with me yesterday when I was playing with Jacob.

Am I right about that?" If your child is conflict avoidant, they'll probably lie and say no. If you're pretty certain of your observation, you could make it easier by saying, "Are you sure? I'm wondering if there was something in that interaction that bothered you that speaks to other things you'd like me to work on. I really want you to feel like you can be open with me about your complaints. Maybe I haven't done a good job of showing that to you in the past."

Note that here I use the phrase "other things that you'd like me to work on." I do that because you're affirming that theirs is a reasonable request and you're affirming yourself as someone open to working on himself or herself, a critical quality in today's parent–adult child relationships.

That said, many adult children have no desire to talk about what happened because they might not completely understand it, they're worried they'll hear more from you than they feel like they can tolerate, or they feel guilty about it and don't want to know how awful it was for you.

Given all of these factors, the following are provided as recommendations:

Don't feel obligated to ask your adult child what happened if you don't know. Instead, say something like the following: "I'm really happy to be back in your life and to have you back in mine. I don't completely understand what happened to create so much time apart, and on the one hand, I don't have to. On the other, it might be helpful, since if it's something that I do or have done, I want to make sure that I don't do it again."

If your child raises issues that created the estrangement that you believe to be false or highly exaggerated, try to listen empathically. The period of time when you are newly reunited is not the time to start arguing about who did what to whom or when. There will be time for that, maybe, but it won't be until you're on more solid ground. Think of the first year or two as a getting-to-know-you-again period in which your goal is to reassure your child that you are able to be with them in a nonthreatening way and that reuniting with you was a good idea.

"But what if they're threatening to me?" I have heard from more than one reunited parent who said that it wasn't as sweet as they thought it would be because the child was still treating them in a disrespectful or contemptuous way. In general, your model should be similar to the one that I recommended in my earlier discussion about handling disrespectful and abusive behavior. You would say something like "I really want to hear what you're telling me and I know that it's important. I also assume that part of the reason you needed a break from our relationship was because there are parts of me that you find really difficult. I do want to work on that and am committed to it, but do you think you could just calmly tell me instead of yelling at me? I guess you feel like I won't hear it unless you hit me over the head with it and maybe that's true, but can we experiment with a different method?" In general, this kind of conversation is better had after the conflict rather than in the heat of the moment. In the heat of the conflict, you can try to defuse it, and if that's not successful, then try to bring it to a close as quickly as possible.

If you have a strong sense that there is residual resentment or distance, it may be useful to raise it at least once. You might say something like "I'm really happy to be seeing you again, but I can kind of tell that you still have some resentment toward me. Is that right? It's perfectly okay if you do. I'm just raising it to let you talk about it." If they say no, then you can follow with "Okay, well, I just want to make sure you know that the door is always open to talk about whatever bothers you in our relationship. I know that all relationships require work and openness."

"How long do I have to keep apologizing?"

You should accept that you may have to hear complaints about you or your behavior for some time. If your child is back in your life and continues to raise the past, then you should assume that they need to keep raising it either because they're still worried that you won't change, they believe that you haven't changed enough, or they're worried that you will revert to earlier behavior. Overall, your best position is to be relaxed, interested, and open to their complaints.

As has been hopefully made clear throughout this book, the rules of estrangement operate in quite a different way and with a different kind of logic than most of your other relationships. I've provided the next chapter as a way to further clarify this territory and provide you with further insight into what your adult child is thinking.

Chapter 12

THE ADULT CHILD'S PERSPECTIVE

NEW RULES FOR PARENT–ADULT CHILD RECONCILIATION

The Estranged Parent's Perspective

Adult Children Are Not the Ultimate Authorities About What Happened in Their Childhoods.

Just Because You Check a Few Boxes on a Survey Doesn't Mean Your Parent Is a Narcissist.

Actually, You Do Owe Your Parents.

Estranging an Involved Grandparent Who Never Abused Your Child Is Child Abuse and Elder Abuse.

Unless Your Therapist Has Met Your Parent, Their Diagnosis of Them May Be Completely Incorrect.

If Your Spouse Requires That You Estrange Your Otherwise Good Parents and You Go Along with It, You Have a Shitty Marriage.

It's Absurd to Blame Your Parent for Not Using Parenting Standards That Didn't Exist When They Were Raising You.

Hurting Your Feelings Is Not the Same as Abusing You.

The Estranged Adult Child's Perspective

Parents Aren't the Ultimate Authorities About What Happened in My Childhood.

Telling Children That You Can Demand Whatever You Want Because You Made Sacrifices for Us Will Always Backfire.

Having Time with Your Grandchild Is a Privilege, Not a Right.

Unless Your Therapist Has Met Me, the Diagnosis You Have Been Given of Me May Be Completely Wrong.

It's Wrong to Not Empathize with My Wish That You Could Have Raised Me Differently.

Threatening to Cut Me Out of Your Will Does Not Make Me Want to Reconcile.

Just Because You Did a Better Job Raising Me Than Your Parents Did Raising You Doesn't Mean That You Didn't Hurt Me.

This is the view of your adult children and your guide to reconciling with them. You don't have to like it or agree with it. You have to understand it. And that's because today, more than at any other time in our nation's history, children are setting the terms of family life in the United States. If it was once the child's job to earn the parents' love and respect, today it is the parents' job to earn the love and respect of their child and to keep earning these throughout adulthood.

ESTRANGEMENT AND THE PURSUIT OF HAPPINESS

Your adult child has adopted a strategy of estrangement in the pursuit of a happy life. At a time when work and personal relationships are more and more fragile, when the traditional markers of a good adult life can be no longer counted on to be there—from a secure job to a secure marriage—it's neither surprising nor unreasonable that this generation of adults are focused on the one thing they can still control: the pursuit of their own growth and life satisfaction.

For example, according to a recent report by economists at the Federal Reserve, "[m]illennials are less well off than members of earlier generations when they were young, with lower earnings, fewer assets, and less wealth." This is despite being the most educated generation to date. In 2018, happiness among even younger adults in America fell to a record low of only 25 percent—the lowest level recorded by the General Social Survey, a key barometric index of American social life. Only 22 percent of young men and 28 percent of young women reported being "very happy" in 2018. At the same time, we're witnessing skyrocketing rates of mental illness, especially among women at the higher-income levels. These results occurred during a period of declining use of alcohol and drug abuse and during an economic expansion. Either way, younger generations have their reasons for wanting to make the prioritization of their happiness an important goal.

When I'm able to get a grown child in the same room as his or her estranged parent—something I try to make happen as often as possible—I want the parent to understand that from the perspective of their adult child, estrangement is every bit as necessary to their psychological survival and well-being as reconciliation is to the parent. That no healing will take place unless there is a radical shift in the dynamic between the adult child and the parent.

FIVE MOST COMMON MISTAKES
OF ESTRANGED PARENTS

Because most of today's parents are unaware how much the ground has shifted beneath their feet in recent decades, they often make matters worse once an estrangement is on the horizon. From that perspective, here is a list of the five most common mistakes of estranged parents.

Mistake #1: Believing That Reconciliation Should Be Based on Principles of Fairness

It's not fair. I get that. With most of the families that I work with, it's really unfair. If it was really fair, the model would be the same that it would be with a best friend, a spouse, or somebody else—you talk about your perspective and he or she talks about theirs. You talk about how you felt hurt or misunderstood. Your kid talks about how she or he feels hurt or misunderstood. You put your heads together and make sense of it, and hopefully you move on and get closer as a result.

That is not the case once there's an estrangement in place. A lot of adult children say they want a relationship of equality, but in reality, it probably isn't going to feel very equal to you. One of the reasons that parents make mistakes with estrangement is that they have never encountered anything like this in their lives. The rules and guidelines required to deal with an estrangement are also ones that you've probably never encountered in any other relationship in your life.

Because if it was fair, you'd get to make demands about how much time you could spend visiting with your children or grandchildren. You could ask for more. You could demand more empathy and forgiveness for whatever mistakes you made with your child growing up or have made over this period of time. You could demand more commitment.

If it was fair, you would get credit for all the money you spent on your child and for the time spent being the more dedicated parent after a divorce.

If it was fair, you'd get credit for being as good of a parent as yours, or an even better parent than yours, and for giving your child opportunities and experiences as a child and young adult that nobody ever gave you.

If it was fair, your child would understand that when you say you did the best you could, you really mean you did the best you could and that people can parent well only to the extent that they were given good role models, co-parents, or the financial and emotional resources to parent.

Finally, *if it was fair*, you'd be able to talk about all the ways that your child themselves might have made parenting difficult—that our children bring their own issues into the world or they marry partners that are really difficult for us to be close to or that pull our children away from us. If it was fair, you'd be able to speak to those issues.

You don't have those options while you're working on an estrangement; and you can't be oriented toward those principles of fairness because they'll get in your way. It will affect how you communicate. It's going to make you more demanding than you should be and more resentful. You're going to talk too much about how hurt, sad, and rejected you feel in ways that aren't going to be that useful.

A better attitudinal framework is the one that you would use when your child was, say, two or three years old—and I don't mean that in any disrespectful way to the adult children. I mean your model shouldn't be one of thinking that it's going to be a relationship between equals where you get to make demands and talk about your feelings—about how imbalanced all this is, and how mistreated, rejected, neglected, and furious you feel, which is of course exactly what you feel if you're like the thousands of other parents I've interacted with around this topic.

Thinking of your child as a younger person is helpful because it requires a proportionate kind of selflessness where you don't expect much in return; where you accept the one-way-street quality of it all. In this sense it doesn't really work with the younger-child model, because at least your toddler will smile at you or crawl into your lap. Your adult child is not going to do that.

It also requires patience, because nothing is more infuriating, humiliating, and devastating than rejection from an adult child. It requires patience, because it's going to take time.

For those of you who are in the midst of an estrangement, you may have already been dealing with this for years. You may well have more years to go. You have to see this as a marathon, not a sprint, and get some acceptance around that, as we'll discuss in the next chapter.

Mistake #2: Trying to Motivate Your Child Through Guilt

It used to be that parents had a right to make demands and to say, "You haven't called me. What's the story?" or express some other form of moral outrage about the fact that the kid wasn't holding up their end of the bargain. That's no longer true, and therefore, that card has been taken out of your hand. Our society and culture are getting more and more individualistic, which means that relationships are evaluated on the basis of whether or not they make people feel good, or good about themselves, or contribute to their self-esteem and personal development.

A recent example from my practice illustrates the way that the use of guilt is contrary to a good parent–adult child relationship.

Daughter (twenty-four): When you were my age, did you call Grandma every day because you wanted to, or because that's what she wanted you to do?

Mother: I guess because she wanted me to. I wasn't that close to her, as you know, but I felt like it was the right thing to do.

Daughter: Yeah, I don't want that kind of relationship with you.

Therapist: What kind of a relationship would you like with your
   mother at this point?

Daughter: If I want to call her, I'll call her. If I don't, then I
   don't want to be made to feel guilty about it.

As this interaction shows, the daughter believes that calling her
mother out of obligation goes against her values of honesty and in-
tegrity. She believes that setting some general guidelines about the
rules of engagement is a healthy expression of her adulthood and individuality. She also believes she's giving her mother a useful and,
arguably, loving perspective on how to have a better relationship with
her—a perspective the mother would be wise to heed.

While her mom was hurt and resentful that her daughter felt burdened by any obligation to her, she also recognized that her daughter
was behaving exactly how she raised her to behave: Be true to yourself, don't do things out of guilt or convention because that will get in
the way of your happiness and success; and honesty, even if it hurts, is
preferable to a false presentation of self.

The mother raised her daughter with those values because, as a
woman growing up in the fifties and sixties, she strongly disliked her
own inclinations toward compliance, dutifulness, and guilt. She had
worked most of her life to feel immune to those pressures and wanted
to make sure that her daughter didn't have to struggle in the same way.
She also observed that her more confident and assertive women friends
tended to do better in the workplace than those who were more reticent.

While the mother was glad she had succeeded in inoculating her
daughter against those constraints, she resented, and not that quietly,
that her daughter wasn't more responsive and sensitive to her needs,
since she had also provided her with a life far richer than her parents
had given her: one that included foreign travel, private schools, tutors,
college tuition, and the kind of loving, dedicated parenting only seen
on the bland TV family dramas or sitcoms of her generation.

The mother had also undergone years of her own therapy so that she could be a better mother to her daughter than hers was to her. She did this in part because she was terrified of making the same mistakes that her parents had made. This comparison of mothering and childhoods, sometimes spoken, always felt—"You have no idea how good you have it compared to what I grew up with"—was a source of conflict with her daughter, since the mother was raised to respect authority and be responsive to the demands of family obligation, while the daughter was raised to see both as constraints to her feelings of happiness and independence.

This mother illustrates the dilemma experienced by many parents who wonder what they're allowed to expect in return for their historically large investment in their children. While we've had other eras in which adult children couldn't find work, moved back in with their parents, or took a long time to leave home, never before have they occurred during an era preceded by such intensive parenting and such concern for socializing children to expect such high degrees of self-fulfillment and empowerment, not only from themselves but from the parent.

There's a very strong sense in our culture that if a relationship doesn't make you feel good about yourself or makes you feel guilty or bad, then completely cutting that person—even a parent—out of your life is not only a reasonable decision, it's a courageous decision. So from that perspective, guilt is your enemy. The more you make your child feel guilty, the more you're going to shut them down and drive them away.

Mistake #3: Returning Fire with Fire

Many parents of estranged children are furious with their adult children, and understandably so. They feel devalued, misunderstood, taken advantage of, kicked to the curb; its as if their child has taken the most innocent and vulnerable part of them, poured gasoline on them, lit a fire, and stood there watching it burn. Parents feel blamed for things that they never did or said, or if they did, should fairly be balanced out by all the loving, dedicated things that the parent did over the many years of parenting.

The previous example with the mother and her twenty-four-year-old daughter illustrates that however positive current relations are between parents and adult children, in many homes, there's still quite a bit of confusion, uncertainty, and conflict.

These cultural differences highlight the shaky ground that today's parents walk upon if their goal is a close and enduring relationship with their adult child. And tragically, nothing causes more parental error than a child's estrangement.

There are a variety of reasons that adult children say really hurtful, cruel things to their parents, and I'm not giving them a pass. I'm appalled, frankly, by some of the things adult children and their spouses say to their parents. But you're better off thinking about it from the perspective of their trying to communicate something that's important about their experience or the relationship that they don't have the skills to do in a more tactful way.

Secondly, and more subtly, they're trying to sort out the past and can only see what's true and what isn't by blaming you and seeing what you do with it. If you get too angry or defensive, it just muddies the water. The more you can address their complaints or observations in a very respectful way—by being investigative and interested in their thoughts and feelings—the more clarity you will bring to the situation.

You don't have to tolerate bad behavior or rubber-stamp it, but if you return fire with fire, you're not really advancing anything or creating the potential for a better relationship, if that's your goal. You're also stirring yourself up. It's much better to work on soothing yourself and responding in ways that you're going to feel better about.

How do you do that? Here are some ideas:

Handling Abusive or Disrespectful Behavior
1. *Decide what you want to say before the interaction.* What are your goals? Are there particular points that you want

to make sure you make? Write out the two or three most important things you want to say. If you're particularly nervous, practice saying them out loud.

2. *Have an exit plan.* How will you get off the phone or away from the interaction if it starts to head south?

3. *Consider prefacing the conversation with some ground rules if prior interactions have gone poorly.* Say something like "I know these conversations haven't gone very well when we've had them in the past, so let's both make a good effort to keep it calm and reasonable, okay? Maybe you should tell me what you'd like to get out of the conversation and I'll tell you what I'd like to get. How does that sound?"

4. *Express good intentions.* "I really do want to understand what you're saying. I would like to have a closer relationship with you." Or "I'm sure these interactions haven't felt very good to you in the past, either."

5. *Start by expressing a belief in the child's good intentions even if you don't like how he or she is saying it.* "I think that you're telling me something that you really want me to understand. Something that you think is very important."

6. *Describe your perception of your child's dilemma that is causing them to talk to you in a disrespectful manner.* "You must feel like I'm not going to understand unless you beat me over the head with it."

7. *Describe your dilemma.* "While I want to understand what you're saying, it's hard to focus on it when you're yelling at me or calling me names. I'm sure you can understand that."

8. *Ask for different behavior.* "Do you think you could try to tell that to me in a calmer way so I can focus on what you're telling me? It's actually hard for me to hear what you want me to hear when you talk to me like that."

9. *Give an example of appropriate behavior.* "You can tell me you're furious with me or even tell me that you hate my guts

if you like, but you can't scream at me and you can't call me names." Stay calm. Take deep breaths. Count to ten.

10. *Set limits.* "If you can't talk to me in a more respectful tone, I'm getting off the phone."

11. *Deliver on your limits.* If your child maintains his or her abusive behavior, hang up.

12. *Follow up within twenty-four hours and engage in a calm, even, friendly manner.* "Calling to check in with you and to see how you're doing. Do you want to try again?" If your child says no or something abusive, calmly say, "Okay, just wanted to see if we could have a more productive conversation. Here when you're ready."

13. *Rinse and repeat.* See if you can have a more productive discussion. If not, maintain the same steps.

After the Fight

Most parents find that the hours or days after a fight with their adult child are the hardest. This is because a fight with an adult child may cause the parent to ask themselves:

- What could I have done differently?
- What should I have done differently?
- Do I deserve this?
- Where did I go wrong?

Self-doubt and self-torment are predictable fallout emotions from a fight with an abusive or disrespectful adult child. The following are some recommendations to help you restore your balance:

- *Remind yourself of your good intentions.* "My goal was to have a closer interaction with my child."
- *Forgive yourself if you blew it.* "I probably shouldn't have

told him or her that they're selfish but I was very provoked. Hopefully next time I'll do a better job. Guess I got caught in the quicksand."

- *Engage in a self-soothing activity.* After a fight, our nervous systems are still poised for fight or flight. It's important to change your body's response to the stress by exercising, meditating, doing yoga, or doing something else to distract yourself.
- *Write out what happened.* It can help to remove yourself from the stress caused by the interaction and provide a way to analyze it when you feel up to it (if you feel like it).

Mistake #4: Assuming That Reconciliations Can Be Quickly Achieved

Reconciliation is typically a long road; more often a matter of years than months, though sometimes much more quickly if parents can catch it early enough. Once an estrangement has already been going on for a while, it's typically going to take longer to resolve, so you have to have the marathon model in mind.

Parents often ask me, "When do I get to say how I feel or say, 'Enough is enough'?" The answer is: Whenever you want. I've supported parents in my practice saying, "I've had enough. I can't deal with it anymore. It's too painful. I feel too disrespected, rejected, and hurt. I'm not doing this anymore." Unless their child is a minor, I think parents have the right to do that and at some point say that they've tried hard and long enough.

However, if you're still on the path toward reconciliation, when you get to say how you feel is probably not until there has been a full, strong reconciliation. Maybe it's a year or two into it. Frankly, depending on the kid, maybe never.

Mistake #5: Assuming That Their Distance or Negativity Is All Because of You

By the time we have adult children our lives are largely set. We may be newly divorced, dating, have new careers—but we're pretty much who we're going to be. There's so much of adult children's behavior that we personalize that has little or nothing to do with us, especially these days when our expectations for closeness are higher than in previous generations. Sometimes we get on a slippery slope and personalize everything they do and then complain about how it makes us feel. Then it *is* about us.

A lot of adult children's behavior has nothing to do with their parents. They're in the process of still figuring out who they are. They're raising children and working on their relationships. They're developing their careers. They may have their own emotional challenges that may or may not relate to our parenting. For most of us, our adult children are our central pleasure or joy if they're being nice to us, our central preoccupation when we're close to them, and our central source of torment when we're shut out.

Either way, they're very much on our minds all the time. We're *not* very much on their minds all the time, and not because they don't love or care about us. A lot of the adult children in my practice who are estranged from their parents say, "I do love my parent. I actually feel guilty about this. I feel bad for the ways that they suffer." They say that in addition to all the complaints that they have about them and their need to maintain the estrangement. But most of the time it isn't that they don't care.

It's so easy when you're in the midst of an estrangement to assume that your adult child only hates you and has completely forgotten about all the good, dedicated things that you did do for them growing up. The reality is that it's in there even if it's not at the forefront of their consciousness. And often we don't know what they're truly thinking or feeling until we carefully try to address their complaints.

So, yes, working on reconciliation is a bit of a minefield requiring a completely new mindset. Given that, here are my

Ten New Rules for Parent–Adult Child Relations

RULE #1: Your adult child has more power than you to set the terms of your relationship because they're more willing to walk away. Basic game theory: *she who cares less has more power.*

RULE # 2: Your relationship with your adult child needs to occur in an environment of creating happiness and personal growth, not an environment of obligation, emotional debt, or duty.

RULE # 3: You are not the only authority on how well you performed as a parent. Your adult child gets to have their own narrative and opinions about the past.

RULE #4: Use of guilt trips or criticism will never get you what you want from your adult child, especially if you're estranged.

RULE #5: Learning to communicate in a way that is egalitarian, psychological, and self-aware is essential to a good relationship with your adult child.

RULE #6: You were the parent when you were raising your child and you're the parent until they die. You brought your child into this world. That means that if your child is unable to take the high road, you still have to if reconciliation is your goal.

RULE #7: A large financial and emotional investment in your child does not entitle you to more contact or affection than that which is wanted by them, however unjust that may seem.

RULE #8: Criticizing your child's spouse, romantic partner, or therapist greatly increases your risk of estrangement.

RULE #9: Criticizing your child's sexuality or gender identity greatly increases your risk of estrangement.

RULE #10: Just because you had a bad childhood and did a better job than your parents doesn't mean that your adult child has to accept all of the ways that they felt hurt by you.

Understanding how to manage the pain of estrangement is one of the greatest challenges most parents will ever face. And that's because estrangement strikes us at our most tender and primitive places. Being a good parent is central to our identities and self-esteem. Being told directly or indirectly that you're not a good parent by your own children creates profound feelings of fear, sadness, worry, rage, guilt, and regret. Each one of these emotional reactions brings its own suite of problems that make healing a far more difficult enterprise.

Chapter 13

HOW DO I HEAL THE PAIN
OF ESTRANGEMENT?

There is no pain so great as the memory of joy in present grief.

Aeschylus

When I became a psychologist, I could not have predicted my practice would one day be filled with parents suffering from ongoing, unrelenting grief. That I would need to grapple with questions like: *What if I never see my child ever again? What if my grandchildren think that I don't love them? Does my son remember any of the wonderful times that we had together? Does my daughter still care about me if she's decided she won't see me? Or does she just hate me?*

I also didn't know that I would have to address heartrending end-of-life issues such as: *Who will bury me? Will I die alone in a hospital bed with no children or grandchildren to comfort me? Will my children even miss me once I'm gone? If I get cancer will they finally end the estrangement? How will I feel if they won't?*

Nobody trained me for these questions, and I'm sure I responded clumsily and ineffectually the first few years that I began to be flooded with referrals after writing *When Parents Hurt*. But after working with so many estranged parents over the past decade, here's what I've learned. To start: *There's nothing I can do or say that will take away your pain.* You're going to see a grandmother push her granddaughter down the street with her daughter smiling by her side and feel pain. You're going to listen to your friend or relative tell you about the fantastic trip they all went on with their three adult children and their grandchildren and feel pain. You're going to wake up from a dream where your son blissfully reconciled with you, remember you're heading into year seven of no contact, and feel pain. Despite your strongest inner warnings, you'll go *again* to your child's Facebook page or Instagram or wherever the hell they post pictures of themselves, their children, their in-laws, their friends—seemingly everybody but you—and feel pain.

Here's what else I've learned: *It's what you do with the pain that will make the difference between a life tethered to constant, implacable sorrow and one that has joy and meaning along with the pain.*

"The path out of hell is through misery," writes University of Washington psychologist and researcher Marsha Linehan, the founder of Dialectical Behavior Therapy. "By refusing to accept the misery that is part of climbing out of hell, you fall back into hell."

The path out of hell is through misery. Excuse me? What is that supposed to mean? It means that you have to start by "radically accepting" where you are right now. Radical acceptance means that you don't fight what you're feeling in this moment. You feel sad? Feel sad. Don't judge it, don't push it away, don't diminish it, and don't try to control its passage. *Turn toward the feeling* rather than turn away from it.

I learned this lesson the hard way. When I was going through my estrangement, I found myself daily rehearsing every parental mistake I'd ever made and winding up in the same pool of sadness, anger, and fear. However, one day, instead of continuing to bathe myself in the deadly font of those feelings, I thought: "Hey, guess what? Your daughter may never talk to you again. Ever! Last time you saw her? That may be the last time you'll ever see her. Deal with it." It wasn't a harsh or critical voice—more like wise and caring counsel from some censored part of me. And the acceptance of that gloomy reality was oddly, paradoxically reassuring. That's radical acceptance. It's accepting what you cannot change in this moment and may never be able to change.

Here's another example: Psychotherapist Megan Devine tragically watched her partner drown at the beach when he was thirty-nine. She knows a lot about the geography of pain. This is what she advises: "Your pain needs space. Room to unfold," she and Mark Nepo write in *It's OK That You're Not OK*: "Maybe your pain could wrap around the axle of the universe several times. Only the stars are large enough to take it on." The path out of hell is through the misery of accepting where you are right now. Right now, you're reading this because you're desperate, you're angry, you're guilt-ridden, worried, ashamed, scared, and scarred. These are powerful messages from your mind: *There's something here you should be attending to and not judging.*

You might think, "But I'm already attending to it. That's the problem!" True, but there's a right and a wrong way to attend to our thoughts and feelings. I've found that it's useful to distinguish between pain and suffering, because pain and suffering are two different things. Pain is the inevitable and unavoidable part of being human and of being an estranged parent. Unfortunately, you have relatively little control over that. However, you *can* gain increasing control and awareness over how long you feel pain. You can reduce the meaning of it, the actions you take that increase it, and the distance the pain travels through other aspects of your life. That's the suffering part.

The difference between pain and suffering is an insight that found its way from Buddhist teachings into contemporary psychotherapy. Psychiatrist Mark Levine, who developed the Mind to Mindful program, gives this example: "Let's say I stub my toe walking across the kitchen floor and it really hurts. That's pain. But then I start telling myself a bunch of things about stubbing my toe such as 'You idiot, why don't you watch where you're going?' Or 'Next time you're going to fall flat on your face or break your hip!' Or 'This is so typical of you to be so clumsy. Just one more example of what a screw-up you are!'"

That's suffering. Suffering lengthens the experience of pain because it creates an endless cognitive feedback loop where pain is always its terminus. Where suffering begets suffering begets suffering.

Here's a more relevant example: You go to a dinner at your friend's house where their adult children are visiting from out of town. These are kids you watched grow up, so you're happy to see them and they're happy to see you. And these are your close friends, so it makes you glad to see them with their thriving, successful children. And devastatingly sad because of the mirror it holds up to all that you've lost. So you end up excusing yourself multiple times throughout the evening to go to the bathroom and sob into your hands so no one will hear you.

Pain in this example are the feelings of sadness and loss. *Suffering* would be any of the following:

- Shaming yourself: I must be a terrible person/terrible parent for my own child to have turned against me.
- Societal shame: Others must think I'm terrible that my own child would turn against me.
- Social isolation related to societal shame: I shouldn't even leave the house if this is what's going to keep happening to me.
- Fear and catastrophization: How can I survive the pain if this never resolves? How can I survive the pain of not seeing my child or grandchild?
- Guilt and rumination: I can't stop thinking of all of the ways that I may have created this problem or what I should be doing to fix it. I also can't stop thinking about how hurt and mistreated I feel by my child.
- Rage: How can my own child do this to me? Who do they think they are?
- Envy: Why do others get to spend time with their children and grandchildren and I don't?

- Vestiges of the past: How can I tolerate the pain of my own child rejecting me when my own parents didn't love me? Doesn't this prove I'm unlovable?

Linehan, whose work was also greatly influenced by Buddhism, lists a number of different images to use as a way to face your pain and then watch whatever thoughts surface in reaction that could lead to suffering. For example, think of your pain and the subsequent thoughts as a leaf falling in a slow-moving stream that gradually moves out of sight.

Think of your emotion as a wave you're going to surf without trying to block or suppress it. Don't grab on to it, just notice where you're feeling it and focus on the sensations as fully as possible. Observe how long it takes before it starts to lessen.

It's also helpful to get into the *granularity* of your emotions. Is it just sadness? Or is it actually despair, grief, misery, agony, rejection, insecurity, sorrow, or defeat? Is it just anger? Or is it actually resentment, rage, irritation, jealousy, annoyance, or bitterness? Why should you get more specific? Psychology professor, and author of *How Emotions Are Made*, Lisa Feldman Barrett found that higher emotional granularity was associated with lowered needs for medication, fewer hospitalization days for illnesses, and greater flexibility regulating emotions. Getting into the specifics of what you're feeling helps you hear the message one part of your mind is trying to deliver to another part. It can guide you to determine the course of action in response to that emotion. It can help you to feel less ruled or controlled by your feelings because you'll know more specifically what you're feeling.

IS THERE A HIERARCHY OF GRIEF?

Part of what makes living with estrangement so challenging is the lack of public awareness and support for estranged parents. There's no shortage of websites, books, and workshops for those struggling with divorce, illness, or death and dying. But is a parent whose child is living and wants nothing to do with them less deserving of our support? Where every day they have to relitigate their right to feel like a decent person who provided their child with a good or reasonable life? Or if they made significant mistakes, is it just that they spend the rest of their years in a purgatory of guilt and sorrow? A life imprisonment where only their children can commute their sentence?

If your child actually dies, everyone will feel sorry for you. If your child stops talking to you, everyone will judge you. At least that's what it feels like. That perception will make your ability to properly grieve and take care of yourself far more complicated and difficult.

Here's something else I've learned that helps estranged parents: *Self-compassion is everything.* Without self-compassion there is no se- renity, no happiness, no resilience, and no future. Your life will be spent in endless infernos of self-loathing, self-doubt, and self-hatred. You will turn away from those you love and those who love you. And if you don't turn away from them, you will drive them away with your inability to take care of yourself.

What's standing in your way? Here are some common obstacles to self-compassion:

YOUR FAMILY HISTORY

My experience as a psychologist shows me that the worse your family treated you growing up, the more challenging your ability to feel self- compassion. This is because if you were raised in an environment where you were abused, neglected, frequently criticized, or shamed, you were likely hard on yourself well before you even had children.

In addition, you may have had other experiences in your life that led you to irrationally believe that you're completely defective, such as being teased or humiliated by peers, siblings, or others. As a result:

- You have less immunity to your child's criticism than is good for you.
- You feel more deserving of rejection or even abandonment.
- You are more likely to blame yourself for things that you didn't do, or you have a hard time sorting out what you caused and what you didn't.
- You struggle with feelings of guilt for things that aren't even related to parenting.
- You struggle with ongoing feelings of anxiety or depression.

MOTHERHOOD AS OBSTACLE

One of the biggest obstacles to your ongoing serenity is the idea that being a good mother means continuing to blame yourself and to feel guilty for whatever mistakes you made; or to blame yourself for whatever mistakes your child thinks you made.

This is not to say that estrangement is any walk in the park for dads, as I can readily attest. In addition, men's tendency to cover our depression with anger, social withdrawal, and compartmentalization may make us look less affected than most of us actually are. However, there is a self-emphasis granted to the identity of masculinity that may cause dads to better defend against the dictates of guilt, to push back more aggressively against the child's rejection, and to feel less obligated to keep trying.

Women are not provided with the same kinds of cultural refuge. For example, common definitions of motherhood may obligate you to:

- Put yourself last, especially where your children are concerned, including grown children
- Give till it hurts
- Sacrifice when you shouldn't
- Worry about your child all the time
- Preoccupy yourself with your child's well-being well past the point of it being useful for anyone

Can you see how these popular notions of ideal motherhood stand in the way of your letting go of self-blame, regret, and sorrow? The constant cultural transmission is that if you DON'T feel all of those things, then you're somehow behaving selfishly, irresponsibly, and unlovingly. That you're being *unmotherly*.

Here's the irony: The skills that made you a good parent are now working against your ability to feel self-compassion. Because in order to feel more self-compassion, you have to embrace the following beliefs (print this out and carry it around as a reminder):

- I am still a good person and a good parent even if I don't think about my child.
- I am still a good person and a good parent if I put my own happiness before everyone else's.
- Putting myself first doesn't mean that I'm putting others last.
- There is a difference between being self-interested (i.e., prioritizing my happiness and thinking about what makes me happy) and being selfish.
- Since my child is choosing not to spend time with me, it is healthy for me to think about how I want to spend my time without him or her in my life.
- Putting my child out of my mind is useful for my happiness and serenity.
- When I punish myself for the past, I perpetuate the myth that I deserve to suffer.

- I have suffered enough and as of today I choose to feel good about myself as a parent and as a person.

Six Common Myths of Estranged Parents

MYTH #1: I can't have a happy life without my child or grandchild in it.

FACT: While the pain of estrangement is enormous, the biggest obstacle isn't just the absence of your child; it's your guilt, shame, and inclination to punish yourself. It's your belief that not only could you have done better but that you should have done better.

MYTH #2: If my own child rejects me, it proves that I'm unlovable.

FACT: Your value isn't for your child or anyone else to determine. Your value is part of your birthright, and you should guard it with your life.

MYTH #3: I should always be thinking about my child. Otherwise, I'm being a neglectful parent and a bad, selfish person.

FACT: It isn't good for your mental health to obsess about the estrangement or the well-being of your child. Putting your child out of your mind can actually be useful for your happiness and serenity. You are still a good person and a good parent even if you don't think about him or her.

MYTH #4: If I hadn't made the decisions or mistakes I made, my child's life would be completely different.

FACT: Perhaps, but parents are only part—and sometimes a small part—of determining how a child's life turns out.

Genetics, class, neighborhood, siblings, peers, culture, their choice of partners, and random luck are sometimes far more important.

MYTH #5: My child is the most appropriate person to say what kind of a parent I am or was.

FACT: Sometimes one's children are the least able for the following reasons:

1) They are too influenced by your ex or the person to whom they're married.

2) Their mental illness causes them to view you through the distorted lens of their illness.

3) Their therapist has changed their perception about what kind of a parent you are or were.

4) They devalue you for reasons that don't have to do with your parenting. They have to combat their fear that they're too dependent and to prove to themselves that they can stand on their own.

MYTH #6: If only I'd raised them differently or gotten them help, I wouldn't be estranged today.

FACT: No one knows who is going to estrange and who isn't. There are many truly abusive parents whose children would never dream of estranging them; conversely, there are plenty of dedicated parents whose children choose to end the relationship. The fact that so many dedicated parents are estranged today shows that this is part of a larger social phenomenon, more than the problem of any one parent.

ANGER AND ESTRANGEMENT

Anger is your friend and anger is your enemy. Anger can let you know that you've been wronged, that your well-being is threatened, and it readies you for action. For estranged parents, it can provide a firewall against someone who has hurt you and may continue to hurt you.

There's a saying that *depression is anger turned inward.* I think depression is more complex than that, but there is a pearl of wisdom there for estranged parents. So maybe you need to write your son or daughter or in-laws or whoever else has poisoned the well against you and get angry so that you can do battle with the voice that's saying you're supposed to suffer for eternity. (Typically, I don't suggest mailing these letters—this is for you alone.)

On the other hand, maybe you're *too* angry and it's negatively affecting your life. This might be true if you're experiencing any of the following:

- You feel so consumed with rage that you can't take any pleasure in anything.
- You find yourself getting mad at the wrong people.
- Your anger interferes with your enjoyment of your other kids if you have them, of your spouse or significant other, or of your friends.

If the above items describe you, it probably means you're working too hard to defend yourself. Typically, feelings of *guilt, self-criticism, and regret are underneath that kind of anger.* If you fall into the too-angry camp, then I recommend you work more on:

- Self-compassion
- Forgiveness of yourself
- Forgiveness of your child

HOW CAN I POSSIBLY FORGIVE MY CHILD, AND WHY WOULD I BOTHER?

You are not obligated to forgive your child. And before you can, you need to understand the following realities:

- You can't forgive your child if you're still attacking yourself.
- You can't forgive your child if you believe that you deserve to be estranged (deserving of your child's anger or hurt is different from deserving their estrangement).
- You can't forgive your child if you don't have enough pleasure, meaning, or support in your life.
- You can't forgive your child if you're confused about your fundamental worth as a person (for example, if you were abused or neglected and struggle with basic feelings of self-worth).

This is because forgiving them means being very, very clear that you don't deserve to have this kind of trauma in your life. That however small or great your mistakes as parents, those mistakes don't mean that living the rest of your lives without your children or grandchildren is a just punishment for whatever complaints they have about what you did or didn't do.

Here's what forgiving your child doesn't mean:

- It doesn't mean that you're excusing their behavior or mistreatment of you.
- It doesn't mean that you're signing on for more in the future.
- It doesn't mean that you deserve to be mistreated.
- It doesn't mean that you don't get to ever give your side of things and how it's impacted you if a reconciliation were to occur (though I would caution you to do that very slowly, and well after a reconciliation has occurred).

So what does forgiveness mean?

- It means that you work hard to understand what is motivating their estrangement.
- Forgiveness means replacing bitterness with a kind of wise affection, a *parental* affection for a child who needs to take this very rigid stance against you.
- Overall, forgiveness can feel better and make you feel more grounded and in control of your life than anger.
- Forgiveness is empowering and more attractive to others, especially your child—assuming that you're not being taken advantage of or taken for granted.

PARENTING AT A DISTANCE

So maybe you're *not* one of those lucky enough to be reconciled with your child, at least not for a while. In this case, your task is to work toward radical acceptance of your role in your child's life. Typically, we think of parenting as an active enterprise engaged through advice, visits, babysitting grandkids, phone calls, etc. But there's also a passive form of parenting where after an active attempt to reconcile the problem, we accept that the child doesn't want to engage. And in not fighting that, not guilt-tripping them, not acting overly victimized or martyred, we parent by accepting their need for the distance, however at odds it is with our own needs.

We accept that being out of contact allows them time to work on feeling separate, more independent, less triggered by whatever ways we annoy them, hurt them, or frustrate them; it allows them time to calm the fuck down about whatever it is they're so upset about, to become more self-reflective about the ways they may be overreacting or blaming us. Time apart also serves as a kind of peace offering to their spouse who makes them feel like they're being weak to be close to you, or a peace offering to their other parent if you're divorced and they know that nothing makes that parent happier than your head on a platter.

So many of the parents that I see, moms in particular, feel that they're being terrible people to accept the limitations of their parenting: "There must be *something* I can do, should do, have to do to resolve this." I sometimes have to say, *No, there really isn't. At least not right now.* At that point I recommend that the parent not do anything at all for at least a year (assuming the child isn't a minor) and then reconsider reaching out after that time. Why a year? Because it has to be long enough for the adult child to feel like they might have gotten what they needed from the parent. And it also gives the parent a leg to stand on if after a year they reach out and say, "It was clear that you needed time apart from me. I'm checking in to see if you're now open to have a different conversation with me?"

Time and acceptance can be powerful agents of healing when we let them. Time can sometimes create enough space for a new perspective to develop. And that's why I call it parenting at a distance: your child is actively engaging with you, just outside of your vision and awareness.

GETTING IN SHAPE TO WORK ON HEALING FROM ESTRANGEMENT

There's a reason that almost every news segment details the importance of regular exercise, getting enough sleep, eating a reasonable diet, having a regular yoga or meditation practice, and developing a supportive network of friends or others: they're all necessary to a balanced life. All of these are especially necessary to work on healing from your estrangement. That's because healing from your estrangement requires that you develop a kind of poise, balance, and resiliency in the face of ongoing pain. Buddhists call this state of mind *upekkha*.

You need the resources drawn from good sleep, a reasonable diet, regular exercise, and people who care about you to be able to exist in the presence of pain and face it head on.

Not everything happens for a reason. You didn't get estranged because you were supposed to be taught some purposeful lesson in order to become stronger, wiser, whatever. God didn't deliver this nightmare to teach you how to become better at suffering. You were probably pretty good at it before you became estranged.

You became estranged because bad things happen to good people. And even if you made monstrously terrible decisions with your children, nothing makes you deserving of a life without them in it. If your kids are unable to see you as worthy of love, acceptance, and forgiveness, then you have to find redemption in that *small crack in the continuum of catastrophe,* as Walter Benjamin put it. And guard it with your life.

AFTERWORD

The truest form of wealth is social, not material.

Jonathan Rauch, *The Happiness Curve*

My parents belonged to the last generation of unworried middle-class parents. They didn't worry about the corruptive power of their authority, didn't base their self-esteem on how they fared as parents, didn't obsess about my future. My brothers and I consumed hours of television and ate a staggering amount of sugar—for breakfast. We vanished in summer mornings—biked back for lunch—and disappeared till dusk. There were no curious and intrusive neighbors offering unsolicited advice about how to be even more restrictive of our whereabouts. It was the gilded age before the concept of toxic parents captured the national imagination.

My parents also had a life. My mother played mah-jongg and bridge weekly with "the girls" (her Temple Sisterhood friends), and Mom and Dad went out every weekend without calling it "date night." My dad played squash on weekends at the downtown YMCA and didn't worry about whether my brothers and I felt neglected. They were as luxuriously removed from our minds as we were theirs. There was no Internet broadcasting a little shop of daily horrors: a kidnapping in Saskatchewan, a child's murder in Booneville, a teen's failure to launch coming to a city near you if you didn't get it right.

As young parents in the mid-1950s, my mother and father were influenced by the more permissive, laissez-faire attitudes of Benjamin

Spock than by the austere, punitive dictates of the behaviorists who preceded him. And while they didn't spank us, we knew the look that told us that we'd better back off or suffer the consequences. They were friendly, but we knew where we stood in the order of things and didn't mistake who had the authority in the household. We were also lucky, since many parents of the day still took parental authority as a license to be controlling or physically abusive.

The move toward a friendlier household began to slowly accelerate in the 1960s. The focus on rights, liberation, and self-expression that animated that era also revolutionized and democratized the American family. Parents, especially in the middle classes, began to be more interested in the inner lives of their children: in increasing their self-esteem, their assertiveness, and their individuality; in helping them be less preoccupied with or motivated by guilt or obligation. Children continued to move away from being seen and not heard to becoming the center of family life, a trend that continues unimpeded to this day.

But a major reason that middle-class mothers and fathers of my parents' generation were less worried is because they had less cause to be worried. There was still heartbreaking poverty in rural areas, and racial discrimination still restricted the opportunities for many. However, there was a sense of shared sacrifice and shared victories from the Depression and the end of the war. Segregation was slowly declining, and income distribution was becoming more equal. Outside of agriculture and temporary work, employers typically provided health care, and many jobs guaranteed a pension. A middle-class family with one breadwinner could put two kids through college, while most blue-collar work paid a living wage, making college less necessary as a pathway to adulthood. And if their sons were able to support families, most parents of the time reasoned, their daughters would be able to be supported by whomever they married.

In the same way that climate change proceeded at an almost imperceptible pace until it suddenly accelerated and intensified, so, too, did the forces undermining the seemingly bright future of the American family. The postwar consensus that every generation would do better than the last is disappearing. As a growing body of new reseach makes clear, this transformation—which has resulted in the decimation of unions, livable wages, pensions, and healthcare along with the social inequality that underlies it—has had a profound impact on family well-being and longevity. Family historian Stephanie Coontz notes that the collapse of the economic safety net of prior generations has created a collapse of the *psychological* safety net. Today's children suffer with higher rates of mental illness, and parents across the classes are far more worried and distressed than prior generations.

And it's small wonder. The number of poor families facing eviction is greater today than it was during the Depression. The average two-parent family now works 26 percent longer, or seven hundred more hours per year, than did the typical two-parent family in 1975—more time than workers in any other Western democracy.

Middle-class parents are especially confused. On the one hand, they have luxuries unthinkable to my parents' generation—nicer homes, better cars, computers, cell phones. On the other, they maintain their position by working longer and harder; by getting more and more degrees and qualifications; and by pushing their children to do the same. The cost of security, from medical insurance to college tuition, has skyrocketed—also raising fears about the prospects for their children's future.

YOU CAN DO IT!

Yale political scientist Jacob Hacker notes that there has been a *great risk shift* since the late 1970s, away from governmental and corporate family supports and onto the backs of parents. Other countries haven't been in such a rush to make that shift. Almost every other Western industrialized nation still provides free or subsidized preschool, school lunches, free or subsidized college, health insurance, job training, and pensions. If countries with low social inequality and greater supports have higher indices of happiness (and they do), it's in no small measure because they have a lot more to be happy about. In spite of having the third-highest GDP per capita, the US ranks an embarrassing twenty-sixth in child happiness. Contrary to the view that it's all up to the parents, most other Western industrialized democracies believe that it's all up to society to help the parents.

While rugged individualism has always been part of the American ethos, it was often animated by a sense of a shared common purpose and struggle. This is also changing. Public deliberations have drifted away from a belief that we're all in this together to one where government is the enemy, personal responsibility is key, and failure to achieve is a personal flaw.

As opportunities have decreased, a narrative of personal responsibility and cultural emphasis on finding happiness has accelerated. There is an increasing emphasis on blaming parents for the outcome of their children's lives rather than the steady erosion of social and economic pathways to a secure future.

The self-help industry has grown into an almost $10 billion enterprise to meet a seemingly insatiable need for guidance about how to have a happy life. A common theme in psychotherapy and self-help is deciding who to be close to and who to get rid of. "As a twenty-first-century individual, you must choose your style of personal life," notes sociologist Andrew Cherlin in *The Marriage-Go-Round.* "You are allowed to—in fact, you are almost required to—continually monitor your sense of self and to look inward to see how well your inner life fits with your marriage or cohabiting life. If the fit deteriorates, you are almost required to leave . . . [A] relationship that no longer fits your needs is inauthentic and hollow. It limits the personal rewards that you can achieve." Cherlin's comments are apt for the way that many think about today's broader family relationships. If it constrains your personal rewards, you need to get out. Failing to do so is a sign of weakness, of existential cowardice, and of failure.

Social media has become an enormous platform to broadcast the sometimes-destructive messages of individualism, as it allows people the experience of being with others without any of the commitment or struggle required of face-to-face relationships. Prior to social media, only siblings or other close family or friends could weigh in on the validity or invalidity of our claims about our families. Today an infinite number of online forums exist at the ready to corroborate a perception that your family is harmful and in need of riddance, good or otherwise—forums that can tell you whether your parent is a *narcissist, a borderline,* or *toxic.* They can tell you whether your adult child is *lazy, a snowflake,* or *overly entitled.*

Today, social media and online forums serve as a kind of unhinged kin, there to offer support and validate our struggles with difficult family members. However, unlike family and close friends who have some degree of data and stakes upon which to base their claims, forums serve more to offer support to our most desperate instincts for validation and reassurance. They exist as a kind of crowdsourcing, conceptually funded from the cultural mood of what is believed to constitute healthy family relationships. Yet the tribal nature of these "communities" often makes their influence as divisive for the American family as it is for the political climate.

Of course, having high expectations of one's family is important. It can make us think carefully about our deepest values and surround ourselves with family members who reflect those principles. It can help us parse the fabric of our identities and call on loved ones to be more considerate of our needs, our emotions, and our aspirations. The high rates of positive contact between many parents and adult children today is testimony to the success of this endeavor, as well as to a more democratized and egalitarian family ethos.

At the same time, high expectations may make family relationships more fragile. They can cause us to expect too much and resent family members for not giving us more. It may instantiate a myth of self-reliance, lionize a go-it-alone mentality, and conceal the ways that we need our connections to others, often including family, for our happiness, our meaning, and our health. The rates of divorce, estrangement, and loneliness testify to that.

Perhaps more important is that searching for happiness using the compass of individualism—online or not—doesn't always point us in the direction of the greatest satisfaction. "Happiness has turned inward and become entangled with the idea of a personal journey and forging ahead alone," notes writer Ruth Whippman in *America the Anxious*. Yet numerous studies have found that the more actively we pursue happiness as an individual quest toward meaning and fulfillment, the more *unhappy* we are likely to become: more lonely and more depressed. By contrast, in those countries where happiness is defined as a form of social engagement rather than an individual pursuit, *more* happiness was the result of actively pursuing it. Which should make us wonder whether a pursuit of happiness built upon the graveyard of discarded relationships is always the most prudent course.

I am often asked in interviews whether I think estrangement is good or bad, justified or unjustified. Sitting in my office every day with sobbing estranged mothers and sometimes fathers, I have concluded that those are the wrong questions. The questions should be, Is it right to end a relationship with a parent when you know that it will ruin their life? When doing so—whatever their flaws or mistakes, serious or trivial, traumatizing or expectable—will bring endless heartache, loss, and shame to them? When that loss, as serious and in some ways *more* serious than the physical loss of a child, will create ongoing depression and suffering?

"Yeah, well, they should've thought of that before they had children" is a common refrain. Perhaps. But that statement assumes a lot. Does *anyone* have the capacity to anticipate the challenges that will befall them or their children before they have them? Can they know that the person that they married may later betray them or turn their child against them? That their own childhood wounds will come roaring into the present, causing them to treat their own inno-cent children as terribly as they were by their own traumatized and traumatizing parents? That their children themselves may bring their own challenges in temperament, personality, or attention that make parenting them a much more impossible endeavor than anyone could possibly have warned them it would be?

Our American love affair with the needs and rights of the individ-ual conceals how much sorrow is left in the wake by those engaging in its pursuit. I know that there are studies showing that many adult children try long and hard before cutting off the parent. I've seen that in my practice as well. But I also see plenty who don't try long *or* hard. Those who refuse to give the parent a single chance, or a second, third, or fourth, to try to repair or make the relationship one that feels healthy and respectful of the adult child or their spouse.

So to answer the question, yes, it's easy to empathize sometimes with adult children who end the relationship with their mother or father. Some parents continue to be so hurtful, so unrepentant, so disrespectful of the adult child's needs that they leave no other option for that adult child than to walk. And some parents have been so destructive when the child was young that there is little left to build a foundation upon, even if the parent is able and willing, later in life, to make amends.

But let's not turn that into some kind of distributive justice. Let's not say that doing a bad job as a parent, in that increasingly difficult-to-quantify way, grants the adult child the right to forever immiserate the life of a mother or father. Let's not claim that the estrangement, however understandable, is the same thing as saying that the parent got what they deserved.

We need a different conversation in our society, one where not only parents are asked to be empathic to the harm that they did to their children, but where adult children are asked to be empathic to the harm that they're doing to the parent by cutting them out of their lives.

Throughout this book I have had two voices in my head: in one ear, the plea of the adult child to be understood and cared about, to assert their need and right to end a relationship with a parent who—however mystifying to the mother or father—they believe harmful to their well-being. I hear a request to not oversimplify their struggles and their aspirations for a life more in line with their values and feelings; and to not cast that aspiration in the simple and harsh light of overentitlement or selfishness.

In the other ear is the parent who feels unjustly cast off, denied a life with children and grandchildren they assumed would be in their lives forever. A wish for me to help them make sense and meaning of a world without those they deem the most crucial to their well-being, if not their survival. A hope that I will stand up for them in a world where they feel vilified and alone.

As a family therapist, I know that both sides can learn to listen to the other. But I also know how much effort it takes. Parents who discover how to communicate in a way that is respectful of the child's needs and perceptions, their feelings and their goals, are more likely to heal the distance between themselves and their children. Those who can make amends, see themselves through the child's eyes, however bleak that reflection, are more likely to invite sympathy and a willingness to keep working on the relationship. Those willing to take the time needed for their adult child to feel understood will fare better than those told to move on or get over it.

Adult children who can accept the parent's claim that they did the best they could as fact, not as dismissal, may gain access to a person they hadn't seen before. Those who are able to empathize with their parent's inability or difficulty communicating thoughts or feelings will find the parent better able to listen than those who remain in a position of criticism or judgment. In the same way that we're constantly growing and changing, discovering new parts of ourselves, our parents may be far more capable of growth and change than we had imagined them to be.

"We need to recognize that to deny people their complications and contradictions is to deny them their humanity," notes Meghan Daum in *The Problem with Everything*. Developing compassion for parents, adult children, intimate partners, and friends is helpful not only because it makes us more resilient, but because it allows us to see them more clearly—their awkward or ineffectual attempts to care for us; the confounding nature of their struggles; the history they carry stumbling into the present. While many say that finding compassion for those who hurt them is one of the hardest things they've ever done, others discover that it's freeing in ways they hadn't imagined. It binds them to a common humanity where we are all in some measure flawed, torn, and hurt. And dying for understanding.

NOTES

INTRODUCTION

Page 1   **estranged parents who all say the same thing:** The word *estranged* means different things to different people, including researchers. For a good review, see Lucy Blake, "Parents and Children Who Are Estranged in Adulthood: A Review and Discussion of the Literature," *Journal of Family Theory & Review* 9, no. 4 (2017): 521–36, doi:10.1111/jftr.12216.

In this context I'm using the framework, with some small revisions in parentheses, proposed in an article by psychologist Richard Conti, "Family Estrangement: Establishing a Prevalence Rate," *Journal of Psychology and Behavioral Science* 3, no. 2 (December 2015): 28–35.

Conti defines estrangement as: "1. A (mostly) complete communication cutoff between relatives, which means little to no intentional direct communication between the estranged parties. Indirect communication may occur, for example, through other family members or lawyers. 2. The communication cutoff is maintained deliberately or intentionally by at least one person. 3. The estranged relatives know how to contact each other unless the estranged party hasn't provided contact information. Neither is considered missing. Consequently, the cousin you simply have not spoken to in many years is not estranged. People who have unintentionally fallen out of touch are not estranged. 4. At least one of the persons involved claims that something specific about the other person justifies the communication cutoff, like something the other person did, does or failed to do."

Page 2   **many of those who contact me are some of the most dedicated, ed-ucated, and loving parents of any generation:** https://www.wsj.com/articles/baby-boomers-and-the-art-of-parenting-adult-kids-11555156800.

Page 2   **experts keep changing what's considered ideal parenting every three or four years:** Timothy Aubry and Trysh Travis, eds., *Rethinking Therapeutic Culture* (Chicago: University of Chicago Press, 2015).

Page 2   **Whatever the cause, rejection from the person whose opinion and love you care the most about:** A growing literature details the psychological stress that occurs to both estranged parents and adult children. See, for example, Kylie Agllias, "No Longer on Speaking Terms: The Losses Associated with Family Estrangement at the End of Life," *Families in Society* 92, no. 1 (2011): 107–13, http://doi.org/10.1606/1044-3894.4055; Kylie Agllias, *Family Estrangement: A Matter of Perspective* (New York: Routledge, 2016); Becca Bland, "I Am Estranged from My Family," https://www.theguardian.com/life andstyle/2012/dec/15/becca-bland-estranged-parents; Lucy Blake, Becca Bland, and Susan Imrie, "The Counseling Experiences of Individuals Who Are Estranged from a Family Member," *Family Relations* (October 2019), https://doi.org/10.1111/fare.12385.

Page 5   **Studies show that divorce is sometimes less hard on children than their parents' remarriage:** William Jeynes, "A Longitudinal Analysis on the Effects of Remarriage Following Divorce on the Academic Achievement of Adolescents," *Journal of Divorce & Remarriage* 33, nos. 1 and 2 (2000): 131–148.

Page 8   **is still a largely closeted problem:** Conti, "Family Estrangement."

Page 9   **I wrote my last book, When Parents Hurt:** *When Parents Hurt: Compassionate Strategies When You and Your Grown Child Don't Get Along* (New York: HarperCollins, 2007).

Page 11   **It is true that some parents have been destructive in how they raised their children:** Joshua Coleman, Philip Cowan, and Carolyn Pape Cowan, "The Cost of Blaming Parents," *Greater Good* magazine, Berkeley, California, 2014; Kristina M. Scharp, Lindsey J. Thomas, and Christina G. Paxman, "'It Was the Straw That Broke the Camel's Back': Exploring the Distancing Processes Communicatively Constructed in Parent-Child Estrangement Backstories," *Journal of Family Communication* 15, no. 4 (2015): 330–48.

Page 13   **I believe reconciliation is better than staying apart:** Debra Umberson, "Relationships Between Adult Children and Their Parents:

Psychological Consequences for Both Generations," *Journal of Marriage and Family* 54 (1992): 664–74.

CHAPTER 1: CAN I SAVE THE RELATIONSHIP WITH MY ESTRANGED CHILD?

Page 19   **women are still held to a higher standard of responsibility for family relationships than are men:** Anne-Marie Slaughter, "Why Women Still Can't Have It All," https://www.theatlantic.com /magazine/archive/2012/07/why-women-still-cant-have-it-all /309020/; Joshua Coleman, *The Lazy Husband: How to Get Men to Do More Parenting and Housework* (New York: St. Martin's Press, 2007).

Page 20   **For some parents, feeling empathy for their child's allegations is a slippery slope:** Selma Fraiberg et al., "Ghosts in the Nursery," *Journal of the American Academy of Child & Adolescent Psychiatry* 14, no. 3 (Summer 1975): 387–421.

Page 23   **Adult children should do it because working through childhood issues:** Philip Cowan, personal communication. See also Joshua Coleman, Philip Cowan, and Carolyn Pape Cowan, "The Cost of Blaming Parents," *Greater Good* magazine, Berkeley, California, 2014.

Page 23   **At the climax of Russell Banks's novel *Affliction*:** Russell Banks, *Affliction* (New York: HarperPerennial, 2004).

Page 26   **In Tara Westover's memoir, *Educated*:** Tara Westover, *Educated: A Memoir* (New York: Random House, 2018).

CHAPTER 2: THE MANY PATHWAYS TO ESTRANGEMENT

Page 30   **Parents typically have to take leadership because they are often more motivated for a reconciliation to occur:** Researchers Lucy Blake and Becca Bland found that the majority of estrangements had been initiated by the adult child, not the parent. Lucy Blake and Becca Bland, University of Cambridge Centre for Family Research and Stand Alone, December 2015. Their findings mirror those in my practice and my survey of 1,600 estranged parents.

Page 30   **In a highly individualistic culture such as ours, divorce may cause the child to see the parents and others in a family less as members of a unit of which they're a part:** Joshua Coleman, *The Marriage Makeover: Finding Happiness in Imperfect Harmony* (New York: St. Martin's Press, 2000); Pamela Webster and A. Regula Herzog, "Effects of Parental Divorce and Memories of Family Problems on Relationships Between Adult Children and Their Parents," *The Journals of Gerontology* Series B, vol. 50B, no. 1 (January 1995): S24–S34.

Page 33   **A majority of parents today are in far more contact with their adult children than were prior generations:** Stephanie Coontz, *Marriage, A History: How Love Conquered Marriage* (New York: Penguin, 2006); Andrew Cherlin, *The Marriage-Go-Round: The State of Marriage and the Family Today* (New York: Vintage, 2010); Eli Finkel, *The All-or-Nothing Marriage: How the Best Marriages Work* (New York: Dutton, 2017); Julie Beck, "Love in the Time of Individualism," *The Atlantic,* September 22, 2017, https://www.theatlantic.com/health/archive/2017/09/love-in-the-time-of-individualism/540474/.

Page 34   **A common thread in the perspective of estranged children are allegations of harm:** Kylie Agllias, "Disconnection and Decision-Making: Adult Children Explain Their Reasons for Estranging from Parents," *Australian Social Work* 69(1) (2016a): 92–104, http://doi.org/10.1080/0312407X.2015.1004355; Blake and Bland, University of Cambridge Centre for Family Research and Stand Alone, December 2015; Kristina M. Scharp and Elizabeth Dorrance Hall, "Family Marginalization, Alienation, and Estrangement: Questioning the Nonvoluntary Status of Family Relationships," *Annals of the International Communication Association* 41, no. 1 (2017): 28–45.

Page 34   **In a recent *New York Times* article, "Generation Z":** Dan Levin, "Generation Z: Who They Are in Their Own Words," *New York Times,* March 28, 2019, https://www.nytimes.com/2019/03/28/us/gen-z-in-their-words.html.

Page 34   **causing a writer in the *Wall Street Journal*:** Peggy Drexler, "Millennials Are the Therapy Generation," *Wall Street Journal,* March 2019, https://www.wsj.com/articles/millennials-are-the-therapy-generation-11551452286.

Page 34   **According to psychologist Nick Haslam, definitions of abuse, trauma, and neglect have grown in the past three decades:** Nick Haslam, "Concept Creep: Psychology's Expanding Concepts of Harm and Pathology," *Psychological Inquiry* 27, no. 1 (January 2016):

1–17; "When those concepts involve harm they're especially prob-lematic because when one person sees harm where the other doesn't that becomes a moral disagreement that reasoned argument will have trouble overcoming." Haslam, email correspondence, Novem-ber 15, 2019; Michele Cascardi, Cathy Brown, Melinda Iannarone, and Norma Cardona, "The Problem of Overly Broad Definitions of Bullying: Implications for the Schoolhouse, the Statehouse, and the Ivory Tower," *Journal of School Violence* 13, no. 3 (2014): 253–76; Allan V. Horwitz and Jerome C. Wakefield, *The Loss of Sadness: How Psychiatry Transformed Normal Sorrow into Depressive Disorder* (New York: Oxford University Press, 2007); Allan V. Horwitz and Jerome C. Wakefield, *All We Have to Fear: Psychiatry's Transforma-tion of Natural Anxieties into Mental Disorders* (New York: Oxford University Press, 2012); Edward Shorter, *How Everyone Became Depressed: The Rise and Fall of the Nervous Breakdown* (New York: Oxford University Press, 2013).

Page 35   **causing some to accuse the authors of the DSM and the field of psychiatry of disease mongering:** For good reviews of the DSM see Anne Harrington, *Mind Fixers: Psychiatry's Troubled Search for the Biology of Mental Illness* (New York: W. W. Norton, 2020); Gary Greenberg, *The Book of Woe: The DSM and the Unmaking of Psy-chiatry* (New York: Plume, published by the Penguin Group, 2014); Ethan Watters, *Crazy Like Us: The Globalization of the American Psyche* (New York: Free Press, 2011).

Page 35   **Stresses, struggles, and painful incidents once viewed as existen-tial problems in families (and something better kept to oneself) are now seen, for better and worse, as life altering and transform-ing:** Eva Illouz, *Cold Intimacies: The Making of Emotional Capital-ism* (Cambridge: Polity, 2017); Jennifer M. Silva, *Coming Up Short: Working-Class Adulthood in an Age of Uncertainty* (New York: Ox-ford University Press, 2015); Greg Lukianoff and Jonathan Haidt, *The Coddling of the American Mind: How Good Intentions and Bad Ideas Are Setting Up a Generation for Failure* (New York: Penguin Books, 2019); Bradley Campbell and Jason Manning, *The Rise of Victimhood Culture: Microaggressions, Safe Spaces, and the New Cul-ture Wars* (Cham, Switzerland: Palgrave Macmillan, 2018).

Page 36   **Studies show that expanding the list of mental disorders to incor-porate more and more experiences:** Matthew Lebowitz, "Biological Conceptualizations of Mental Disorders Among Affected Individu-als: A Review of Correlates and Consequences," *Clinical Psychology:*

Science and Practice 21, no. 1 (2014): 67–83, doi:10.1111/cpsp.12056; Haslam, "Concept Creep."

Page 36   **"blank slate" musings of Locke and Rousseau:** Richard I. Aaron, *John Locke* (Charleston, S.C.: Nabu Press, 2011); Jean-Jacques Rousseau, *The Social Contract* (New York: Penguin, 1968); Richard Webster, *Why Freud Was Wrong: Sin, Science and Psychoanalysis* (Oxford: The Orwell Press, 2005); Abraham Maslow, *The Farther Reaches of Human Nature* (New York: Arkana, 1993).

Page 37   **Contemporary research challenges this received wisdom:** Alison Gopnik, *The Gardener and the Carpenter* (New York: Picador, 2017); Robert Plomin, *Blueprint: How DNA Makes Us Who We Are* (Cambridge: MIT Press, 2019).

Page 37   **As cultural sociologist Eva Illouz writes:** Illouz, *Cold Intimacies*; Lillian Hellman, *Pentimento* (Boston: Little, Brown and Company, 2000).

Page 38   **As family historian Stephanie Coontz observes in *The Way We Never Were*:** Stephanie Coontz, *The Way We Never Were: American Families and the Nostalgia Trap* (New York: Basic Books, 2016).

Page 38   **"How to 'Break Up' with a Narcissistic Parent":** Brittany Wong, "How to 'Break Up' with a Narcissistic Parent," *HuffPost*, December 7, 2017, https://www.huffpost.com/entry/what-its-like-to-break-up-with-your-narcissistic-parent_n_5a1f1d16e4b037b8ea1f3f0f.

Page 39   **According to the Hofstede cultural dimensions model:** Hofstede Cultural Dimensions National Culture (n.d.). Retrieved from https://www.hofstede-insights.com/models/national-culture/.

Page 39   **Why are so many young adults claiming:** A recent Google search found 7,050,000 pages with the entry "narcissistic parent" and 11,200,000 for "borderline personality parent."

Page 39   **parents are more worried:** Marianne Cooper, *Cut Adrift* (Berkeley: University of California Press, 2014); Matthias Doepke and Fabrizio Zilibotti, *Love, Money & Parenting: How Economics Explains the Way We Raise Our Kids* (Princeton: Princeton University Press, 2019).

Page 39   **In addition, many ways that technology:** Catherine Saint Louis, "In the Facebook Era, Reminders of Loss After Families Fracture," *New York Times*, June 14, 2012, https://www.nytimes.com/2012/06/15/us/facebook-complicates-family-estrangements.html; S. R. Cotten, B. M. McCullough, and R. G. Adams, "Technological Influences on Social Ties Across the Life Span," in ed. K. L. Fingerman et al.,

Handbook of Life-Span Development (New York: Springer Publishers, 2012), 647–72.

Page 40   **today's parents are more likely to be *highly* involved:** Madeline Levine, *Ready or Not: Preparing Our Kids to Thrive in an Uncertain and Rapidly Changing World* (New York: Harper, 2020); Karen L. Fingerman, PhD, "Millennials and Their Parents: Implications of the New Young Adulthood for Midlife Adults," *Innovation in Aging*, 1, no. 3 (2017): igx026, https://doi.org/10.1093 /geroni/igx026; C. J. Bowan, "Holding Them Closer," *The Hedgehog Review: Critical Reflections on Contemporary Culture* 15, no. 3 (2013): 8–23; Jeffrey Arnett and Joseph Schwab, "The Clark University Poll of Emerging Adults: Thriving, Struggling, and Hopeful," 2012, http://www2.clarku.edu /clark-poll-emerging-adults/pdfs /clark-university-poll-emerging-adultsfindings.pdf.

Page 40   **Sociologist Paul Amato found:** Paul R. Amato, *Alone Together: How Marriage in America Is Changing* (Cambridge: Harvard University Press, 2009).

Page 40   **Sociologist Robert Putnam made a similar observation:** Robert D. Putnam, *Bowling Alone: The Collapse and Revival of American Community* (New York: Simon & Schuster, 2020).

Page 40   **"Childhood has become the last bastion of kindness":** Adam Phillips and Barbara Taylor, *On Kindness* (London: Picador, 2010).

Page 42   **a large international study of nearly 2,700 parents over the age of sixty-five:** Merril Silverstein et al., "Older Parent-Child Relationships in Six Developed Nations: Comparisons at the Intersection of Affection and Conflict," *Journal of Marriage and Family* 72, no. 4 (2010): 1006–21.

Page 42   **Sociologist Amy Schalet observed:** Amy Schalet, *Not Under My Roof: Parents, Teens, and the Culture of Sex* (Chicago: University of Chicago Press, 2011).

Page 43   **In earlier generations, a parent's job, however affectionate:** Steven Mintz, *Huck's Raft: A History of American Childhood* (Cambridge, Mass.: Belknap, 2006); Paula S. Fass, *The End of American Childhood: A History of Parenting from Life on the Frontier to the Managed Child* (Princeton: Princeton University Press, 2017).

Page 43   ***Habits of the Heart:*** Robert N. Bellah, *Habits of the Heart: Individualism and Commitment in American Life,* with a New Preface (Berkeley: University of California Press, 2008).

Page 43   **British sociologist Anthony Giddens:** Anthony Giddens,

Modernity and Self-Identity: Self and Society in the Late Modern Age (Cambridge, U.K.: Polity Press, 2010).

Page 44   **Social psychologist Eli Finkel's observation:** Finkel, *The All-or-Nothing Marriage.*

Page 44   **sociologist Annette Lareau:** Annette Lareau, *Unequal Childhoods: Class, Race, and Family Life,* with an update a decade later (Berkeley: University of California Press, 2011).

Page 45   **However, recent research by sociologist Jennifer Silva:** Silva, *Coming Up Short.*

CHAPTER 3: MARRIED, DIVORCED, ESTRANGED

Page 47   **her constant complaints about him, as well as her portrayal of being victimized by him:** E. Mavis Hetherington and John Kelly, *For Better or for Worse: Divorce Reconsidered* (New York: W. W. Norton, 2003); Wednesday Martin, *Stepmonster: A New Look at Why Real Stepmothers Think, Feel, and Act the Way We Do* (Boston: Houghton Mifflin Harcourt, 2009); William Bernet, Amy J. L. Baker, and M. C. Verrocchio, "Symptom Checklist-90-Revised Scores in Adult Children Exposed to Alienating Behaviors: An Italian Sample," *Journal of Forensic Sciences* 60 (2015): 357–62, http://dx.doi .org/10.1111/1556-4029.12681; Sanford L. Braver, Diana Coatsworth, and Kelly Peralta (n.d.), "Alienating Behavior Within Divorced and Intact Families: Matched Parents; and Now–Young Adult Children's Reports," retrieved from https://archive.uea.ac.uk/swp /iccd2006/Presentations/tues_pm/ps12%20High%20conflict%20 &%20Enforcement/Braver%20summary.

Page 52   **It's not uncommon for new wives to have strong opinions:** Based on her thirty-year Virginia Longitudinal Study of life postdivorce, Hetherington concludes that stepmothers are frequently singled out for very bad treatment indeed by stepchildren, who pick up on their mother's anger and resentment and become her proxy in their father's household. Hetherington and Kelly, *For Better or for Worse;* Martin, *Stepmonster.* However, researcher Marilyn Coleman told me in an email: "If stepdaughters live with their stepmothers, there are more chances to build a close relationship. In addition, if the stepmother attempts affinity building with the stepdaughter, it only works if the stepdaughter realizes the stepmother is trying to develop a relationship with her in doing activities that she wants to do."

Page 52   **For most, their wives are their best friends, if not their only friend:** Keith E. Edwards and Susan R. Jones, "'Putting My Man Face On': A Grounded Theory of College Men's Gender Identity Development," *Journal of College Student Development* 50, no. 2 (2009): 210–28, doi:10.1353/csd.0.0063; Michael E. Addis and James R. Mahalik, "Men, Masculinity, and the Contexts of Help Seeking," *American Psychologist* 58, no. 1 (2003): 5–14; Raven Saunt, "One in Five Men Have No Friends as Loneliness Epidemic Leaves Thousands Living in Isolation," Daily Mail Online, Associated Newspapers, September 21, 2019, https://www.dailymail.co.uk/news/article-7488709/One-five-men-no-friends-loneliness-epidemic-leaves-thousands-living-isolation.html; Melanie Hamlett, "Men Have No Friends and Women Bear the Burden," *Harper's Bazaar*, May 2, 2019, https://www.harpersbazaar.com/culture/features/a27259689/toxic-masculinity-male-friendships-emotional-labor-men-rely-on-women/.

Page 52   **In addition, many men come into marriage:** Michael S. Kimmel, *Guyland: The Perilous World Where Boys Become Men* (New York: Harper Perennial, 2018); C. J. Pascoe, *Dude, You're a Fag: Masculinity and Sexuality in High School* (Berkeley: University of California Press, 2012). In Tey Meadow's book *Trans Kids: Being Gendered in the Twenty-First Century* (Oakland: University of California Press, 2018), she observes the following: "Feminine boys face much harsher scrutiny than their masculine female peers. Indeed the category 'male' reveals itself to be more fragile than 'female' does; while masculine girls needed to assert fully a male identity, invoking a categorical shift for their femaleness to be in question, maleness, as a social category, was brittle, called into question by smaller infractions that were not, in and of themselves, declarative. While ample evidence exists in and beyond the sociological canon for the stricter assessment of masculinity, this demonstrates that the category male itself is paradoxically both accorded high value and highly fragile," p. 51.

Page 52   **This inability to navigate their emotional worlds:** Peggy Orenstein, "The Miseducation of the American Boy," *The Atlantic*, December 20, 2019, https://www.theatlantic.com/magazine/archive/2020/01/the-miseducation-of-the-american-boy/603046/.

Page 52   **parents, even today, use less emotion language with boys:**

Kristina Dell, "Mothers Talk Differently to Daughters than Sons: Study," *Time*, November 13, 2014, https://time.com/3581587 /mothers-emotion-words-girls-boys-surrey-studymothers-encourage -emotions-more-in-daughters-over-sons-study-says/; Ana Aznar and Harriet R. Tenenbaum, "Gender and Age Differences in Parent-Child Emotion Talk," *British Journal of Developmental Psychology* 33, no. 1 (December 2014): 148–55, doi:10.1111/bjdp.12069.

Page 52   **The fragile nature of male identity:** Kimmel, *Guyland*; Pascoe, *Dude, You're a Fag.*

Page 53   **Finally, many courts weaken the attachment between fathers and their children:** Jennifer J. Harman, Edward Kruk, and Denise A. Hines, "Parental Alienating Behaviors: An Unacknowledged Form of Family Violence," *Psychological Bulletin*, 144, no. 12 (2018): 127-99, doi:10.1037/bul0000175; Luiza Lopes Franco Costa et al., "Gender Stereotypes Underlie Child Custody Decisions," *European Journal of Social Psychology* 49, no. 3 (2019): 548–59, https://doi.org /10.1002/ejsp.2523.

Page 53   **On the other hand, being a stepmother is no small task:** Hetherington and Kelly, *For Better or for Worse.*

Page 53   **Studies show that the mother-daughter dyad:** Kira S. Birditt, Laura M. Miller, Karen L. Fingerman, and Eva S. Lefkowitz, "Tensions in the Parent and Adult Child Relationship: Links to Solidarity and Ambivalence," *Psychology and Aging* 24, no. 2 (2009): 287–95, doi:10.1037/a0015196; V. L. Bengtson and J. A. Kuypers, "Generational Differences and the Developmental Stake," *Aging and Human Development* 2, no. 4 (1971): 249–60 [Google Scholar].

Page 53   **This matrilineal advantage:** Karen L. Fingerman, "The Role of Offspring and In-Laws in Grandparents' Ties to Their Grandchildren," *Journal of Family Issues* 25, no. 8 (2004): 1026–49, doi:10.1177/0192513x04265941.

Page 54   **Gray divorce:** H. Wu, "Age Variation in the Divorce Rate, 1990 & 2015," National Center for Family & Marriage Research, Bowling Green State University, 2017, doi:10.25035/ncfmr/fp-17-20.

Page 57   **Most adult children don't choose estrangement lightly:** Kristina M. Scharp, Lindsey J. Thomas, and Christina G. Paxman, "'It Was the Straw That Broke the Camel's Back': Exploring the Distancing Processes Communicatively Constructed in Parent-Child Estrangement Backstories," *Journal of Family Communication* 15, no. 4 (2015): 330–48; Kylie Agllias, "No Longer on Speaking

Terms: The Losses Associated with Family Estrangement at the End of Life," *Families in Society* 92, no. 1 (2011): 107–13, http://doi.org /10.1606/1044-3894.4055.

Page 59   **People rarely know how powerful sorrow:** Karen L. Fingerman et al., "Ambivalent Reactions in the Parent and Offspring Relationship," *The Journals of Gerontology Series B: Psychological Sciences and Social Sciences* 61, no. 3 (2006), doi:10.1093/geronb/61.3.p152.

Page 59   **As journalist Ruth Whippman observed:** Ruth Whippman, "The Power of the 'Little Comment' in Mother-Daughter Relationships," *New York Times*, December 20, 2018, https://www.nytimes .com/2018/12/20/well/family/the-power-of-the-little-comment-in -mother-daughter-relationships.html.

Page 68   **For her, the affair was a stopgap measure:** Esther Perel, *The State of Affairs: Rethinking Infidelity* (London: Yellow Kite, 2019).

Page 69   **courts often defer to the desire of younger teens:** https://www .divorcewriter.com/child-preference-in-custody.

Page 70   **Developmental psychologist Amy Baker:** Amy Baker, "Parental Alienation: A Special Case of Parental Rejection," *Parental Acceptance* 4, no. 3 (2010): 4–5; Amy Baker and N. Ben Ami, "Adult Recall of Childhood Psychological Maltreatment in Adult Children of Divorce: Prevalence and Associations with Outcomes," *Journal of Divorce and Remarriage* 52, no. 4 (2011): 203–19.

Page 70   **Treatment for parental alienation is often difficult to obtain:** Demosthenes Lorandos and J. Michael Bone, "Child Custody Evaluations: In Cases Where Parental Alienation Is Alleged," *Handbook of Child Custody* (2015): 179–232, doi:10.1007/978-3-319-13942-5_16.

Page 71   **would have also encouraged her lawyer to ask the court for reunification therapy:** Kathleen M. Reay, "Family Reflections: A Promising Therapeutic Program Designed to Treat Severely Alienated Children and Their Family System," *The American Journal of Family Therapy* 43, no. 2 (2015): 197–207, doi:10.1080/01926187.2015 .1007769.

Page 72   **studies show that Native American and African American parents are far more at risk:** Christopher Wildeman, Frank R. Edwards, and Sara Wakefield, "The Cumulative Prevalence of Termination of Parental Rights for U.S. Children, 2000–2016," *Child Maltreatment*, doi:10.1177/1077559519848499.

Page 72   **According to attorney Brian Ludmer, coauthor of *The High-Conflict Custody Battle*:** Amy J. L. Baker, J. Michael Bone, and

Brian Ludmer, *The High-Conflict Custody Battle: Protect Yourself and Your Kids from a Toxic Divorce, False Accusations, and Parental Alienation* (Oakland: New Harbinger Publications, Inc., 2014).

Page 74   **In addition, your child isn't aware that their memories are false:** Henry Otgaar, Mark L. Howe, Peter Muris, and Harald Merckelbach, "Dealing with False Memories in Children and Adults: Recommendations for the Legal Arena," *Policy Insights from the Behavioral and Brain Sciences* 6, no. 1(2019):, 87–93, doi:10.1177/2372732218818584.

CHAPTER 4: DEALING WITH MENTAL ILLNESS AND ADDICTION

Page 78   **In the past few decades there has been a significant increase in mental illness:** R. P. Auerbach et al., "World Health Organization World Mental Health Surveys International College Student Project (WMH-ICS): Prevalence and Distribution of Mental Disorders," *Journal of the American Academy of Child & Adolescent Psychiatry* 57, no. 10 (2018), doi:10.1016/j.jaac.2018.07.723; Rebecca Bitsko et al., "Epidemiology and Impact of Health Care Provider–Diagnosed Anxiety and Depression Among US Children," *Journal of Developmental & Behavioral Pediatrics* 39, no. 5 (2018): 395–403, doi:10.1097/dbp.0000000000000571.

Page 82   **While the US ranks next to last in social mobility:** Richard Wike, "Five Ways Americans and Europeans Are Different," Pew Research Center, April 19, 2016; Elise Gould, "U.S. Lags Behind Peer Countries in Mobility," October 10, 2012, retrieved from https://www.epi.org/publication/usa-lags-peer-countries-mobility/.

Page 82   **Psychologist Martin Seligman:** Martin Seligman, *Learned Optimism, How to Change Your Mind and Your Life* (New York: Vintage Press, 2014).

Page 82   **As historian Stephanie Coontz notes:** Molly Langmuir, "The Rise of the Mom-Shaming Resistance," *Elle*, October 24, 2019, retrieved from https://www.elle.com/culture/a26826429/mom-shaming-resistance/.

Page 83   **As sociologist Matthew Desmond wrote in *Evicted*:** Matthew Desmond, *Evicted: Poverty and Profit in the American City* (New York: Crown/Archetype, 2016). See also Richard Rothstein, *The Color of Law: A Forgotten History of How Our Government Segre-*

gated America (New York: Liveright Publishing Corporation, a Division of W. W. Norton & Company, 2018); and Dale Russakoff, *The Prize: Who's in Charge of America's Schools?* (New York: Mariner Books, 2016).

Page 83   **This lack of social capital puts enormous strain on working-class and poverty-stricken parents:** Robert D. Putnam, *Our Kids: The American Dream in Crisis* (New York: Simon & Schuster Paperbacks, 2016).

Page 83   **Since the radical defunding of mental health services and legal aid to the poor during the Reagan administration:** D. Pan, "Timeline: Deinstitutionalization and Its Consequences: How Deinstitutionalization Moved Thousands of Mentally Ill People Out of Hospitals—and into Jails and Prisons," *Mother Jones,* April 29, 2013, retrieved from http://www.motherjones.com/politics/2013/04/timeline-mental-health-america; Joel John Roberts, "Did Reagan's Crazy Mental Health Policies Cause Today's Homelessness?" Poverty Insights, October 14, 2013, retrieved from http://www.povertyinsights.org/2013/10/14/did-reagans-crazy-mental-health-policies-cause-todays-homelessness/.

Page 86   **"Everybody talks about the weather . . .":** Attributed to Mark Twain, though it doesn't appear in anything he wrote or in any of his recorded speeches. It's also credited to Twain's friend, Charles Dudley Warner, and there is a published source for that attribution but the provenance of that quote is also debated.

Page 87   **According to geneticist Robert Plomin:** Robert Plomin, *Blueprint: How DNA Makes Us Who We Are* (Cambridge: MIT Press, 2019).

Page 87   **Even traits such as lack of empathy and disregard for others, known as callous-unemotional traits:** Plomin, ibid.

Page 92   **Research by Paul Costa and Robert McCrae:** Mark D. Kelland, "Paul Costa and Robert McCrae and the Five-Factor Model of Personality," retrieved from https://socialsci.libretexts.org/Bookshelves/Psychology/Book:_Personality_Theory_in_a_Cultural_Context.

CHAPTER 5: PSYCHOTHERAPY AND THE CURATED CHILDHOOD: "MY THERAPIST SAYS YOU'RE A NARCISSIST"

Page 96   **If you were a therapist in the 1950s:** Stephanie Coontz, *A Strange Stirring: The Feminine Mystique and American Women at the Dawn of the 1960s* (New York: Basic Books, 2012).

Page 96   **This example is just one in a long history where psychotherapy:** Anne Harrington, *Mind Fixers: Psychiatry's Troubled Search for the Biology of Mental Illness* (New York: W. W. Norton, 2020); Gary Greenberg, *The Book of Woe: The DSM and the Unmaking of Psychiatry* (New York: Plume, published by the Penguin Group, 2014); Ethan Watters, *Crazy Like Us: The Globalization of the American Psyche* (New York: Free Press, 2011).

Page 96   **In 1850, Dr. Samuel Cartwright reported in *The New Orleans Medical and Surgical Journal*:** Cited in Greenberg, *Book of Woe*.

Page 97   **While the family was once where individuals:** Eva Illouz, *Cold Intimacies: The Making of Emotional Capitalism* (Cambridge: Polity, 2017), p. 156.

Page 100   **"This is what it feels like to be young now":** Michael Hobbes, "Generation Screwed," *Huffington Post*, December 14, 2017, retrieved from https://highline.huffingtonpost.com/articles/en/poor-millennials.

Page 100   **As historian Steven Mintz told me:** email correspondence, December 2018.

Page 102   **Communications professor Kristina Scharp:** Kristina M. Scharp, Lindsey J. Thomas, and Christina G. Paxman, "'It Was the Straw That Broke the Camel's Back': Exploring the Distancing Processes Communicatively Constructed in Parent-Child Estrangement Backstories," *Journal of Family Communication* 15, no. 4 (2015): 330–48.

Page 102   **British journalist and researcher Becca Bland:** personal communication, January 3, 2020. See also Becca Bland, "I Am Estranged from My Family," https://www.theguardian.com/lifeandstyle/2012/dec/15/becca-bland-estranged-parents.

Page 105   **being raised by a depressed parent:** Bizu Gelaye et al., "Epidemiology of Maternal Depression, Risk Factors, and Child Outcomes in Low-Income and Middle-Income Countries," *The Lancet Psychi-*

atry 3, no. 10 (2016): 973–82, doi:10.1016/s2215-0366(16)30284-x; Elena Netsi et al., "Association of Persistent and Severe Postnatal Depression with Child Outcomes." *JAMA Psychiatry* 75, no. 3 (January 2018): 247, doi:10.1001/jamapsychiatry.2017.4363.

Page 105   **though there's other research that shows that the strengths learned from that role can also be a positive:** Paula S. Fass, *The End of American Childhood: A History of Parenting from Life on the Frontier to the Managed Child* (Princeton: Princeton University Press, 2017).

Page 105   **Studies show:** Sam Harris, *Free Will* (New York: Free Press, 2012).

Page 106   **Depressed mothers can be more needy, anxious, and sometimes disparaging:** Leslie J. Sim, *Depression in Parents, Parenting, and Children: Opportunities to Improve Identification, Treatment, and Prevention* (Washington, D.C.: National Academies Press, 2009).

Page 107   **Carl Jung wrote:** Claire Dunne, *Carl Jung: Wounded Healer of the Soul* (Watkins Media, 2015).

Page 107   **Andrew Solomon, *Far from the Tree*:** *Far from the Tree: Parents, Children and the Search for Identity* (New York: Scribner, 2013).

CHAPTER 6: FLASHPOINTS: GENDER IDENTITY, SEXUALITY, RELIGION, POLITICS, AND PERSONALITY CLASHES

Page 112   **From this perspective, announcing their desire to transition:** Diane Ehrensaft and Norman Spack, *The Gender Creative Child: Pathways for Nurturing and Supporting Children Who Live Outside Gender Boxes* (The Experiment New York, 2017); Tey Meadow, *Trans Kids: Being Gendered in the Twenty-First Century* (Oakland: University of California Press, 2018).

Page 112   **On the other hand, parents who haven't seen signs of gender dysphoria:** Ehrensaft and Spack, ibid. Ehrensaft notes that children who later transition were often consistent, persistent, and insistent in their identity of not being their assigned gender.

Page 116   **Accepting the adult child's viewpoint:** Joshua Coleman, "'Radical Acceptance' After Wrongful Accusations," *Psychology Today*, https://www.psychologytoday.com/us/blog/the-rules-estrangement/201911/radical-acceptance-after-wrongful-accusations.

Page 117   **As Columbia sociologist Tey Meadow notes:** Meadow, *Trans Kids*.

Page 118   **Consider, for example, that the dating app Tinder lists thirty-seven custom gender options:** Ibid.

Page 118   **As psychologist Diane Ehrensaft writes:** Ehrensaft and Spack, *The Gender Creative Child*.

Page 120   **Researchers Becca Bland and Lucy Blake found that "clash of personality or values":** Lucy Blake and Becca Bland, University of Cambridge Centre for Family Research and Stand Alone, December 2015.

Page 120   **Megan Gilligan, Jill Suitor, and Karl Pillemer found that:** Megan Gilligan, J. Jill Suitor, and Karl Pillemer, "Estrangement Between Mothers and Adult Children: The Role of Norms and Values," *Journal of Marriage and Family* 77, no. 4 (2015): 908–20, doi:10.1111/jomf.12207.

Page 121   **many people who feel rejected by their parents over sexuality or gender identity are much more at risk for depression:** "Many Parents Struggle for Years to Adjust After Learning a Child's Sexual Orientation." *ScienceDaily*, June 18, 2019, https://www.sciencedaily.com/releases/2019/06/190618224055.htm.

Page 123   **Christopher Ojeda and Peter Hatemi found:** Christopher Ojeda and Peter K. Hatemi, "Accounting for the Child in the Transmission of Party Identification," *American Sociological Review* 80, no. 6 (2015): 1150–74.

Page 124   **Marital researcher John Gottman:** John Mordechai Gottman and Nan Silver, *The Seven Principles for Making Marriage Work: A Practical Guide from the Country's Foremost Relationship Expert* (New York: Harmony Books, 2015).

Page 125   **Mary Catherine Bateson wrote that marriage requires a constant rhythm:** Mary Catherine Bateson, *Composing a Life* (New York: Grove Press, 2010).

CHAPTER 7: SONS-IN-LAWS, DAUGHTERS-IN-LAW, AND THE CULT OF ONE

Page 126   ***My Brilliant Friend:*** Elena Ferrante, trans. by Ann Goldstein, *My Brilliant Friend* (Melbourne: The Text Publishing Company, 2018).

Page 130   **to act like a powerful cult leader, enforcing absolute obedience:**

E. A. Bates, "'Walking on egg shells': A Qualitative Examination of Men's Experiences of Intimate Partner Violence," *Psychology of Men & Masculinities* 21, no. 1 (2020): 13–24, https://doi.org/10.1037/men0000203.

Page 131   **It's interesting how similar these characteristics:** Glenn Collins, "The Psychology of the Cult Experience," *New York Times*, March 15, 1982, https://www.nytimes.com/1982/03/15/style/the-psychology-of-the-cult-experience.html.

Page 132   **As Stanford researcher Philip Zimbardo wrote:** Philip Zimbardo, *The Lucifer Effect: Understanding How Good People Turn Evil* (New York: Random House, 2013).

Page 135   **Leon Festinger:** Leon Festinger, *A Theory of Cognitive Dissonance* (New York: Row, Peterson, 1957).

Page 140   **According to family historian Rebecca Jo Plant:** Rebecca Jo Plant, *Mom: The Transformation of Motherhood in Modern America* (Chicago: University of Chicago Press, 2012).

Page 140   **Historian Stephanie Coontz writes that, by the 1920s:** Stephanie Coontz, *Marriage, A History: How Love Conquered Marriage* (New York: Penguin, 2006).

Page 141   **Women, in contrast, often have the role of being *kinkeepers*:** Dawn O. Braithwaite, Jaclyn S. Marsh, Carol L. Tschampl-Diesing, and Margaret S. Leach, "'Love Needs to Be Exchanged': A Diary Study of Interaction and Enactment of the Family Kinkeeper Role," *Western Journal of Communication* 81, no. 5 (2017): 1–19.

Page 143   **French branch of psychoanalysis referred to:** Jean Laplanche and Jean-Bertrand Pontalis, *Language of Psychoanalysis* (Philadelphia: Routledge, 2019).

Page 144   **a poem by Melanie Gause Harris:** "The Art of Losing My Daughter," unpublished.

CHAPTER 8: WHEN SIBLINGS ESTRANGE: THE IMPACT ON THEIR LIVES AND THOSE AROUND THEM

Page 150   **Studies show that differential treatment:** Karl Pillemer et al., "Mothers' Differentiation and Depressive Symptoms Among Adult Children," *Journal of Marriage and Family* 72, no. 2; Jennifer S. Williams et al., "A Typology of Childhood Sibling Subsystems That May Emerge in Abusive Family Systems," *The Family Journal* 24, no. 4 (2016): 378–84, doi:10.1177/1066480716663182.

Page 150   **And yet sibling relationships are not influenced by parents as much as we believe:** Alison Gopnik, *The Gardener and the Carpenter* (New York: Picador, 2017); Robert Plomin, *Blueprint: How DNA Makes Us Who We Are* (Cambridge: MIT Press, 2019).

Page 150   **today's parents have less influence:** Claire Cain Miller, "Stressed, Tired, Rushed: A Portrait of the Modern Family," *New York Times*, November 4, 2015, https://www.nytimes.com/2015/11/05/upshot /stressed-tired-rushed-a-portrait-of-the-modern-family.html.

Page 151   **As family historian Steven Mintz notes:** personal communication, 2017.

Page 151   **In the early national period, Euro-American siblings:** C. Dallett Hemphill, *Siblings: Brothers and Sisters in American History* (New York: Oxford University Press, 2014).

Page 151   **Historian Peter Stearns observed:** Peter N. Stearns, "The Rise of Sibling Jealousy in the Twentieth Century," *Symbolic Interaction* 13, no. 1 (1990): 83–101, doi:10.1525/si.1990.13.1.83.

Page 152   **Research on couples shows:** John Mordechai Gottman and Nan Silver, *The Seven Principles for Making Marriage Work: A Practical Guide from the Country's Foremost Relationship Expert* (New York: Harmony Books, 2015).

Page 152   **Developmental psychologist Lucy Blake observed:** Lucy Blake, B. Bland, A. Rouncefield-Swales, 2020, Estrangement Between Siblings in Adulthood. Submitted manuscript undergoing peer review.

CHAPTER 9: THE RULES OF MONEY AND ESTRANGEMENT: SHOULD I CUT MY CHILD OUT OF MY WILL?

Page 167   **what psychologist Terry Real refers to as offending:** Terry Real, "The Awful Truth: Most Men Are Just Not Raised to Be Intimate," https://www.terryreal.com/the-awful-truth-most-men-are-just-not -raised-to-be-intimate/.

Page 172   **I have heard plenty of stories in my office:** See, for example, Catherine Pearson, "What It's Like to Grieve a Parent You Didn't Like," *HuffPost*, August 5, 2019, https://www.huffpost.com/entry/hat-like -grieve-parent-you-didnt-like_l_5d484b13e4b0aca34121b147.

Page 176   **But that's different from thinking that they're able to become anybody other than who they already are:** For a good discussion about the illusions of free will, see Robert M. Sapolsky, *Behave: The Biology of Humans at Our Best and Worst* (New York: Vintage, 2018); Sam Harris, "Free Will." https://samharris.org/books/free-will/.

Page 177   **Psychologist Mike Riera advises:** Michael Riera, *Uncommon Sense for Parents with Teenagers* (New York: Ten Speed Press, 2012).

Page 178   **According to Peter Myers:** personal communication, October 19, 2019.

CHAPTER 10: ABANDONED GRANDPARENTS AND THE WEAPONIZING OF GRANDCHILDREN

Page 187   **For most estranged grandparents, not knowing:** Margaret Sims and Maged Rofail, "The Experiences of Grandparents Who Have Limited or No Contact with Their Grandchildren," *Journal of Aging Studies* 27, no. 4 (2013): 377–86, doi:10.1016/j.jaging.2013.09.002.

Page 190   **This is probably why arranged marriages:** Paul Bentley, "Why an Arranged Marriage Is 'More Likely to Develop into Lasting Love,'" *Daily Mail*, March 4, 2011.

Page 190   **In contemporary marriage:** Stephanie Coontz, *Marriage, A History: How Love Conquered Marriage* (New York: Penguin, 2006); Eli Finkel, *The All-or-Nothing Marriage: How the Best Marriages Work* (New York: Dutton, 2017).

Page 190   **when couples marry and become parents:** Carolyn Pape Cowan and Philip A. Cowan, *When Partners Become Parents: The Big Life Change for Couples* (New York: Basic Books, 2000).

Page 190   **wives have much clearer ideas:** Michael E. Lamb, *The Father's Role: Cross-Cultural Perspectives* (Philadelphia: Routledge, 2017).

Page 190   **Wives are also more likely to import:** Karen L. Fingerman, "The Role of Offspring and In-Laws in Grandparents' Ties to Their Grandchildren," *Journal of Family Issues* 25, no. 8 (2004): 1026–49, doi:10.1177/0192513x04265941.

Page 191   **"The side that knows when to fight":** Sun Tzu, *The Art of War* (London: Luzacs and Co., 1910).

Page 192   **working mothers today:** Oriel Sullivan and Scott Coltrane, "Men's Changing Contribution to Housework and Childcare," 2008, https://contemporaryfamilies.org/mens-changing-contribution-to-housework-and-childcare-brief-report/.

Page 192   **They create that extra time by giving up time for sleep:** Suzanne
Bianchi and Melissa Milkie, "Work and Family Research in the
First Decade of the 21st Century," *Journal of Marriage and Family*
72, no. 3 (2010): 705–25.

Page 194   ***The Country of "Giant Babies":*** Wu Zhihong, *The Country of
"Giant Babies": A Domestic Psychologist Examining the Chinese
National Character* (Chinese edition) (Beijing People's Publishing
House, 2016).

Page 195   **Amy Chua's controversial book, *Battle Hymn of the Tiger
Mother*:** Amy Chua, *Battle Hymn of the Tiger Mother* (London:
Bloomsbury Publishing, 2014).

Page 195   **In "The Last of the Tiger Parents":** Ryan Park, "The Last of the
Tiger Parents," *New York Times*, June 22, 2018, https://www.nytimes
.com/2018/06/22/opinion/sunday/asian-american-tiger-parents.html.
See also K. Kim et al., "Relationships Between Adults and Parents
in Asia," in ed. S. T. Cheng et al., *Successful Aging: Asian Perspectives* (New York: Springer, 2015), 101–23.

Page 195   **"Tiger mom has become a shorthand to describe parents, usually Asian, with rigorous discipline":** Michelle Kuo, *Reading with
Patrick: A Teacher, a Student, and a Life-Changing Friendship* (New
York: Random House, 2018).

Page 196   **"How to Disobey . . .":** Michelle Kuo, "How to Disobey Your Tiger
Parents, in 14 Easy Steps," *New York Times*, April 14, 2018, https://
www.nytimes.com/2018/04/14/opinion/sunday/disobey-your-tiger
-parents.html.

Page 196   **writes historian Paula Fass in *The End of American Childhood*:**
Paula S. Fass, *The End of American Childhood: A History of Parenting
from Life on the Frontier to the Managed Child* (Princeton: Princeton
University Press, 2017).

Page 197   **studies show that the relationship between grandparents and
grandchildren:** Aalyia F. A. Sadruddin et al., "How Do Grandparents Influence Child Health and Development? A Systematic
Review," *Social Science & Medicine* 239 (2019): 112476, doi:10.1016/j
.socscimed.2019.112476.

Page 205   **Pat Hanson, author of *Invisible Grandparenting*:** Pat Hanson, *Invisible Grandparenting: Leave a Legacy of Love Whether You Can Be
There or Not* (Pacific Grove, Calif: Park Place Publications, 2015).

Page 207   **I spoke with James Karl:** phone conversation, September 2019.

CHAPTER 11: COPING STRATEGIES, INTERVENTIONS, AND YOUR NEW NORMAL

Page 220   **We need community because:** Jonathan Rauch, *The Happiness Curve: Why Life Gets Better After 50* (London: Picador, 2019).

Page 222   **Psychological trauma has the potential to negatively impact your romantic relationship:** Benjamin R. Karney, "Keeping Marriages Healthy, and Why It's So Difficult." PsycEXTRA Dataset, 2010, doi:10.1037/e554752011-002.

Page 222   **Studies show that almost any stress outside of a couple:** Justin A. Lavner and Thomas N. Bradbury, "Protecting Relationships from Stress," *Current Opinion in Psychology* 13 (2017): 11–14, doi:10.1016/j .copsyc.2016.03.003.

Page 222   **There's also an idea, especially in our soulmate culture:** Joshua Coleman, *The Marriage Makeover: Finding Happiness in Imperfect Harmony* (New York: St. Martin's Press, 2000); Joshua Coleman, "Americans Put Too Much Weight in Romantic Love" in https:// www.nytimes.com/roomfordebate/2016/01/25/hillary-clinton -deals-with-her-husbands-transgressions/americans-put-too-much -weight-in-romantic-love.

Page 224   **Avoid what marital researcher John Gottman refers to:** John Mordechai Gottman and Nan Silver, *The Seven Principles for Making Marriage Work: A Practical Guide from the Country's Foremost Relationship Expert* (New York: Harmony Books, 2015).

CHAPTER 12: THE ADULT CHILD'S PERSPECTIVE: NEW RULES FOR PARENT–ADULT CHILD RECONCILIATION

Page 235   **"[m]illennials are less well off":** Derek Thompson, "Millennials Didn't Kill the Economy. The Economy Killed Millennials," *The Atlantic,* retrieved at Quartz, https://qz.com/co/1288601/millennials -didnt-kill-the-economy-the-economy-killed-millennials/.

Page 235   **the lowest level recorded by the General Social Survey:** W. Bradford Wilcox and Lyman Stone, "The Happiness Recession," *The Atlantic,* April 8, 2019, https://www.theatlantic.com/ideas/archive/2019/04 /happiness-recession-causing-sex-depression/586405/.

Page 235   **skyrocketing rates of mental illness:** Tara Bahrampour, "Mental

Health Problems Rise Significantly Among Young Americans," *Washington Post*, March 16, 2019, https://www.washingtonpost .com/local/social-issues/mental-health-problems-rise-significantly -among-young-americans/2019/03/14/5d4fffe8-460c-11e9-90f0 -0ccfeec87a61_story.html.

Page 238   **It used to be that parents had a right to make demands and to say, "You haven't called":** Paula S. Fass, *The End of American Child- hood: A History of Parenting from Life on the Frontier to the Managed Child* (Princeton: Princeton University Press, 2017).

Page 238   **A recent example from my practice illustrates:** Joshua Coleman, "The Changing Landscape of Parent–Adult Child Relations" in Michelle Yvonne Janning, *Contemporary Parenting and Parenthood: From News Headlines to New Research* (Westport: Praeger, 2019).

CHAPTER 13: HOW DO I HEAL THE PAIN OF ESTRANGEMENT?

Page 249   **"The path out of hell is through misery":** Marsha Linehan, *DBT Skills Training Manual* (New York: Guilford, 2017).

Page 250   **Psychotherapist Megan Devine tragically watched her partner:** Megan Devine, *It's OK That You're Not OK: Meeting Grief and Loss in a Culture That Doesn't Understand* (Boulder, Colorado: Sounds True, 2017).

Page 250   **Psychiatrist Mark Levine, who developed the Mind to Mindful program:** personal communication, November 2019.

Page 252   **Psychology professor, and author of *How Emotions Are Made*, Lisa Feldman Barrett:** Lisa Feldman Barrett, *How Emotions Are Made: The New Science of the Mind and Brain* (Boston: Houghton Mifflin Harcourt, 2016).

Page 254   **In addition, men's tendency to cover our depression with anger:** Terrence Real, *I Don't Want to Talk About It: Overcoming the Secret Legacy of Male Depression* (New York: Scribner, 2003).

Page 261   **Buddhists call this state of mind *upekkha*:** In Devine, *It's OK That You're Not OK.*

Page 262   **small crack in the continuum of catastrophe:** Richard Wolin and Walter Benjamin, *An Aesthetic of Redemption* (Berkeley: University of California Press, 1994).

AFTERWORD

Page 263   **The truest form:** Jonathan Rauch, *The Happiness Curve: Why Life Gets Better After 50* (London: Picador, 2019).

Page 263   **My parents belonged to the last generation of unworried middle-class parents:** Historian Stephanie Coontz wrote the following email to me about this era: "Right up through the 1920s the majority of Americans had a lot of worries: little discretionary income, high accident rates for workers and for children, then the Depression and WWII. Parents of the 1950s and 60s were uniquely confident about their future. They were living much better than their parents and grandparents. They had far fewer immediate worries about their kid being safe or not having enough to eat. And they were not yet obsessive about whether they were making all the right choices to do even better by their kids. So, it was a gilded age in between such life-and-death worries and before all the new therapeutic ones."

Page 264   **The focus on rights, liberation, and self-expression that animated that era:** Matthias Doepke and Fabrizio Zilibotti, *Love, Money & Parenting: How Economics Explains the Way We Raise Our Kids* (Princeton, NJ: Princeton University Press, 2019).

Page 265   **As a growing body of new research makes clear:** Marianne Cooper, *Cut Adrift* (Berkeley: University of California Press, 2014).

Page 265   **Family historian Stephanie Coontz notes that the collapse of the economic safety net:** Personal communication.

Page 265   **Today's children suffer with higher rates of mental illness:** Jean Twenge., et al. "Age, Period, and Cohort Trends in Mood Disorder Indicators and Suicide-Related Outcomes in a Nationally Representative Dataset, 2005–2017," *Journal of Abnormal Psychology*, 128, no. 3 (2019), 185–99.

Page 265   **The number of poor familes facing eviction:** Between 2007 and 2010, while the average white family experienced an 11 percent reduction in wealth, the average black family lost 31 percent, and the average Hispanic family lost 44 percent. As Harvard sociologist and Pulitzer Prize winner Matthew Desmond observed, "the number of poor families who faced eviction each year was a fraction [during the Depression] of what it is today. During the recession, many working class families were thrown into poverty, and many who were in poverty became homeless." Matthew Desmond, *Evicted: Poverty and Profit in the American City* (New York: Crown/Archetype, 2016).

Page 265   **The average two-parent family:** Cooper, *Cut Adrift*.

Page 265   **Yale political scientist Jacob Hacker:** Jacob S. Hacker, *The Great Risk Shift: The Assault on American Jobs, Families, Health Care and Retirement and How You Can Fight Back* (Oxford: Oxford University Press, 2008).

Page 266   **In spite of having the third-highest GDP per capita:** Matthias Doepke and Fabrizio Zilibotti, *Love, Money & Parenting: How Economics Explains the Way We Raise Our Kids* (Princeton, NJ: Princeton University Press, 2019).

Page 266   **The self-help industry has grown into an almost $10 billion enterprise:** Eva Illouz, *Saving the Modern Soul: Therapy, Emotions, and the Culture of Self-Help* (Berkeley: University of California Press, 2017).

Page 266   **"As a twenty-first-century individual:** Andrew Cherlin, *The Marriage-Go-Round: The State of Marriage and the Family Today* (New York: Vintage, 2010).

Page 267   **The high rates of positive contact:** Karen L. Fingerman and Frank F. Furstenberg, "You Can Go Home Again," *New York Times*, May 30, 2012, https://www.nytimes.com/2012/05/31/opinion/the-parent-trap.html; Karen Fingerman, Kyungmin Kim, Patrick S. Tennant, Kira S. Birditt, and Steven Zarit, "Intergenerational Support in a Daily Context," *Gerontologist* 56, no. 5 (2016): 896–908; Karen Fingerman, Jori Sechrist, and Kira Birditt, "Changing Views on Intergenerational Ties," *Gerontology* 59, no. 1 (2013): 64–70.

Page 268   **"Happiness has turned inward":** Ruth Whippman, *America the Anxious: Why Our Search for Happiness Is Driving Us Crazy and How to Find It for Real* (New York: Griffin, 2017).

Page 268   **Yet numerous studies have found that the more we actively pursue happiness:** Iris B. Mauss et al., "Can Seeking Happiness Make People Unhappy? Paradoxical Effects of Valuing Happiness," *Emotion* 11, no. 4 (2011): 807–15; Iris B. Mauss et al., "The Pursuit of Happiness Can be Lonely," *Emotion* 12, no. 5 (2012): 908–12.

Page 269   **I know that there are studies:** Kristina M. Scharp, "'It Was the Straw That Broke the Camel's Back'": Exploring the Distancing Processes Communicatively Constructed in Parent-Child Estrangement Backstories," *Journal of Family Communication* 15, no. 4 (2015): 330–48.

Page 271   **"We need to recognize that to deny people their complications":** Meghan Daum, *The Problem with Everything: My Journey through the New Culture Wars* (New York: Gallery Books, 2020).

ACKNOWLEDGMENTS

I want to start by thanking my fabulous editor at Harmony, Michele Eniclerico, for seeing the value of a book where theory, research, self-help, and a touch of memoir all meet at one place. I am grateful for her ability to show me how and where to pull back when I most needed it and to allow me to stretch out where I wanted to. Heartfelt thanks also to my agent, Helen Zimmerman, for her ability to quickly shape my massive book proposal into something that publishers would find compelling rather than overwhelming. I appreciated her availability and guidance throughout the process of finding the right home for this book.

My friends and colleagues at the Council on Contemporary Families have been an ongoing source of inspiration and support for the past twenty years. Historian Stephanie Coontz not only read every chapter but provided her famous "ruthless edits" for those places that desperately needed it in the early drafts. She was a careful watchdog to ensure that the historical assumptions I made were grounded in fact, and I can't think of a better person to have had review this. Phil and Carolyn Cowan were helpful in many ways. First by helping me construct my survey, which was completed by 1,621 estranged parents. As important, they individually gave me detailed notes on every chapter. Phil and Carolyn have contributed enormously to the field of psychology and I am forever grateful to have had their help. Frank Furstenberg also generously read through the manuscript and met with me to discuss it. He also helped me to address and correct those places in the book where my clinical opinions were sometimes at odds with the sociology research. Sociologists Paula England, Eva Illouz, Barbara Risman, Jennifer Silva, Judith Stacey, and Amy Schalet provided valuable insight and perspectives by either meeting with me in person or speaking on the phone. Historians Paula Fass, Steven Mintz, and Steven Vincent also generously gave of their time to help me locate the problem of estrangement from a historical perspective. I feel so fortunate to have received their help.

Michelle Kuo gave me unstinting support and critical feedback throughout the manuscript. I am grateful for her ideas and encouragement to put more of my own experience on the page. I am in awe of her writing and am so grateful that she was part of my team.

Profound gratitude to Virginia Roosevelt of the Donner Foundation, who approached me about funding a study on parental estrangement. As a result of their generous grant I was able to create and run my survey, which is currently one of the largest ever done on parental estrangement. Big thanks to Kelly Elver, John Stevenson, and Nathan Jones at the University of Wisconsin Survey Center for helping me with the study. Especially to Nathan who helped me to structure and administer my questionnaire and manage the 1,621 completed surveys. He tirelessly answered and addressed my many, many questions, and I learned a lot from him.

My science book club with Hal Cox, John Ericson, Chris Knudsen, and Bruce Onisko has been going on for fifteen years and is a great source of ongoing support for ideas and discussion. The UC Berkeley Family Book Group, which has been meeting for over thirty years, welcomed me as a member several years ago, and I have benefited from the wealth and diversity of ideas and the scholarship of its members.

I am grateful to Becca Bland for reading through the whole manuscript and providing feedback and friendship. And for partnering with me on our project to increase public awareness about family estrangment. Deep thanks to developmental psychologist Lucy Blake for her overnight feedback about my chapter on siblings as my deadline was looming—I am grateful to have had her input. Also to Liz E. Bates for speaking to me about her research on "intimate terrorism" in romantic relationships. Special thanks to psychologist Diane Ehrensaft for her priceless feedback about my section on gender identity and transitioning. She is a leader in the field, and I am grateful for her clarity and scholarship. Attorneys Brian Ludmer and James Karl provided insights into the legal challenges for parents trying to counter parental alienation, while attorney Peter Myers provided valuable insight into the many complications of estate planning in the context of estrangement. Amanda, who founded Grandparent Alienation Anonymous, has been an ongoing source of inspiration and education for grandparents who are faced with the trauma of being cut off from their grandchildren. Thank you for your tireless advocacy. Deep thanks to Marsha Mayer and Helen Wilson for providing their unique perspectives on estrangement and alienation.

I have learned so much from psychologist Jamie Edmund, whom I mention in my introduction. She has been a consultant to my practice for over twenty years, and we continue to have weekly meetings. Her wisdom and ideas are woven through all of my books. She consistently provides me with a unique angle into humanity grounded in understanding, compassion, and empathy.

They say that you're a composite of your closest friends, and if that's the case, it's a rich tapestry to draw from. Massoud Badakshan, Jessica Broitman, Tommy Cramer, Dan Fitting, Joel Kramer, John Kunze, Mark and Lisa Levine, Seth Neiman, Jennifer Palangio, Paul

Pilliterri, Richard Sullivan, Shari Bashin-Sullivan, Mary Sylvia, and Katherine Vincent are family to me and make my life so much more fun, rich, and meaningful.

Many thanks to my older and younger brothers for their ongoing friendship and companionship, and to my cousin who has been like a sister to me.

Of course, profound love and gratitude to my wife of over thirty years, Ellie Schwartzman. She listened patiently to my obsessions about what should or could be included, deleted, reframed, or considered for the book. It's helpful to have a fellow psychologist in the family—especially one who's so kind and perceptive.

To my three grown children and my grandson for all the obvious reasons. Especially to my daughter for our reconciliation. As any formerly estranged parent knows—there is no greater gift that a child can provide a parent, and I'm forever grateful.

And to the reader, may you find a way back to your child, your grandchild, and your happiness.

INDEX